The Fates of Privilege

The Life and Times of a Harvard Man

Dean O. Smith

Annandale Press

Published by Annandale Press

Spokane, WA 99224

Copyright © 2025 Dean O. Smith

All rights reserved

Many of the real names of characters portrayed in this book have been changed to protect their privacy. Some names of well-known individuals have been retained; in those cases, no information about the individual has been added that is not available from public sources.

No part of this book may be reproduced, or stored in a retrieval system, or transmitted in any form or by any means, electronic, mechanical photocopying, recording, or otherwise, without express written permission of the publisher.

ISBN-13: 978-1-7364534-6-9

Printed in the United States of America

Other Books by Dean O. Smith

Smith, Dean O. (2011). *Managing the Research University.* New York: Oxford University Press.

Smith, Dean O. (2015). *Understanding Authority in Higher Education.* Lanham, MD: Rowman & Littlefield.

Smith, Dean O. (2018).*University Finances: Accounting and Budgeting Principles for Higher Education.* Baltimore, MD: Johns Hopkins University Press.

Smith, Dean O. (2019). *How University Budgets Work.* Baltimore, MD: Johns Hopkins University Press.

Worth, Ellis. (2021). *The Sonora Springs Tales: A Collection of Ellis Worth Short Stories,* edited by Dean O. Smith. Spokane, WA: Annandale Press

Worth, Ellis. (2021). *Once upon a Farm: Tales of Discovery,* edited by Dean O. Smith. Spokane, WA: Annandale Press.

Smith, Dean O. (2023). *The Man I Didn't Know: My Father's Hidden Struggle with PTSD.* Spokane, WA: Annandale Press.

Contents

Acknowledgments v
Prologue 1
The Traveling 3
The Beginning 5
Harvard-I 29
Boulder and Fort Collins 54
Harvard II 60
Stanford 69
Gothenburg 84
Munich 94
UCLA 111
Madison-I 119
Madison-II 144
Africa 158
Madison-III 163
Hawaii-I 171
Hawaii-II 196
Lubbock-I 210
Heidelberg 219
Colorado Springs 224
Lubbock-II 227
Huntsville 238
Lubbock-III 242
Bozeman 245
Spokane-I 259
Tulsa 274
Spokane-II 281
Epilogue 291

Acknowledgments

I should like to thank everybody mentioned in this book. Wittingly or not, they all contributed to my life, always in positive ways. If this book were an encyclopedia, I could write a chapter on nearly every one of them. But it's not. So, I'll simply repeat my expression of appreciation for them.

Most significantly, I wish to thank my wife, Karlene. She has stood by me throughout this project. Fate smiled upon me when we first met many years ago. Also, I should like to acknowledge our beagle, Barney, who has brought us immense comfort and pleasure. He is indeed, our "best friend."

And, finally, I should like to acknowledge the editorial staff at Annandale Press for their help in the production of this book.

Prologue

Lots of people write autobiographies, the history of their lives from beginning to end. Likewise, lots of people write their memoirs, abbreviated autobiographies that concentrate on the history of a specific time period or sequence of events in their lives. Either genre seeks to lay out the significant events in the authors' lives. What made them the persons they are today. And so forth. Most are narcissistic. Why not? Most people enjoy talking about themselves, whether anybody listens or not. Furthermore, most autobiographies are intended to confer immortality on their authors. Again, why not? Most people enjoy thinking that they will be remembered long after their demise.

I'm no different. I chose to write this autobiography to memorialize the events that shaped my life. And, speaking narcissistically, it has been a privileged life. My life didn't begin that way; I wasn't born with a silver spoon in my mouth. But fate favored me time after time. Not all the time, but enough times to embolden me to assert that my life has been privileged. Of course favorable genes and supportive parents come into the mix, and, looking backwards, they provided the necessary foundation for success in life. But fate made a decisive difference in many situations.

The most consequential event in my life occurred when I was admitted to Harvard as an undergraduate. Fate's sometimes grim expression turned into a bright smile on that occasion. As a Harvard undergraduate (a "Harvard man" in the vernacular), I was inducted into an elite class, a very privileged class. This privilege manifested itself in many ways during my lifetime, all of them favorable. Over the years, I have asked myself: Why did I receive this honor? Did I deserve it, or did fate simply play a cruel trick on the many unsuccessful Harvard aspirants? I seek explanations to these questions throughout the book.

For those who choose to read this autobiography, I hope to answer these and more fundamental questions about myself: Who is this person? How did he become who he is? Is he one of a kind or can I learn something inspirational from his experiences? Good questions, all of them. So, let's get on with the search for answers.

The Traveling

My wife Karlene says that I'm doing the traveling. Old people do that when they sleep, during the night when they sleep or during the day when they nap. They venture out and come back. But, someday they just don't come back. In those cases, their traveling during this lifetime is over. I asked her where the term "traveling" came from. She explained that it was Jamaican but maybe British. You see, she was born of Chinese ancestry in colonial Jamaica which, at that time, was governed by Great Britain. That explains her very English turns of phrase: "Where's me bloody shoe?" and so forth. Regardless of its origin, I understood what she meant by "the traveling."

Usually I do the traveling in one of two places: our bed and my easy chair, the bed at night and the chair during the day. The queen-sized bed is an ideal place for the traveling. Our dog, a 30-pound beagle named Barney, Karlene, and I share it, with the dog occupying about one-half, and Karlene and me splitting the other half. For whatever reason, I always sleep in the middle, sandwiched between Barney and Karlene. This provides me with the comfort commonly associated with the middle seat on an airplane, limiting my opportunities for deep sleep, keeping me in the realm of shallow REM (rapid eye movement) sleep where dreaming occurs. Perfect for the traveling. The chair, a classic recliner, is also an ideal place for the traveling. It belonged to Karlene before our marriage, but I quickly claimed de facto ownership of it (although the dog disputes my hegemony over this wonderful chair). With the chair reclined and often the warm dog in my lap, the conditions are just right for drifting into the realm of shallow REM sleep conducive for the traveling.

Whenever I do the traveling, I inexorably go back in time, sometimes as far back as my early childhood. Along the way, I encounter memories of particular events or thoughts. Sometimes I dwell on them, sometimes I move on, continuing the traveling. At some encounters, a companion made its presence known. Call the companion fate. Or, call it destiny. I'm not sure which term is appropriate. But that pedantry aside, I realized that this companion had directed my life in one way rather than another. Traveling isn't the occasion to ask the question "What if I had gone the other direction?" I had no interest in that question. Besides, it can't be answered with any certainty whatsoever.

These memories don't comprise my entire lifetime of experiences and thoughts. The traveling is more selective. And, I have no understanding about how it selects which memories to visit and which to ignore. Moreover, when I am awake, I paid little heed to those memories ignored during the traveling. They were there somewhere in my past and could be retrieved, I'm sure. But, I see no reason to recreate a lifetime. One passage is enough.

I have gone out of my way to verify dates and other factual aspects of the memories chronicled here, to present the truth as I know it. Nonetheless, some individuals may dispute my memories of particular interactions or events: "No, that's not how it happened. That's not true." At best, I can simply suggest that they write their own memoirs of those disputed interactions and events to set the record straight, to present their version of the truth.

Although I have no obligation to reveal the memories encountered during the traveling, I feel compelled to share them with my family and any interested observers (if there are any). At least, these readers can understand what "this man" did with his allotted days of life on Earth.

The Beginning

It all began with a series of fateful mishaps. Oh, perhaps that exaggerates my beginnings a bit, but not everything went as planned. To clarify this exaggeration, I'll start before the beginning, going back to a couple of years before my birth.

In 1942, World War II was ravaging the planet. Young, and not so young, Americans enlisted or were drafted into the country's military to combat the forces of evil. My father, Everett E. Smith, a thirty-two year old attorney for the United States government in Washington, D.C., was included among those patriots, those defenders of freedom who joined the Army. For basic training, he was assigned to Camp Carson (now known as Fort Carson) in Colorado Springs, a far outpost for a Washington lawyer. Although my father was not particularly religious, while there he ventured into the local Unitarian church for occasional services. And that was where he met my mother, Margaret E. Kelley, who played the violin during the Sunday morning services. They were married a year later, in 1943.

Shortly after their marriage, my father was assigned to San Antonio and then Ann Arbor for Officer Candidate School. My mother accompanied her new husband as he prepared to go to war in Europe with the Third Army under the leadership of General George Patton. At the time, many of the women chose to get pregnant, since they were unsure whether their husbands would ever return. My mother joined the crowd, and my father presumably obliged, for I was conceived shortly before his departure for Europe. My venture into this world had just begun.

Pregnant, my mother returned to her family's homestead in Colorado Springs to be with her parents and extended family. It was there, in Glockner Hospital (now known as Penrose Hospital), that I departed my mother's protective womb. Not without mishaps, however. For starters, my mother's obstetrician showed up for his helpful role in my birth on schedule but not in sobriety. That is, he was drunk, so drunk that my mother fired him on the spot. Another doctor was found to assist with my birth. But that, too, was beset with a challenge: I was a breech presentation, meaning that I was positioned to come out bottom first instead of head first. The ersatz doctor was up to the challenge, however, for he turned me around in time for a normal delivery. Thus, on May 28, 1944, I was born into this world with the name Dean Orren, after my father's younger brother and my mother's father, respectively.

As an only child with an absent father, I was now the sole recipient of my mother's love and attention. Furthermore, I was the beneficiary of comforting support from my mother's parents, aunts, uncles and other family relatives who lived in Colorado Springs. Additional attention was bestowed by my paternal grandmother who, according to my mother, came from her farm in Minnesota to help care for me shortly after my birth. I inferred from my mother's telling of the visit that her mother-in-law was not particularly welcome; she hardly spoke English and insisted on Old World baby-rearing traditions that were foreign to my mother. In short, there was friction between the two. Although the mother-in-law had come for an extended stay of a couple of months, she returned disgruntled to Minnesota after only a couple of weeks.

After two years as the sole recipient of my mother's attention, things changed. Two more people intruded into our lives. First, my father returned from the war. My mother

The Beginning

and I joined him in Washington D.C., where he was offered the position as Deputy Counsel of the National Gallery of Art. I was no longer the sole object of my mother's love and attention. How did I adapt to sharing my mother with this stranger? I don't have any memories in that regard. Second, my younger brother was born. I remember the arrival of my mother from the hospital with newly born brother Curtis in her arms. Now I shared her attention with two other people. I must have been unsettled by this brotherly intrusion, for I remember my mother cuddling him, kissing him, cooing gently to him while I simply watched from a distance, probably with an older, less lovable boy's envy. Oh, she may have given me the same loving attention when I was at that age, but I have no memories of that. Nonetheless, I don't remember harboring any blatant jealousies; from his beginning, my brother and I have always been very close.

With the birth of my brother Curtis, our family was complete. My memories of those early years are scant, but I suspect that we were perceived as a storybook family, living in a very nice house in Silver Spring, Maryland. We boys had ample toys and yard space to play in, our mother stayed at home caring for us, and our father, who had been highly decorated during the war, had a prestigious job at the National Gallery of Art. He commuted to work daily in a car pool. Occasionally, my mother would drive us in our car, a 1947 Hudson sedan, into the city for shopping at Garfinkel's downtown department store or simply visiting Rock Creek Park or some other part of the city. Curtis would usually snuggle into her arms as she drove. Dangerous, yes, but my mother managed to handle the awkward situation well, for she was quite a good driver. By and large, we were a happy family.

But our happiness was interrupted by a most serious misfortune. In the spring of 1949, as I turned five years of age, my mother took Curtis and me with her on a vacation to visit her family in Colorado Springs. While we were there, my father had an acute nervous breakdown. He was committed to a local mental hospital at Perry Point, Maryland, where he was diagnosed with paranoid schizophrenia. Nowadays the diagnosis would most probably be post-traumatic stress disorder (PTSD). My mother with us two children rushed back to Washington, D.C. to attend to this unfortunate episode. She encountered my father seriously ill in the hospital, where he was under suicide watch and given regular insulin- and electro-shock treatments. I remember visiting him once; he was slow, dull-witted, concentrating on assembling a simple cubical box made of colored plastic. He was a stranger, not the father I knew.

With my father in the hospital, at age five I entered kindergarten at a neighborhood school in Silver Spring. I enjoyed school. Miss Colletti was the teacher; I adored her. She always had us working on some engaging project of one sort or another. One of my favorites was a paper bus large enough for us children to enter and sit on seats that we had brought in. My mother gave me a four-barrel money changer like the ones carried by city bus drivers that I took to school, which added to my enjoyment of our bus. Yes, I enjoyed school.

That enjoyment was short-lived. My father's illness frightened my mother. In his delusional state, he had threatened to kill his two boys. Frightened for our safety, my mother pulled me out of school (literally out of the bus) one afternoon and fled with Curtis and me from my father to the safety of her parents in Colorado Springs. We boarded a train in Washington's Union Station and en route rode in a Pullman sleeping car, which allowed us to sleep overnight in a small compartment. That experience began my lifelong fascination with trains. Along the way, we stopped in Midway, Kentucky, where, about ten years earlier, my mother had taught music at Midway College. We stayed in a house in town that had no running water, indoor plumbing, or electric refrigeration, relying on a pump-handle well, an outhouse, and an ice box respectively. I was five years old then, certainly old enough to remember these quaint details of our visit.

In Colorado Springs, we were met by my maternal grandfather, Orren Green Kelley, commonly known as O.G. Kelley, who was station agent for the local Railway Express Agency adjacent to the main Rio Grande train depot. I noticed immediately something that I hadn't noticed before: he carried a revolver—a six shooter—on his hip. That was my introduction to the Old West. He drove us to his house, which was one of nine houses comprising two city blocks on the far west side of town owned by the extended family. My mother, Curtis, and I moved into a small cottage in this compound, across the street from my grandparents.

This proximity to my extended family provided me an opportunity to learn about the family's history. Indeed, I have fond memories of sitting on my great aunt's screen porch as the adults sipped mint juleps and Coors Banquet beer on warm summer evenings, telling stories about the "old days."

In a nutshell, my grandmother's side of the family were Quakers who had emigrated to the United States with William Penn seeking religious freedom. They settled in Indiana, where the family lived for many generations. In the late nineteenth century, several members of the family came down with tuberculosis. Thus, a branch of the extended family moved to Colorado Springs seeking a cure for the dreaded disease in the high dry climate. Several generations later, I appeared on the scene. Notably, going back in history, that side of the family emphasized the importance of higher education, with a couple of them earning their Ph.D.s. This historical interest in higher education probably explains why my mother simply assumed that Curtis and I would go to college. We carried on that tradition. It's in our blood, so to speak.

I learned fewer details about my grandfather's side of the family. They were Scotch-Irish who settled in the South, with roots extending back to antebellum Georgia where the family owned a plantation near Macon. They bore old Georgia family names such as Kelley and Lumpkin. And, yes, they were slave owners. My relatives had no problem with that: "We were good to our Darkies." I never learned how my grandmother, the Indiana Quaker, met my grandfather, the Georgia cracker. Was he a Quaker, too? I don't know. Did she fall off the train while passing through Macon, Georgia? I don't know. My efforts to track down how they met have yielded no information in that regard, except that my mother was born in Meridian, Mississippi, in 1914.

Sometime after its formation in 1929, several family members, including my grandfather, went to work for the Railway Express Agency. This venerable company, which preceded modern package delivery services such as United Parcel Service and Fedex, had a near monopoly on the transportation of goods across America, with iconic branch agencies at many railroad stations across the country. It was tightly woven into the railroad infrastructure of the time. My family members' stories about Railway Express, the railroads, and train-hopping hoboes, remnants of the Great Depression, reinforced my interest in the railroad industry.

Apropos hoboes, my grandmother pointed out coded chalk etchings on neighborhood houses, garden walls, and so forth ostensibly left by hoboes to communicate to their colleagues whether the owner of the house was generous with money or food, whether they had a vicious dog, and other important pieces of information. I was fascinated whenever I saw these etchings. My favorite stories were about hoboes stealing freshly baked fruit pies left in an open kitchen window to cool. Damn hoboes.

The Beginning

After about a year of living in the cottage, we moved into the main house which was right next door when the tenants' lease expired. This house was ideal for our small family: separate bedrooms for each of us, a front sun porch, and one centrally located bathroom with a bathtub. No showers in those days. Moreover, the house sat on about two acres of land, with plenty of room for two young boys to play. And, the entire property backed up to the Garden of the Gods, with its spectacular red rock formations. Of course, my brother and I were climbing up those iconic rocks in no time. Fortunately, my mother had done the same thing as a child, so she never seemed to worry about our safety in these adventures. The land was covered by native grasses and other native plants: prickly pear cactus, yucca, scrub oaks, and the like. And they provided a home for a multitude of animals, big and small: mule deer, golden eagles, magpies, rabbits, horned ("horny") toads, grasshoppers, and so forth. Moreover, we had several cats and two rambunctious dogs. All in all, this was a wonderful place for young boys.

Several other features of that time period stick in my mind. Our trash went into an old beehive-shaped concrete incinerator in the back yard. During the first couple of years or so in the cottage and the house, we relied on an ice box for refrigeration. So, once or twice per week (I don't remember exactly how often), the iceman delivered a large block of ice coated with sawdust which he put into the top cabinet of the small ice box. And the milkman made regular deliveries of fresh milk, cream, butter, and eggs. Occasionally, he would also deliver freshly squeezed orange juice. Also, there was the paperboy, really a grown man, who delivered the morning paper every day. The kitchen stove and hot water were heated by natural gas. Furthermore, the house was heated by a single pot-belly shaped natural-gas heater located in the center of the house. In the winter, we spent many afternoons and evenings huddled around this heater. The rest of the house simply got cold. After three years or so, my mother had a central heating system installed, with a gas-heated furnace in the unfinished basement and hot air ducts in the main-floor rooms, but not the attic where my bedroom was. Rising hot air from downstairs provided the only heating up there. Consequently, in winter, I spent most of the day downstairs, going upstairs only to spend the night under warm blankets.

After settling into the new home in Colorado Springs, my mother needed a job. Although my father had agreed to send her $75 per month for child support, she needed more to make ends meet. Indeed, she would have needed roughly $165 per month just to reach the poverty level in 1950. Where was the money going to come from? Three sources: private violin lessons, gigs as a violinist, and, most importantly, teaching violin lessons in the public schools. In this latter job, she drove from one school to another, giving lessons all day long. Together, the income from these sources was sufficient for us to have a modest living. At least that was my perception of the situation. We were not wealthy by any means, but we were not destitute.

These various jobs often required my mother to work until late in the evening. For example, after a day of teaching in the schools, she would teach private lessons for another two or three hours in a downtown studio provided by a local music store. Then, on at least two evenings each week, she would have evening rehearsals with the Colorado Springs Symphony. My brother and I were on our own during these long days. Well, not completely on our own; we weren't abandoned. My mother arranged for us to eat at a nearby diner where she kept a running tab, and we often stayed with our grandmother, who lived across the street, for the night.

During overnight stays with my grandmother, I learned a fundamental truth about women: they remove one leg at night before going to bed. Yes, I witnessed this many times. You see, my grandmother lost her right leg from above the knee down when she was run over by a trolley car in her youth. Since that fateful accident, she wore an artificial leg that gave her the ability to walk, albeit with a limp. Before going to bed at night, she sat on the side of the bed, took off the artificial limb, and shoved it under the bed. And, of course, the next morning, she reversed the process, putting on the limb for the day. Keenly observant of everything that my grandmother did, I watched her do this every night.

But there's more to the story. My grandmother's sister, Aunt Margaret as we called her, had also lost her right leg from above the knee down due to tuberculosis. And, she wore an artificial leg just like my grandmother's. Occasionally, I would spend the night at her house, which was right next door, and watch her do the same thing: sit on the side of the bed, take off her artificial limb, and shove it under the bed. Aha, so that's what all women do at night, I surmised. And so it was my belief for several years in my childhood.

The critical mind may wonder if I ever saw my mother take off one of her legs before going to bed. Good question. The answer is simply "No. I never saw her do it." But in a child's mind, just because I didn't see her do it certainly doesn't mean that she didn't sit on the side of the bed, take off her leg, and shove it under the bed. After all, that's what my grandmother and Aunt Margaret did. In my mother's case, it must have occurred after I had gone to sleep. Oh, the naive workings of a child's mind.

A major issue needed attention: my schooling. I was now six years old and ready for the first grade. For some reason, however, my mother didn't enroll me in the fall, when the school year began. To this day, I don't understand the reasoning for the delay. Perhaps she thought that we might return to live with my father. Regardless, she enrolled me starting in the second semester. Mrs. Burgess, the teacher, took me under her wing and quickly brought me up to speed in "reading, writing, and 'rithmetic." She provided a wonderful introduction to formal schooling, and I did very well in her class. Indeed, I received top grades in all subjects, despite my late entry into the class.

My success in the first grade set the stage for continued success for the rest of my academic life. I quickly became recognized as the "brightest" student in my class, at least by the teachers. There was only one hiccup along the way, when my fifth grade teacher claimed that I had uncontrollable behavior problems and required psychiatric counseling. Well, my mother nixed that suggestion, defending her precocious son. Somehow, I regained my teacher's confidence and, in fact, became her "pet," and once again received top academic honors in her class. Those early successes in school inculcated an expectation by my teachers and me that I would excel academically, would be the best in the class, an expectation that persisted throughout my entire life.

Now and then, I ponder my early academic prowess. Why did I stand out academically at such an early age? For starters, I suspect that fate conferred me with a good set of genes; in that regard, I was privileged intellectually from the get-go. I attended good public schools and, for the most part, had good teachers. My parents didn't tutor me, but in their own ways they provided a well-rounded foundation for academic success. Moreover, they were both college graduates, unlike most of the parents in the neighborhood. That may have made a big difference.

At home, my mother provided strong support, usually manifest as a big hug when I brought home a stellar report card. In addition, she bought a set of the *Encyclopedia Britannica*, which I consulted frequently (despite its ridiculously small print and erudite tone) and an accompanying set of beautifully illustrated geography books, which I pored over every evening, reading about faraway lands and people. Moreover, I spent many hours studying notebooks of detailed plant drawings from botany courses my mother had taken as a student at Colorado College. And, I attended numerous symphony concerts and operas where she played, which added to my cultural education. To make a long story short, my home learning environment was a rich supplement to my formal education in school.

While my mother encouraged me in these endeavors, my father showed little enthusiasm for my interest in academics. Sure, he had been a good student throughout his schooling, but now he disparaged formal education. Inevitably, he just scoffed when I showed him my excellent report cards from school. Nonetheless, he introduced my brother and me to the fine visual arts—paintings, sculptures, and the like—by taking us routinely to museums and galleries in Colorado Springs and Denver. His birthday and holiday cards were always reproductions of a fine arts masterpiece, usually from the collection at the National Gallery of Art, where he had worked at one time. In this way, he instilled in us an appreciation for the classics of art. Plus, he often spoke to us in French. Not enough to teach us to speak the language, but enough to familiarize us with the French culture.

I was an egghead. No getting around that. Even my after-school pleasures had an academic component to them. Many after-school hours were spent huddled next to the heater while reading books about one thing or another in the dim light. Most of all, I enjoyed comic books. My favorite series was *Classics Illustrated*, which introduced me to great literature (*Moby Dick*, *Hamlet*, *The Iliad*, et cetera) in comic-book simplicity. Whenever the downtown news stand got in any new comic book, I bought it right away. My desire for them was insatiable. Similarly, I thrived on facts—important and trivial. My primary source was *The World Almanac and*

Book of Facts, which came out with updated editions annually. I memorized baseball trivia, mountain heights, Kentucky Derby winning times, and scads of other arcane details from that bible of generally useless information.

    As the son of a professional musician, I was exposed to music during these early years. In the second grade, my mother arranged for piano lessons on a weekly basis, where I learned not only to play but also to read music fluently. And, I learned to recognize the classical music of the great composers: Bach, Beethoven, Brahms, and so forth. About the same time, my mother asked me what other instrument I wanted to play—something that I could play in the school band or orchestra. The trombone with its long slide appealed to me, but I was uncertain about its name. So I said the "long straight thing." She thought that I referred to a clarinet, so that was what I got. Although I was disappointed, I began taking clarinet lessons at age seven. Before my musical career came to an end, I had taken lessons on the oboe and French horn as well. I excelled on the French horn and played it in school and community orchestras through my high school years. I was on my way to becoming a musician like my mother (and her two sisters, my aunts).

    The only problem was that I loathed practicing. Oh, I made progress but only because of my ability to read music well. My teachers would complain to me and my mother about my failure to practice; for example, at one point, my frustrated piano teacher said "Mrs. Smith, you're not a wealthy woman. I suggest that you save your money by discontinuing Dean's private lessons." Ignoring this advice, my mother simply arranged for another piano teacher, a younger man who assigned light popular music of the time as well as the classics. She thought that the lighter music might entice me to practice. But that didn't help; I still eschewed practicing, no matter what the music was. Practicing simply wasn't in my constitution. Consequently, I never became really good at any instrument: certainly competent, but not good enough to consider music as a career option.

Athletically, I was adequate. My father encouraged my participation in various athletic activities, such as little league baseball, ice hockey, tennis, rock climbing, skiing, and so forth. He was a good ice skater (after all, he grew up in Minnesota) and baseball player (he had been a catcher). So, he joined us in those activities. For the others, he patiently sat on the sidelines watching us.

My favorite sport was baseball. My brother and I played it in the back yard regularly, often having to pick sharp spines out of our gloves and hands whenever a baseball rolled into a cactus plant. Although I was recognized as one of the better players in grade school and even into junior high school, my skills were limited by my astigmatism. I couldn't see a straight line, and as I got older and the pitches got faster, that made it increasingly more difficult for me to hit a pitched baseball or to catch a sharp line drive. My baseball career ended in high school when I failed to make the varsity team.

Also, I played ice hockey with some skill, since I could ice skate with ease. Indeed, I was an excellent ice hockey skater, mainly because my father, who was an accomplished figure skater, had taken Curtis and me to skate at the Broadmoor ice arena or, for that matter any other frozen outdoor rink in town or beaver dam in the mountains, on many Saturdays. But I never could master shooting the puck with any force or accuracy; I just couldn't do it, and that limited my future in the sport. Figure skating could have been an alternative to hockey, but it never interested me. Many of the world's best figure skaters practiced at the Broadmoor, but despite their obvious athleticism, the males all seemed effeminate. That's not for me. I could go on and on about my limited successes in other athletic activities, such as tennis, basketball, track and the like. Looking back, I could play many sports with a modicum of competence, but I wasn't a gifted athlete in any of them. No; my gifts lay in academics.

Although I wasn't particularly impressive in athletic ventures, Curtis quickly demonstrated natural talent in many sports. Significantly, I was not jealous. Indeed, I was proud of his skills. I loved my brother, although I should add that he and I had the usual brotherly squabbles during our early years. One day, however, during a quarrel about who knows what—I don't remember exactly when or any other details—we looked at each other, communicated nonverbally, and just stopped our bickering. It was as if somebody had thrown a switch. We never quarreled since then, nearly 75 or so years later. Our father contributed to this detente by insisting always that my brother and I were loved equally; he had no favorite son. Accordingly, when we played catch with the baseball, it was always three-cornered. Moreover, he had us both sit together with him in the front seat of his car during our drives with him. At least until we were too big to fit comfortably. Then, usually we both sat together in the back seat. And he always encouraged both of us equally as we played baseball, shot pool, climbed rocks, and so forth. As the older brother, I was often better at most sports at that young age, but as we grew up, the tables quickly turned. Curtis became an excellent bowler, table tennis player, golfer, and participant in whatever other sport interested him at the time. I looked on in proud amazement.

As I got older, I enjoyed driving cars. This enjoyment began at the age of 14, when my mother taught me how to drive. One winter day, she took my brother and me to the top of a snow-capped mountain pass and told me to drive us the 100 miles back home. I protested that it was snowing—indeed, we were in the midst of a blizzard. But she said that "You're growing up in Colorado, so you have to know how to drive under these conditions." So, I drove us home. From that time onwards, whenever we went into the mountains, I was tasked with the driving. Shortly after this initial drive down the mountain, my mother bought me a car, a 1951 Dodge, which sat in my grandmother's yard until I was old enough for a license to drive it legally (15 ½ in those days). I spent many hours just sitting in it, waiting for the freedom that it would bring.

Besides sitting in my own car, I sat for many hours in our neighbors' car. It belonged to Mr. and Mrs. Townsend, a retired couple who lived in the cottage next door. Mr. Townsend usually spent his time sitting in his old car (a 1939 or so Ford coupe), smoking a pipe and reminiscing on "the old days." After school, I would frequently join him. Besides teaching me how to clean a pipe and load it with tobacco, he taught me how to shift the car's gears using the clutch (to "double clutch" in those days before synchromesh transmission), use hand signals for turning and stopping, change the oil, repair a punctured tire inner tube, and myriad other details of car driving and maintenance. Moreover, he supplemented what our father had taught us about playing baseball: hitting, throwing, catching, and the like. After school and during the summer, he would often hit balls to us so we could practice catching flies and grounders. And, he taught me how to paint houses (his profession before he retired). It's safe to say that Mr. Townsend played an influential role in the non-academic aspects of my upbringing. He took the place of our father during the week.

Curtis and I had only one playmate about our age nearby — that is, within less than a mile or so from our house. I shall call him Timmy. He was a year older than I was but looked much older mainly because of his height. He came from an impoverished family comprised of his father and mother and two older sisters. Timmy took odd-jobs at local diners and so forth to earn money for clothing and shoes, while his mother took care of the housework. His father owned a dump truck and made a meager living hauling dirt and so forth at construction projects. Most of the time, he just sat at home. But, occasionally, he would disappear for weeks at a time to work on a road construction project somewhere in the state and then return to wait up to six months or so for another job.

Curtis and I played regularly with Timmy, usually at dangerous games involving hunting knives, B-B guns, sharp-tipped darts, and bows and arrows with razor-sharp hunting tips. One of our favorite pastimes involved throwing a dart or shooting an arrow as high as we could straight up into the air and then watching it come back down. They usually landed perilously close to where we had thrown them, but somehow we all escaped serious injury. Okay; there was one exception. Once a dart landed on Timmy's head and stuck in his skull. He rushed home, with the dart in place, where his mother tended to the wound. The dart had not gone completely through the skull, so no serious brain damage was done.

Now and then, Timmy brought us cigarettes purloined from one of his family members. We would climb into a cave hidden in the nearest large red rock where we could smoke unseen by the outside world. Except for his mother, that is. One time, she surprised us by climbing up into our retreat, snatched the cigarettes, and hauled Timmy back home for his "comeuppance." Curtis and I quickly fled to the protection of our house, hoping that she wouldn't tell our mother. That hope was shattered when she came to the back door, "spilling the beans." After Timmy's mother left, our mother simply smiled at us and said nothing. We were lucky to have such an understanding mother.

As we entered our teenaged years, Timmy developed a keen interest in girls before Curtis and I did. To attract girls, he managed to earn enough money to buy a 1951 Chevrolet sedan which he modified by moving the gear shift from the steering column to the floor on his right side. Thus whenever he had to shift gears, he had the opportunity to rub his hand along a young girl's thigh if she sat close enough, which girls usually did on dates in those days of bench (not bucket) seats. Using the back seat of his car as a makeshift bedroom, Timmy became quite skilled at "deflorating" young virgins; in his terms, he "popped their cherry." Indeed, he occasionally showed me the newest blood stain in his back seat. I was just on the cusp of puberty and only marginally understood what he meant.

Fate interrupted Timmy's sexual pleasures, however. This occurred when, at the age of sixteen, he popped the cherry of a young girl whom I shall call Marie. At the age of fifteen, she became pregnant. Soon after she broke the news to Timmy, her father appeared at his doorstep, figuratively with shotgun in hand, and demanded that he marry Marie. Timmy agreed to the proposition but argued that he should be allowed to finish high school first (he had two years to go) if he were to be able to support Marie and the child with an adequate job. Okay; the father agreed with the importance of finishing high school. So, unmarried, Marie moved in with relatives in rural Kentucky for those two years, where she could give birth without the scrutiny of her classmates in Colorado Springs. The shotgun was set aside, but Timmy should expect to see it in Colorado Springs the day after his graduation.

But, Timmy had other plans. Immediately after the graduation ceremony, he jumped into his car and fled Colorado Springs to take refuge with his older sister in Louisville. According to Marie's older sister, who kept me abreast of this drama, Timmy and Marie (with her father and child) must have unknowingly passed each other along the highway between Colorado and Kentucky. With his departure to Kentucky, I lost track of Timmy for several years, and I never again saw Marie (or her sister, for that matter).

Timmy had been a good friend. Growing up together, I had learned informally from him the challenges of near poverty. Besides a shortage of money, Timmy had limited horizons for his future. To be sure, Timmy was a good student. Good enough to be accepted with financial aid into Colorado State College in Greeley. However, he was not inclined to enter college; a college education was beyond his horizon. The last time I saw him was when I was home from college one summer. He worked as a laborer for the City street department and had married a popular woman in his high school class, who promptly bore two children. They lived in a shabby World War II-surplus trailer house behind his parents' house. He invited me in to meet his wife and kids but promptly began arguing with her. In anger, he struck her several times, and she fled with her young children to Timmy's mother's house for protection. I left quickly and never saw him again, although I heard many years later from high-school classmates that he lived in the western part of the state and worked as a manual laborer.

Memories of Timmy lead inexorably to memories of my own sex education. Sometime in every young man's life, he learns about the birds and the bees. I was no different. I learned a few prurient facts from Timmy, but this was a topic not taught in the Colorado Springs school system. Thus, when I was about twelve years old, my father took it upon himself to provide the necessary education in these matters. (My mother was of little help, for she was clearly uncomfortable with the topic. Her main advice was to stay away from strange men). So, every Saturday for what now seems like nearly a year, my father explained the critical details. Remember, he had grown up on a farm, so all of this appeared to come easy to him. Curtis and I listened attentively, although we often forced a disinterested yawn. But we learned all about the female anatomy, the copulatory act, and so forth. Thanks to our father, we were well schooled in these matters when our classmates had something to say about the opposite sex.

Several years later, I received supplementary instruction in sex education in my high school gym class, which was all male. The teacher (the varsity basketball coach) assumed that we knew the basics of human intercourse: foreplay, copulation, et cetera. But, did we know about the potential side effects? No, he wasn't talking about pregnancy. He was talking about venereal disease. Rather than tell us directly, he showed us a film produced by the Army to educate young recruits about the dangers of sexual encounters. Gruesome! The film showed close-ups of syphilis-infected penises and other gory details. And it showed the treatment for syphilis: injection of a large syringe-full of penicillin into the spinal fluid in the lower back region. The class was horrified by these scenes. Indeed, two boys passed out during the injection scene. The teacher simply dragged their limp bodies out into the hallway where they could get fresh air. One thing was sure: none of us would ever forget this film.

Now here's the curious part of these memories. Neither my father nor the gym teacher told us much about contraception. Pregnancy was the girl's problem, not the boys'. Yes, the use of a condom was mentioned in the context of syphilis but only briefly. None of this mattered much, because condoms were quite exotic in those days. They were kept behind the pharmacist's counter, out of sight. Thus, the customer had to ask for them ("rubbers" as they were usually called), which usually required waiting until nobody was within earshot of the counter. And, if the clerk was female—well, forget about it. Come back some other time.

Our father's tutorials and the gym teacher's film constituted the extent of our sex education. Except for what we heard from schoolmates outside the classroom. Even there, in conservative Colorado Springs, the topic of sex seldom came up. At least not in my circle of friends. Although I had many dates as a teenager that involved kissing, sex wasn't the ultimate goal. No fondling, no sly attempts to remove an article of clothing. In that regard, despite my education in these matters, I was quite naïve.

My academic education continued through junior and senior high school. And, I continued to excel academically. By then, I expected—and was expected by the teachers—to be the smartest student in class, no matter what the subject might be. Likewise, these expectations carried over to music. I was first chair in the French horn section of the band and the orchestra, lead singer in the school choirs and operettas (usually by Gilbert and Sullivan), et cetera. And, for that matter, I was expected to be a leader in most other extracurricular activities. All except those that required election by the student body. I simply lacked the personality that attracted votes from my peers. To be sure, I was popular and got along well with most classmates, but my popularity simply didn't translate into endorsements for any school office. But for any role appointed by a teacher, I was almost always the chosen one.

With advancement into junior high school and then high school, my circle of friends grew accordingly. My junior high school was on the west side of Colorado Springs, and most of the students were from lower to middle class backgrounds. I didn't come from a wealthy family either, so that didn't matter much to me. But, I became aware of the intellectual limitations of many of these families. Like Timmy, my classmates' parents had not gone to college. A small gap between me and them began to open slowly. One exception was Larry. Larry was the youngest of thirteen children. Although his parents had not attended college, half of his siblings had gone onto college and, in fact, earned advanced degrees, while the other half had slid into the lower socioeconomic class, which, for a couple of them, included stints in prison. Fortunately, Larry was destined to attend college. We had similar interests and became best friends. Larry, by the way, was good at the very things that I wasn't: he was elected class president in both junior and senior high school and was a superb athlete, becoming the starting pitcher on the baseball team, and so forth. I was proud to be his friend.

High school further enlarged my social world. New friends, new teachers, new opportunities. The school drew students from not only my side of town but also the north side, where most of the wealthy doctors, lawyers, and other professionals lived. I developed a new set of friends from this pool of generally well-educated peers. Their fathers were a college president, a hospital director, a doctor, a lawyer, and other professionals. I felt quite comfortable with them. Besides enjoying the usual camping and other outdoor activities in Colorado, we enjoyed reading and talking about highbrow topics such as Newton's law of motion, Maxwell's equations, and the principles of neurochemistry. I was in my element. And I continued to thrive in class. Again, my teachers were supportive, for they appreciated students who had such willingness, such eagerness to learn. And, again, I received top grades. Oh yes…again, I was adequate in sports but not good enough to earn a varsity letter. That coveted kudo eluded me.

It had always been assumed by my family that my brother and I would go to college. After all, both of our parents were college graduates, with distinction I might add. My mother was inducted into Phi Beta Kappa at Colorado College, and my father was inducted into the Order of the Coif at the University of Minnesota Law School. So, I knew that I was going to college after high school; the only question was where.

That question was answered in a most unusual way. It all began on a fishing trip with my mother when I was about ten years old or so. Once or twice every summer, she took us to her favorite fishing spot on Chalk Creek, at the base of Mt. Princeton, about 100 miles west of Colorado Springs. I loved the spot, and especially Mt. Princeton. In my mind, it was the most beautiful and majestic mountain in Colorado. On one fateful trip, my mother explained that Mt. Princeton lay within the Collegiate Range, along with Mt. Harvard and Mt. Yale and that these mountains were named after the eponymous three Ivy League universities. Well, then, I'm going to Princeton for college. It was decided at that young age. That is, until I learned a few months later that Mt. Harvard was the highest of the three mountains. I changed my mind: I'm going to Harvard instead. When I explained this decision to my mother, she smiled and said "Good choice." But when I explained it to my father, he simply frowned and said nothing.

Despite my enthusiasm, my father was skeptical of Harvard. He made that quite clear. Many times, he had tried to convince me to apply for one of the Service academies. He preferred the Coast Guard or Merchant Marine academies because they were generally not involved directly in military conflicts. Occasionally, I thought about the Air Academy, which had been newly established in Colorado Springs. But, I realized that I wasn't cut out for military service. Indeed, marching in a straight line with the high school marching band was repulsive to me. How could I possibly thrive in a setting that insisted on marching in straight lines? Furthermore, I had no interest in a Colorado school. I didn't consider them academically rigorous. That's where my classmates went when they couldn't get into any better college. This attitude was the first real indication of my innate elitist tendencies.

Several years later, when it came time for college applications, I applied to Harvard, of course, along with Yale and Swarthmore as my only backups. No colleges in Colorado, although I did apply for a Boettcher Foundation scholarship which would pay all expenses if I went to any college within the State. The decision letters all arrived on the same day in April, 1962. I opened them while sitting in the car with my father. "Look at this, Dad. I got into all of them. I'm going to Harvard!" My father stopped the car, slammed his hand against the dashboard and said "You fool! Do you think you're too good to go to a college in Colorado? You know that we can't afford Harvard. Take the Boettcher and hope that it's not too late to get into a state school." "But Dad, Harvard has offered me a full scholarship—tuition, room and board, everything. I'm going there." Sullenly, my father said okay, "But you're on your own. Expect no financial help from me. And don't expect any from your mother, either. She's in no better shape financially to support you in this folly." That ended the discussion. And it never came up between us again.

I should point out that Harvard's "full scholarship" covered tuition and room and board. I was on my own for books, laundry, snacks, and other incidental expenses. By Harvard's reckoning, those items would cost about $400 per year, so they offered me two possible ways of getting that money as part of my financial aid package: part-time work as a janitor cleaning dormitory-room toilets or a loan. I took the loan. That sure beats cleaning toilets.

My senior year in high school came to an end. I graduated at the top of my class, the valedictorian. I was proud of that accomplishment. My valedictory address was met with more yawns than applause, but at least I was the one giving it. With that, high school was over: now off to college. Most of my closer friends were also off to college, primarily schools in the East: Yale, Dartmouth, Wellesley, and so forth. Collectively, we took pride in the academic accomplishments of our class of 1962 at William J. Palmer High School.

Oh yes, lest I forget one unfortunate incident. Traditionally, each graduating class donates a "class gift" to the high school: a bench, a flagpole, a water fountain, or something like that for the betterment of the school.

Accordingly, many members of my class donated a few dollars into a fund to pay for this gift. A day before the graduation ceremony, some overzealous soon-to-be graduates celebrated by throwing cherry bombs (powerful firecrackers) down the three outhouses in Acacia Park, right across the street from the high school. The cherry bombs did their job, blowing the roof and doors off the outhouses and sending their contents sky-high. Of course, these contents returned to Earth, spread over much of the surrounding lawn and sidewalks. The culprits were caught but not punished. But, somebody had to pay for new replacement outhouses, and that obligation fell on the entire senior class. There was only one place to get the necessary money: the class-gift fund. So, the class gift from the Palmer High School senior class of 1962 was three new outhouses in Acacia Park, with no brass plaques identifying them as class gifts. At the time, none of us was particularly proud of this legacy.

Harvard-I

The time came for me to leave the state of Colorado, my family, my foundation, for Cambridge, Massachusetts. Except for my very early years in Maryland and a brief trip to Dallas to visit my aunt, I had never been outside the borders of Colorado. Thus, I had no idea about what awaited me. Fortunately, my good friend Larry, who was going to Wesleyan University in Middletown, Connecticut, helped ease the transition. We arranged to take the train from Colorado Springs to Pittsburgh, where his older sister and her husband (both professors at the University of Pittsburgh) would pick us up and drive us to Cambridge. They would drop me off, and then continue onto Middletown to drop off Larry. So, I packed two suitcases and a footlocker for the journey. The footlocker was too big for the car, so I sent it to Cambridge separately via Greyhound Bus.

The cross-country train ride was spectacular for us, with the bridge over the Mississippi River, its layovers and station changes in Chicago, and the final stretch along the Ohio River into Pittsburgh with the massive steel mills aglow at night. After a night in Pittsburgh, we drove to New York City, where we stayed in a midtown Manhattan hotel. I was awestruck at the towering skyline, the busy harbors, the eclectic peoples, and the diverse architecture. One day wasn't enough for this magnificent city. I knew that I would have to return.

After a day of sightseeing in New York City and a night in the hotel, they drove us all the way to Cambridge. Late that afternoon, we pulled into Harvard Yard and stopped in front of Matthews Hall, my home for the freshman year. After unloading my suitcases, they said goodbye and drove off immediately, en route to Middletown to drop off Larry before evening. I stood alone, beset with homesickness. But there was no time to dwell on that, for I still had to carry my luggage up the steps and into my room, Matthews 8, wherever that might be in this imposing building. When I got there, behold! It wasn't just a room, it was a three-room furnished suite, with a fireplace, to be shared with two roommates. The other two, Bob and Paul, had already arrived and decided the sleeping arrangements: we would keep the largest room with the fireplace as a common room with our separate desks; Bob, who had arrived first, would get a private bedroom; and Paul and I would share a bedroom with a bunk bed. As the last person there, I was assigned the bottom bunk of the shared room. That was quite acceptable, for I had expected far less spacious accommodations.

I quickly assessed my roommates. Harvard had carefully chosen us based on common interests. They did a pretty good job. One roommate, Bob, played clarinet and appreciated music; in fact, he had already been accepted into the marching band, which was preparing for the upcoming football games. For financial aid, Bob had accepted a job on the janitorial crew that cleaned toilets in the undergraduate housing rather than take out a loan. Whether it was this distasteful job or simply his innate personality, Bob was mostly acerbic and generally verged on being downright unpleasant at times. Nonetheless, despite his prickly personality, we got along without any rancor. The other roommate, Paul, didn't play an instrument, but he was appreciative of classical music. In fact, he was appreciative of anything classical and went on to major in Classics. I spent many evenings listening to him recite Homer and other Greek and Latin writers in their original languages as we went to bed. Like me, he had turned down any job on campus; he simply took out loans to cover his discretionary needs. By and large, like three castaways on a raft in the middle of the Pacific Ocean, we supported each other as we learned to get along in this new environment.

Right off the bat, I encountered several surprises. Most disconcerting was the realization that I had unforeseen incidental expenses. At Harvard, all students were required to wear a coat and tie for all three meals. Practically speaking, that meant wearing a coat and tie all day long. Fortunately, I had brought a well-worn sports coat and tie with me, but I needed another one or two. So, my first week there, I went to the Coop (the Harvard Cooperative Society), which sold clothing, textbooks, and other school needs. I bought a new sports coat, a three-piece suit, four dress shirts, and two ties to supplement the meager wardrobe that I had brought from Colorado. Plus, I needed dressier shoes, so I bought two new pairs of Bostonian shoes, one black and one brown. All of these items cost nearly $200, half of my discretionary money for the entire year. But that wasn't the end of my clothing needs. As I learned within a week or so, Boston's weather could be quite unpleasant, which meant that I needed a good overcoat to withstand rain, snow, and cold. A London Fog top coat with a zip-in liner fit the bill, costing another $50. Add a water-repellent hat and an umbrella, and I was prepared for the year.

All of these clothes needed cleaning now and then, specially the cloth handkerchiefs, which most students used instead of Kleenex. Harvard provided coin-operated laundry facilities in the basement of Matthews Hall, and I used them for underwear, socks, handkerchiefs, and the like that didn't need ironing. But for shirts, I used a commercial laundry service; once a week, its valet service would pick up my shirts, wash them, and return everything neatly pressed and folded. For a cost, of course.

And then there were the textbooks. I had anticipated the need to buy a few textbooks. However, to my dismay, many Harvard courses in the social sciences and the humanities assigned numerous books to read—not just a single comprehensive textbook or two but as many as 100 or more books covering the classroom material. Many of these were inexpensive paperbacks, but some of them were costlier hardbacks. Of course, they were all available in the library to be shared with all other members of the class. But, compulsively, I bought all of them to read and re-read at my leisure. Fortunately for my budget, science and math courses usually assigned only two or three textbooks, along with supplementary books that helped clarify difficult concepts. Altogether, the cost of books consumed most of the remainder of my discretionary money. Thus, early in the first semester, I was nearly broke. Realizing my financial plight, both my mother and father sent me occasional (every other month or so) checks ranging from $35 to $50, for which I was most grateful. Despite Harvard's generous financial aid, I simply needed that additional support from home.

With that modest boost from my parents, I was able to broaden my experiences in this new setting. I could attend occasional theater productions in downtown Boston, a Celtics game, or a luxurious roast beef sandwich from Elsie's diner right off of Harvard Square. In addition, I could afford to hitchhike down to New York City, where my mother's cousin Wilbur (of the Railway Express clan) would pay for my hotel room in downtown Manhattan and evening dinners at classy restaurants, with cocktails and wine. (At that time, the drinking age in New York was 18 years). His favorite, and mine, too, was the Playboy Club. At the end of these evenings of drinking and carousing, Wilbur would take the train back home in nearby Bronxville, and I would stumble drunkenly into my hotel room near Grand Central Station. After a couple of days in Manhattan, I would hitchhike back to Cambridge, fully recharged for the academic rigors at Harvard. I should add parenthetically that in those days, hitchhiking was not considered particularly dangerous. I would always wear a coat and tie to look respectable. Sometimes I had to wait up to an hour or so to get a ride, but I was never "stuck" somewhere along the way.

For a naive Colorado boy, the various backgrounds among my classmates were quite enlightening. At Harvard, I realized that I wasn't unique academically; most of my classmates had also graduated at the top of their high school class. Moreover, many of them had been students at the nation's elite preparatory schools: Exeter, Andover, Deerfield, and the like. These "preppies" tended to form exclusive cliques. I realized right away that I was not included in their groups. And, the Jews: although there were reputedly Jews in Colorado Springs, I didn't recognize them as such. But at Harvard and in New York City, I was introduced to Orthodox Jews, with their accoutrements, and the less orthodox Jews who wore the traditional yarmulke. They, too, seemed to form an exclusive clique. In effect, I was simply a public school "hick." This wasn't a major source of concern for me, however, because nearly half of the class fell into the same category.

Right off the bat, I discovered anther trait of Harvard students: they attracted the attention of non-Harvard people when the Harvard affiliation became known. This was not entirely a matter of envy or awe; it was also a matter of cachet. "Ooh. You go to Harvard." I, and most of my Harvard colleagues, young and old, have experienced this attention our entire lives. In fact, there have been numerous articles written about the so-called "H-bomb." We weren't celebrities like movie stars or professional athletes, but we were clearly in a unique, privileged social class. Often, to avert this attention, and the social distance it created, when we were asked where we went to college, we said simply "Oh, back East," and then quickly changed the subject. Of course, that patronizing reply just made matters worse if the Harvard connection became known.

Across the street from Harvard Yard, there was a Unitarian Church. With my Unitarian upbringing, I was comforted to see that church so nearby; it relieved my homesickness a bit. So, shortly after my arrival in Cambridge, I went to a Sunday morning service. As I entered the church, I was surprised to see the words "God Is Love" written in huge gold letters on the front wall. Although the Colorado Springs Unitarian church certainly acknowledged some people's belief in God, it didn't impose that belief on its members. As I listened to the service, I was further surprised by the strong Christian bias. By and large, I found the service dissatisfying and never went again. That wasn't the eclectic Unitarian Church that I knew. It was more like a traditional Christian church. And, intellectually, I could not embrace Christianity.

Harvard had its own signature church, Memorial Church, located prominently in the center of the Yard. Although it was supposedly non-denominational, it was decidedly Protestant Christian. I went to one or two Sunday morning services but quickly decided against going again. Unless, that is, a celebrated theologian came to speak. For example, I went to hear the renowned Harvard theologian Paul Tillich on several occasions and Reinhold Niebuhr on one occasion, but they were not part of the ordinary Sunday service. My goal was simply to see and hear the famous scholars. Otherwise, I could not relate to the Christian religion promulgated by the regular minister.

Of course, I went to Harvard to attend classes, not to buy clothes or go to church. Thus, the most pressing question was what classes to attend. The standard load was four classes per semester, so I had to choose four. As I quickly learned, the choices depended pragmatically on when the final exam occurred. Grades were determined entirely by performance on the three-hour final exam, so it was important to leave sufficient time between exams to allow for last-minute "cramming." Fortunately, the final exam schedule was printed in the course catalogue, which afforded the opportunity to choose courses with maximal time between their final exams. Naturally, other factors played a role in determining which courses to take: general education and concentration (major) requirements, and, for me, the fame of the professor. I always gravitated to courses taught by famous professors whom I had read about in the news, regardless of the subject: professors such as John Kenneth Galbraith, David Riesman, Mark Van Doren, and other luminaries.

Another surprise at Harvard was that students were not required to attend classes. The rationale was that students registered for a course to learn the subject. If they could pass the final exam, then they presumably had learned the material covered in the class. I always attended classes, mainly because I feared that I might miss something important that would appear on the final exam. But, often many students came to the first class and then disappeared until the final exam. In a sociology course offered by Professor Riesman, for example, the lecture hall was filled with well over 100 registered students on the first day but only about 20 showed up for class during the rest of the semester. I wondered why students wouldn't take advantage of this opportunity to listen to this famous professor.

Early in the first semester, the intense pressures of studying for these courses induced me to take up two habits: drinking coffee and smoking cigarettes. While sitting in the library late nights, I noticed that many students drank numerous large cups of coffee brought in from a nearby coffee shop in Harvard Square. Although I had not previously been a coffee drinker, I followed their example and quickly learned the benefits of caffeine during these late evenings. Similarly, I noticed that many students smoked cigarettes almost non-stop. I had not smoked cigarettes since the occasional puffs during my early childhood in Colorado Springs, but I began to smoke in earnest shortly into the first semester. And, I quickly learned the benefits of nicotine as I pored over difficult reading assignments and mathematical problems. No wonder students drank coffee and smoked cigarettes. They became a staple of late nights in the library.

Although the meals provided by the university were usually quite good, I (and most other students) often needed a midnight snack while studying. Several all-night diners in and around Harvard Square offered just what we needed: hot coffee and sweet pastries. My roommate Bob was particularly needy in this regard. Rather than interrupt his studying late at night, he would toss me a quarter to go buy him a cup of coffee and a Danish pastry at the Hayes Bickford cafeteria in Harvard Square and then add another quarter for me to buy the same for myself. Since I was beginning to feel pinched financially, I would always accept the offer regardless of the weather. I felt a modicum of shame when I did this, but I also felt that I needed the money to satisfy my hunger for midnight snacks and coffee. They became a staple of my existence at Harvard.

Also early in the semester, Harvard made sure that we understood that the final exams were considered not just an assessment tool but also a teaching tool. In that latter regard, they showed the student what the most important learning points of the course were. That is, the questions addressed only the most significant points, not the less significant tidbits. To help students judge what those important points might be, the university posted each course's final exam for at least the last five years in the undergraduate library. Understandably, those exams became important study guides when preparing for the final exams, especially for students who hadn't attended the classes.

With so much at stake in the dreaded final exams, Harvard went to great efforts to thwart cheating. In those days, there were no cell phones, pocket calculators, or other modern electronic devices that could help in an exam. But, of course there were the traditional ways: looking over somebody's shoulder, sneaking a peek at notes hidden up a sleeve or written on a shirt cuff, et cetera. To minimize any cheating in those ways, Harvard had students sit far apart and assigned a small army of proctors to walk among the seats, on the lookout for any "mischief." Furthermore, to ensure that no student could ghost write exam answers for another classmate, Harvard counted the number of exams and "blue books" (where the answers were written) issued at the beginning and turned back in at the end of the exam period. If the numbers failed to match, everybody was kept in their seat until the numbers were reconciled. Thus, no student could submit a "doctored" answer book after the exam. Harvard may have had an honor code for something or another, but it certainly didn't apply to final exams. One final note: if a student missed an exam for some reason, the exam could not be taken later. I'm sure there must have been some compelling excuses, but Harvard made it clear to us that there were none as far as it was concerned. Missing the exam meant failing the course. This was not debatable.

I should point out that some courses, usually core general education courses such as the history of western civilization, comparative literature, introductory foreign languages, and so forth, extended over two semesters. Those courses had a three-hour final exam at the end of each semester. And, making life a bit more stressful, the second semester's exam also included questions about material covered during the first semester. The grades from both exams were combined to determine the final grade. Only this final grade for the course was entered onto the official transcript.

Final exam period was preceded by a three-week "reading period." During this time, there were no classes or other assignments. This time was for reflection and consolidation of material covered during the semester or, in the spring, during the full year. In that regard, reading period was not a vacation. For students who had not attended classes or kept up with the classroom assignments, this was an invaluable time to catch up. The past exams were in constant use during reading period, for it was generally thought but never proved that professors re-used questions from past years.

In fall semester, reading period extended over the Christmas and New Year's holidays. During this week, undergraduate housing closed, so I had to find somewhere else to stay. In my freshman year, Harvard helped me by offering to pay for my round-trip airfare home to Colorado Springs for the holidays. Of course I accepted the offer. In fact, I was homesick and could certainly benefit from a week with my family and friends, sharing our freshman experiences.

So, Harvard paid for the tickets, and I packed my suitcase for the trip. Now, I had never flown before, so all of this was new to me. The adventure started off quite auspiciously: a major winter storm had snarled air flights in and out of Logan airport. Consequently, my first flight in an airplane departed eight hours late. Nonetheless, off we went, en route to Chicago, where I would change carriers, from American to Continental, for the continued flight to Denver. Along the way, the airlines served three-course meals accompanied by a packet of three cigarettes. The meals were good, and the cigarettes were a welcome accompaniment to several cups of coffee. Everybody seemed to smoke, and nobody seemed particularly distraught about the smoke filling the cabin. The air quality was no different from that in a restaurant or bar in those days. People smoked. That was that.

The vacation week went by quickly. With the pressure of pending exams on my mind, I had to organize my time: during the days, I studied, and during the evenings, I went out with my friends. We usually went to taverns, where we drank copiously and compared college experiences. One evening, I went ice skating with a high-school acquaintance, Jane. We "hit it off," so to speak, and she joined my friends and me every evening for the remainder of the week. I was sad leaving her when the time came for my return to Cambridge.

Exams came and went, and the new semester began. About the time of spring break, my father developed a kidney infection. I must have mentioned that to the right person at Harvard, for once again the university offered to pay for my round trip airfare to Colorado Springs over spring break to be with my father during his illness. Of course I accepted the generous offer and flew back home for the week. My father didn't seem particularly ill, but he appreciated my presence. That was clear. Every evening for the week, I got together with Jane, who was finishing her senior year in high school. I was becoming very fond of her. I had hoped that she would consider coming to the Boston area for college, but she had been offered and had accepted a full scholarship to the University of Denver. Oh well. I would certainly enjoy being with her in the meantime. The week went by quickly, and I returned a bit despondent to Cambridge for the remainder of the semester.

Near the end of the second semester, I was required to declare a tentative major—or, field of concentration as Harvard called it. I was at a loss. I had decided halfheartedly to take the pre-medical school curriculum, but Harvard didn't have a pre-med concentration. So, I had to choose a traditional liberal arts area. Initially, math came to mind. I enjoyed calculus, but I worried that I couldn't handle the more advanced courses. I thought about a science field. The only science course I had taken so far was geology, "The

History of the Earth." Although I did well in that course, I found it a bit "dry," except for the paleontology (dinosaurs and so forth). Other possibilities came to mind: social relations (that is, sociology) and psychology, among others. Finally, I decided on philosophy, mainly because I had read an enticing book on mathematical logic (*Methods of Logic*) by the famed Harvard Professor of Philosophy Willard Van Orman Quine during spring break. Naively, I thought that his approach to philosophy would address my interest in mathematics with ostensibly less demanding rigor than the traditional mathematics courses. So, I signed up for philosophy.

Once again, the spring reading period provided an opportunity to catch up in my coursework and to reflect on what I had learned during the semester. The final exams came and went with somewhat less stress than I had experienced the first semester. In fact, I enjoyed the challenges posed in several of them. I did okay, and ultimately attained B's and a few A's for the two semesters. I was satisfied with my performance, for all of my grades were better than average, which was a C in those days before grade inflation. In that context, some of my classmates were satisfied to get a "gentleman's C." Yes, I had done okay during my first year at Harvard. No gentleman's C.

Immediately after the last final exam, I packed my belongings and rushed to the airport for the flight to Denver. I rushed, because I had arranged to accompany Jane to her high school senior prom that evening. On the drive from the Denver airport down to Colorado Springs, I changed clothes in the back seat of the car, putting on a tuxedo that my mother had rented for me. Needless to say, Jane and I enjoyed the drama and thrill of the evening.

Besides Jane, I had another interest that summer: getting a job. I wanted to save at least $400 for the next year at

Harvard. I found an ideal position as a surveyor for the United States Forest Service. I was assigned to a four-person survey crew: Bill, John, Gary, and me. We spent the week together in the national forest living in a Forest Service Airstream trailer. It was a tight fit, but we made it work. A priori, I knew nothing about surveying, but the other three, who were several years older than I was, had been working together for at least five years and knew the job well. Initially, with great patience and a lot of "ribbing," they taught me how to handle the rod, chain, and transit. And they taught me where to pound the requisite wooden stakes into the ground, marking the boundaries of a potential road or campsite. I wanted to learn how to enter the survey data into the log book, but they insisted that I lacked the experience and, for that matter, the intelligence to master such a complicated task.

After work, we made dinner on a propane stove inside the trailer. John, who picked up groceries from a supermarket on our way out of town to the trailer, appointed himself chef and prepared mainly hot Mexican food that required cold beer, lots of cold beer, to wash it down. Afterwards, we would often play cards until bedtime, telling the tallest of tales. One night, they took me on a snipe hunt. I was given a burlap bag, taken to a spot about a mile from the trailer, and told to wait while the others beat the bushes to rouse a snipe that would run into my bag seeking safety. After an hour or so, no snipe had come by, and I couldn't see or hear the others. Slowly, I realized the joke and returned embarrassed to the trailer, where they sat playing cards and laughing raucously at my expense.

At least one night during the week, we drove to the nearest tavern, usually located in some small town 30 or more miles away. We generally drank more beer than I had considered humanly possible and then managed to drive home. Upon arrival, each of us quickly went to our corner outside the trailer for relief. Needless to say, the grass grew very high on those corner sites. When Friday came, we put in a half day's work surveying, packed our dirty laundry, and drove back to Colorado Springs, where we got our weekly paycheck. I would cash mine at the nearest grocery store, go home to wash up, and then pick up Jane for an evening of dinner and carousing. Although this summer job prevented me from seeing my friends during the week, it allowed me time to enjoy the mountains and to learn a possible trade, namely land surveying. I enjoyed the summer and was sad when it came to an end.

Back to Cambridge for my sophomore year. The previous spring, all freshmen had self-sorted themselves into groups of two or three, and each group applied for housing in the upper class Houses. There were nine of these Houses, each with a traditional stereotype; Adams House was for those interested in the theater, Kirkland House was for athletes, and so forth. A friend from down the hall, Jack, and I agreed to apply together as roommates. We got along well together. He was from the mountains in Vermont and was interested in skiing and other outdoor activities. Moreover, he and I were both interested in medical school and accordingly applied to Dunster House, which was stereotypically for scientists. We were assigned a two-room suite on the third floor, furnished with a single bed in one room and a bunk bed in the other. I took the single bed, and Jack took the top bunk of the other bed. We had separate bedrooms, which gave us privacy. My only problem with this arrangement was the noise from the adjoining suite. Every night, there was loud talking and laughing—an ongoing party. Worst of all were the repetitive thuds of a soccer ball kicked against our common wall. My complaints had no effect. So, Jack graciously offered me the bottom bunk in his room, where the noises could not be heard. Every evening, Jack would leap into the top bunk with the agility of a monkey, and I would simply lie down in the bottom bunk, thankful for the quiet. That worked out well, for we spent many hours late at night putting each other to sleep with tales of skiing, mountain adventures, and so forth.

Refreshed by the summer's break and enriched by the extra money I had saved from my job (although I still took out another $400 loan from Harvard), I looked forward to the year. At the outset, I had two goals. The first goal was to get into the Harvard Glee Club. Typically, only two or three sophomores were invited to participate. The rest of the members were juniors or seniors. With my musical background, I successfully passed the audition and became a member as a first tenor. I was very proud of that accomplishment. Many rehearsals were held jointly with the Radcliffe Choral Society, which added sopranos and altos; more importantly, it added women to the mix, which delighted most of the Harvard students.

The Glee Club consumed valuable study time. I had to attend two-hour rehearsals two nights per week and occasional concerts during the year. One of those concerts, by the way, was with the Boston Symphony Orchestra, conducted by Erich Leinsdorf. Under his direction, we recorded Wagner's Grand March from Tannhäuser for RCA Victor in Boston's Symphony Hall. Needless to say, I was thrilled by this experience. Another scheduled concert was not so thrilling. The Club had traveled to Washington D.C. for a concert. The downtown hotel where we were scheduled to spend the night refused to accommodate our assistant conductor, who was African American. It was too late to arrange the required number of rooms in another hotel, so we spent the night on a New York Central train to our next scheduled concert in Albany, New York, skipping the Washington, D.C. concert altogether.

The second goal was to find a girlfriend. (Jane was simply too far away). That proved more difficult than I had anticipated. For example, a couple of Jewish Radcliffe students went out with me for an evening in Boston, but on both occasions, at the end of the evening they told me that they wouldn't go out with me again. The reason was the same for both of them. "My parents won't allow me to date goys." That was a hard lesson in Jewish culture. I dated several other Radcliffe students but none of them appealed to me. Thus, several weeks into the semester, I resigned myself to a life without a girlfriend in Cambridge.

Another concern quickly preoccupied my mind: importantly, I had to rethink my choice of concentration, because philosophy wasn't going to work out. Why not? Well, each Harvard student meets weekly with a faculty advisor in his field of concentration. Accordingly, I went to my first meeting in the asthmatic depths of Widener Library. My advisor asked me what times I would be available for a one-hour tutorial. "Every afternoon except Wednesday. That's when I have a chemistry lab." Okay. "We'll meet every Wednesday afternoon at 2 p.m." I was stunned at his disregard of my schedule. Indeed, I decided on the spot to change my field of concentration. But to what? I pondered landscape architecture or visual studies (because of an enjoyable course in visual studies that I was taking). No; I needed a science field to prepare me for medical school. I hadn't taken biology yet, so I didn't know what to expect from that. Consequently, I decided on geology, with an emphasis on paleontology, which I had enjoyed freshman year.

With that decision behind me, the coursework began. I enjoyed my courses, although they seemed even more demanding than the year before, and, because of Glee Club, I had less time to study.

The traveling took me to one particularly embarrassing experience that semester in a visual studies course taught by a famous professor of architecture, Professor Eduard Sekler. The class met in the newly completed Carpenter Center, a modern concrete building designed by the Swiss architect Le Corbusier, in the midst of the traditional brick, ivy-laden buildings in Harvard Yard. One class assignment was to "describe" this controversial building. The professor called on me first. I stood before the other fifteen or so students, hemmed and hawed, and generally fumbled for words. Finally, I said that "It's hard to describe." Wrong answer! Professor Sekler shot back: "If you can't describe something, then you don't understand it." Embarrassed, I returned to my seat. Many times after that experience, I have cogitated on the professor's assertion and have concluded that he was absolutely right. Consequently, I have adhered to this tenet throughout my academic career.

Despite this embarrassing moment, the semester proceeded without any significant issues. That is, until late November when two tragic events occurred that indelibly marked my sophomore year.

The first occurred on Friday, November 22, 1963: the assassination of President John F. Kennedy. I learned about it while driving with three friends into New Haven, Connecticut, for a Glee Club concert that evening preceding the Harvard-Yale football game. At several stoplights, we heard radio reports of the assassination through the open windows of a nearby car. When we got to the Yale campus, we were told that the concert, the football game, and our arranged housing with Harvard alumni in the area had been canceled. There was a state of public confusion and uncertainty. Was the assassination a prelude to an attack by the Soviet Union? Nobody knew. All I knew was that I needed a place to spend the night before hitchhiking back to Cambridge the next day. Fortunately, a high-school classmate who was a Yale sophomore agreed to let me sleep on the floor in his suite. The next morning, I struck out for Cambridge. Getting rides was understandably difficult due to the pervasive public anxiety, but eventually I made it back to Harvard.

The second tragic event occurred about a week later, on Saturday, November 30, 1963: the death of my close high-school friend Joel, who was a sophomore at Dartmouth. Joel had invited me up to join him for Thanksgiving break. According to the plan, I would hitchhike up to Hanover on Thanksgiving, November 28. We would improvise for Thanksgiving dinner because of the imprecise timing inherent in hitchhiking. But, on Friday, we would drive a rental car to the home of one of his professors in Vermont for a belated formal Thanksgiving dinner. Oh, I looked forward to that. However, fate intervened. On Wednesday evening, I realized that I needed the weekend to finish a particularly difficult chemistry assignment. So, I called Joel and canceled my visit. No problem. Joel would go alone to his professor's house for dinner anyway. After that dinner, on the way back to Hanover, Joel encountered a farmer trying to pull a dead cow off the road and stopped to help the man. While they were working on this task, a car came over the hill and struck both of them. They died instantly. When I learned about this tragedy the next morning, I was stunned. "There but for the grace of God go I." Or, more profanely, "There but for the grace of a chemistry assignment go I."

These two tragedies cast a sullen spell over the remainder of the semester. I looked forward to Christmas break when I could return to the comfort of home. When Christmas break rolled around, I flew to Colorado for two weeks' vacation and picked up where I had left off with Jane. The time went very quickly; I wasn't ready emotionally to return to reading period and final exams. I was quite despondent when boarding the flight to Boston for exams and spring semester. Quite simply, I missed Jane.

A third less significant tragedy awaited me back in Cambridge. I flunked the laboratory portion of my first-semester structural geology course. Fortunately, I did well enough on the lecture portion to earn a B in the course. But, I got the message: I wasn't prepared for the academic rigor of upper-level geology laboratories. Nor was I particularly interested in the upcoming course in mineralogy, which required me to take advanced physical chemistry as a co-requisite. So, I switched my field of concentration to biology; that was as close as I could come to paleontology outside of the Department of Geology. Although I hadn't yet taken a college-level biology course, I had run out of alternative concentrations. This need to change concentrations once again to a field that didn't particularly excite me amplified my overall despondent frame of mind.

Notably, as a biology major I had an immediate need to begin taking biology courses. So, I took a one-semester introductory course that spring, Biology 2, my first biology course at Harvard. At the beginning, I had little enthusiasm for the material. I found it dull. But then, about two-thirds of the way through the course, a remarkable turn of events occurred. In context: although I had taken biology in high school, the concepts of heredity, evolution, and genetics were never mentioned in deference to the very conservative religious groups in Colorado Springs. Now, here in Biology 2, the topic of genetics and evolution arose. My first introduction to them. The instructor was Professor James D. Watson, a somewhat imposing young man. He handed out mimeographed draft copies of a book that he had written called *The Molecular Biology of the Gene.* This book later became the definitive textbook on the subject. In it and the accompanying lectures, he told us about DNA, RNA, the double helix, gene structure, and heredity. Within a few days after his lectures started, word got around that Watson and his colleague Francis Crick had won the 1962 Nobel Prize for their discoveries of the mechanisms of DNA replication and gene expression. Wow! I was hearing about genes and heredity for the first time from a Nobel laureate. "This is Harvard for you," I thought proudly.

Despite the distracting rigors of classwork my overall despondency didn't subside. About a month into the semester, at my father's suggestion, I went to a counselor at the student health service, hoping to find a cure for my malaise. The counselor listened to my woes for about five minutes and then pronounced: "What you need is a girlfriend." Hmm. Okay. So I asked the only female in my calculus class, Ruth, for a date. At the outset, we were quite attracted to one another, and a romance flourished. We would get together every evening to study or, more often than not, simply sit on the bank of the Charles River or in Radcliffe Yard snuggled in a wool blanket to keep warm, enjoying each other's company. The counselor was right; my despondency quickly dissipated. I enjoyed the remainder of the semester, which went by quickly.

Ultimately, the semester came to an end, and Ruth and I parted ways with promises of getting together again next fall. I missed Ruth, but Jane quickly displaced her romantically. (Out of sight, out of mind). One day midsummer, however, I telephoned Ruth, who lived on the East Coast, simply to say hello, but the woman who answered the telephone, presumably her mother, said that she was unavailable at the moment. "When would be a good time to call her?" "I'm not sure." "Well, please tell her I called." End of conversation. I got the distinct impression that I would have to wait until next fall in Cambridge to speak to her again. Why the cold shoulder, I didn't know. But I certainly felt her mother's chill.

The return to Colorado Springs for the summer brought me back to a familiar problem: getting a summer job. I could have returned to the Forest Service, but I chose, instead, a job at Colorado Engineers, a small surveying company in town. At first, I went out with the survey crew, handling the rod and chain. But, within a couple of weeks, I was transferred into the office to prepare mortgage plats. These are maps of all permanent structures, including sidewalks, concrete foundations, driveways, et cetera, drawn from the survey notes. I had learned drafting techniques in the structural geology laboratory course at Harvard, so I was adequately prepared for the assignment. I enjoyed this job for two main reasons: I learned even more surveying skills, and I joined my older colleagues after work in the neighboring tavern (The Wagon Wheel) for a "beer and a boiler," maybe even three or four. (I was underage, but one of my older colleagues at work had helped me make a fake identification card using an expired temporary driver's license.) And, there was a third reason: I could see Jane during the week.

I had not returned alone to Colorado Springs. My Harvard roommate, Jack, came with me, intending to stay for the summer. He had lined up a job driving tour buses up Pikes Peak for the Broadmoor Hotel. The initial plan was for him to stay at my house, sleeping in the glassed-in front porch. With three teenaged boys and my mother sharing one bathroom, however, that quickly proved inconvenient, so Jack moved into a dormitory for bus drivers provided by the Broadmoor. I didn't see him as often as I had hoped, but regardless, whenever he was available, Jack joined my friends and me on outings of one sort or another. He was one of the gang.

On one memorable outing, a group of my high-school friends, Curt, Jack, and I drove a rugged "Jeep road" to an abandoned mining cabin in the nearby mountains, which we called "Fred's shack" for lack of a better name. We built a fire for cooking hot dogs, placed a case of beer in a nearby cave to keep cool, and began our evening of partying—our "woodsie," as these parties in the mountains were called. This party included firing guns (several 0.22 rifles and a couple of .357 magnum revolvers) from Fred's shack down into the canyon. Perhaps a bit reckless, but we didn't see any lights or other evidence of human activity down there. But our firing didn't go unnoticed. After about an hour, we saw headlights slowly approaching us. Uh oh. It was a deputy sheriff. He rounded us up, took our driver's licenses, and ordered us to follow him to the sheriff's office in downtown Colorado Springs. Of course, we complied meekly: "Yes sir." The officer on duty shuffled through our driver's licenses and then looked up: "There are three of you from 3402 West Kiowa; what is that, a fraternity house?" I replied that no, it was my mother's house where my brother, my Harvard roommate, and I lived for the summer. The officer looked sternly at all of us and then said: "Well, you have to have somewhere to blow off steam. I know that. But the man living down the canyon was worried about guns fired in his general direction. I don't blame him. So, go back to your partying but without the guns." With great sighs of relief, we all drove back to Fred's shack and, indeed, resumed our woodsie without the guns. There's no question about it: we got off easy.

As usual, the summer passed by quickly. All too soon, I was on a flight back to Boston for my junior year at Harvard. The fall semester started with a thud. No, two thuds. The first thud occurred shortly after my arrival in Cambridge when I contacted my girlfriend, Ruth, hoping to restore our romantic relationship. She agreed to get together for a cup of coffee but for nothing more. Initially, we talked about our romance last spring, but the conversation quickly turned to the toll it took on both of us. I had gotten my only C at Harvard, a C+, in the calculus class. Unfortunately, Ruth didn't fare that well. As I learned, our time together took a worse toll on her academic performance. I never learned the sad details, but she told me that her grades had plummeted, causing her to lose her scholarship. Moreover, she came down with mononucleosis from exhaustion, causing her to cancel a planned trip to Europe with her Radcliffe roommate. For Ruth, the romance had been costly, indeed.

That explained her mother's chilliness on the telephone call. So now, starting her sophomore year without scholarship help, Ruth's father (a Presbyterian minister who could not easily afford Harvard's tuition) had forbidden her to associate with me. In his eyes, I was responsible for her misfortunes. Perhaps. Regardless, our romance was over. She had been the pillar of my stability last semester, but now I must get along without her.

The second thud occurred when Jack announced that he was moving out of our suite into a suite with two of his colleagues on the Harvard Nordic ski team. Suddenly, I was alone: no girlfriend, no roommate. Harvard abhors a vacuum, so they soon assigned another Colorado student, Norman, to replace Jack. I knew Norm and had no objection to rooming with him. Indeed, we enjoyed talking about the Colorado mountains and so forth. The only problem was that after about three weeks into the semester, Norm had a nervous breakdown while on a geology field trip. He entered a mental hospital for the remainder of the year. Meanwhile, I was once again without a roommate. I was lonely.

A student who lived across the hall, Brad, became my main companion, which alleviated my loneliness a bit. He grew up on a chicken farm in Rutland, Vermont, which I visited once that fall. Despite this rural background, Brad got along well with many more "sophisticated" students. He looked like a "preppie" and didn't seem to take life all too seriously. Within several weeks, I realized that Brad was bisexual; he dated (female) Radcliffe students but also went regularly with his male Harvard friends to a renowned Boston homosexual bar, the Punchbowl. I had no experience with homosexuals and generally shied away from Brad's male friends. And, they paid little attention to me; their attention focused on Brad. Despite his homosexual proclivities, I enjoyed Brad's friendship.

Despite these thuds, I quickly dove into the fall semester. I took four difficult courses, including the legendary organic chemistry course taught by Louis Fieser, the inventor of napalm. This course was hard, very hard, and I was not doing very well in it. A couple of other courses were also quite hard, with lots of reading and numerous difficult problem sets. And then there was the Glee Club, with its regular rehearsals and concerts. The Glee Club had awarded me a scholarship for weekly private voice lessons, which entailed more practice time. Topping off all of this, I joined the Dunster Dunces, a small singing group in Dunster House that performed popular music, such as Cole Porter songs, for weddings, bar mitzvahs, and so forth. More rehearsals. I was overburdened with my musical time commitments; they didn't leave sufficient time for studying, and I began to sense an academic disaster looming ahead. But I had these singing commitments that I could not abrogate.

Once again, fate intervened. About midway through the semester, I accidentally violated one of Harvard's parietal rules: on the night of a home football game, women could not be in a man's room after 8 p.m. The penalty for violating this rule was a year's leave of absence. Well, on a Saturday evening after the Dartmouth football game, I had a blind date in my room until about 8:30 p.m. Oops. When I realized the time, we rushed out the door into the courtyard. A janitor saw our exit and reported it to the House Senior Tudor. That was Saturday night. On Monday morning, I met with the Senior Tudor and took the initiative, explaining that I wanted a leave of absence until the beginning of next summer. He readily agreed to the arrangement, assuring me that this leave would not impact my financial aid package. When I brought up the parietal rule violation, he simply pooh-poohed it; my voluntary withdrawal rendered it a moot point. I was relieved by that. The next day, I was on a plane back to Colorado Springs, with my tail between my legs.

Boulder and Fort Collins

When I arrived in Colorado Springs, I wasn't sure what to expect. After all, to many observers, I might be considered a Harvard dropout. Fortunately, my parents were both very understandings and supportive. Although neither of them mentioned money, I knew they expected me to get a job for the year. I wanted a job that contributed to a nascent career. With my surveying background, maybe I could become a civil engineer. So I went to Colorado Engineers, hoping to take up where I left off at the end of the summer. But, behold. They weren't there. I learned that they had gone out of business shortly after I left for college that fall. I tried several civil engineering firms in town, but none of them was hiring at the time. I tried the Forest Service surveying office, but they weren't hiring until the next summer. So, what was I to do?

I decided to look for a job at the University of Colorado in Boulder. So, I borrowed my father's car and drove up there for a day. It felt good to be back in a university environment. It felt so good, in fact, that my first visit was to a math professor who taught advanced calculus. I wanted to audit his course. At the very least, I could resume studying a course that I had been taking when I left Harvard. I told him my story—dropped out of Harvard for the year and now sought a job. He agreed to my auditing the course and recommended a colleague at the Institute of Arctic and Alpine Research, Bill Osburn, who might have a job for me.

Bill (as he insisted on being called) ran a research program tracking radioactive fallout from Chinese high-altitude nuclear testing and needed somebody to collect samples from various stages in the ecosystem (snow, melting runoff water, sphagnum moss, various plants, animal feces, and so forth), measure their radioactivity, analyze these data statistically using the university's new computing facilities, and prepare summary reports. Although I had no experience with computers or applied statistics, I felt prepared to do the job. And so I was hired. I would learn computers and applied statistics on the job. I drove back down to Colorado Springs excited about the immediate future.

The next day, reality intruded on my excitement. I needed a car to get back and forth between Boulder and Colorado Springs and, more importantly, Boulder and Denver where Jane was a student. Cars cost money, of course, and I had only about $450 in savings to keep me going until my first paycheck. Fortunately, my father stepped in to help me; he offered to sell me his car, a 1962 Pontiac, for $400, considerably less than its market value. I thanked him and paid him in full. Now, at least I had a car. Next, I needed a place to live in Boulder. Fortunately, I found a basement room in a house near campus. For meals, I began to try several of the numerous eating clubs catering to students living off-campus. They usually had a two-week trial period before collecting their fees. I took advantage of the free trial period at several clubs, right up through the end of the year. By the end of the semester, I had earned enough money to rent an apartment with a kitchen and laundry facilities, sharing it with a high school friend of mine who had recently dropped out of Northwestern and moved to Boulder.

I enjoyed Boulder. Socially, I enjoyed the student taverns, where I spent several hours every night after work. And, I enjoyed the companionship of several female students whom I had met at one of the eating clubs. On weekends, I drove to Denver to visit Jane. I stayed overnight in the cellar apartment of a high-school friend, Henry, who lived near the University of Denver campus. He gave me my own key to the apartment and never seemed to care when I came in late. Yes, I enjoyed the carousing, the carefree pleasures, unburdened by the stresses of Harvard. And, I enjoyed my job at the university. Some days I would go with Bill into the mountains to collect snow, scat, and plant samples to analyze in the lab for radioactivity. Bill taught me the principles of ecology along the way. Moreover, I learned how to program computers: to enter data onto punch cards, to write FORTRAN programs for analyzing the data statistically, and to enter the data and programs into the computer (an IBM 7090) for processing.

At the beginning of March, Bill moved his research program to Colorado State University in Fort Collins. I moved with him, settling into a cheap boarding house near campus. Although I had to give up my partying lifestyle in Boulder, Colorado State offered me the opportunity to learn how to use other types of computers and, importantly, to learn more about applied statistics from one of Bill's collaborators, a professor of statistics, who took me under his wing. No more carousing, but I was learning skills that satisfied me academically. I felt that I was moving forward with my education, even though I wasn't at Harvard for the time being.

    At that time, Colorado State University was a new, raw research institution. In 1957, only eight years before my move to Fort Collins, the state legislature changed the name and mission of the state's agricultural college from Colorado A&M to Colorado State University, dubbing it the state's second major research institution. However, in those early days of its existence as a research institution, Colorado State University was a far cry from the University of Colorado in Boulder. For example, many mornings when I drove onto campus, the veterinary students would be on the front lawn castrating horses, with blood dripping down their white shirts and ties. Yes, it retained many of its A & M attributes. Even I, a young Harvard dropout, could tell that.

And I wasn't the only person who could tell. While I was there, the university opened a new main library, the university's academic focal point. To christen the new library, the university invited the celebrated historian Arnold J. Toynbee, who was a visiting professor of history at the University of Denver, to deliver the inaugural speech. On the morning before his talk, Professor Toynbee toured the library. To his dismay, there were few scholarly books or journals on topics other than agriculture. Poultry Science, The Horse Encyclopedia, and other agricultural staples of the Colorado A & M legacy. Professor Toynbee was appalled. How could he, a most distinguished scholar of Western civilization, tarnish his reputation by dedicating this poor excuse of a library? Well, he couldn't and didn't; he simply walked away, returning to Denver without delay. Naturally, this embarrassed the university, but, of course, it recovered and went on to become quite a respectable research institution.

Fate intervened in a momentous way while I lived in Fort Collins: Jane got pregnant. For background: I continued to visit her every weekend after the move from Boulder to Fort Collins. The only difference in my routine was the longer drive: 90 miles each direction instead of 30. As always, we enjoyed our time together. In fact, we enjoyed it a bit too much. About the first of April, Jane's physician announced "Young lady, you're pregnant." Oops!

How could that happen? In those days, birth control relied mainly on diaphragms and condoms. Although we knew about them, we naively didn't use either one. There's no need to ask why not; it just never occurred to us. Birth control pills were still on the cusp of being legal for unmarried couples, so they were unavailable. And, furthermore, abortion was illegal, so that was not an option—even if Jane had wanted one (which she didn't). Thus, without hesitation, we decided to get married at the first opportunity, which was about three weeks later.

Each of our parents reacted differently to the news of Jane's pregnancy and our planned wedding. When I told my mother about our situation, she looked despondent and silently walked away, presumably to think about what I had told her. Fortunately, she liked Jane and seemed quick to accept her as a future daughter-in-law. My father reacted with disgust: "What did you think was going to happen?" And that was the end of that. We never discussed the situation again. I'm not sure how Jane's mother reacted to the news when Jane told her. But she was clearly quite angry with me for "knocking up" her daughter. In fact, she proposed cutting off a certain part of my body—the one that caused this problem in the first place. A former battle-tested Army nurse, she was quite prepared to perform the surgery, not necessarily with any anesthesia. Needless to say, I didn't care for her proposal at all. But, after her initial anger subsided, she began to accept me as a trusted member of her family.

The wedding was not an easy undertaking. Because I was younger than 21, I required my parent's permission to get married. Okay. They both signed the required paperwork and wished us well. (For females, the age limit was 18, so Jane didn't need her mother's permission). We lined up a minister at a small church in Idaho Springs, a quaint town in the mountains west of Denver. All we needed was a marriage license. So, early on Saturday, April 23, 1965, we drove to Idaho Springs and then onto the Clear Creek county courthouse in nearby Georgetown to obtain the necessary document. When I showed the clerk my parental permission form, she refused adamantly to issue the license. "We had trouble with one of those forms several years ago." There was no room for debate on this matter.

"Okay, okay," we told her. "We'll just go to Gilpin County." So, we drove an hour to Black Hawk, the county seat in adjacent Gilpin County. Unfortunately, the Clear Creek clerk had called her counterpart there, alerting her not to issue the license; that would only mean trouble. Thus, the Gilpin County clerk also denied us. Enough of these small-town courthouse clerks. We drove back to Golden, the populous county seat of Jefferson County on the outskirts of Denver, where we were issued the license without question. After driving back to Idaho Springs, we were married that afternoon and took off for a two-day honeymoon with nights in Breckenridge and Evergreen. On Sunday evening, we drove to Denver, and Jane returned to her dorm room, where she lived for the rest of the semester. I spent weekends in Denver, staying in the cellar apartment, with very few opportunities to enjoy the perquisites of marriage.

Harvard II

My leave of absence from Harvard came to an end. During the first week in June, Jane and I piled our belongings into the car and drove back to Cambridge, with a two day stop-over in Minnesota to visit my father's family on the farm. In Cambridge, Harvard promptly re-activated my enrollment and financial aid and offered us a one-bedroom apartment in its married-student housing complex, Peabody Terrace. In Peabody Terrace, we paid no rent and had negligible other expenses. Harvard paid for most of whatever costs we might have incurred in housing. That was fortunate, for we had very little money—enough for food, gas and car insurance but little more. In fact, we couldn't afford a telephone. We borrowed the use of a neighbor's phone whenever a call was necessary. We were poor, yes. But, we weren't desperate by any means.

That summer, I enrolled in a course on intermediate calculus and got a full-time job as an applications programmer at the Harvard computing center. As an applications programmer, I was expected to assist members of the Harvard community, including faculty, students, and staff at all levels, with computer-based statistical analyses of their data. Although I had learned to code in FORTRAN and run simple statistical-analysis programs in Colorado, I soon discovered that my computer and statistical skills were usually inadequate to provide the more sophisticated (that is, more complicated) tasks expected of me. So, I would rely on help from my fellow applications programmers. Some of them were generous with their time and patience, but others brusquely said "Read the manual." Despite my shortcomings, I managed to keep my job through the summer and into the fall. In fact, I continued working at the center for the next year. Gradually, my computer and statistical skills improved to the point where I felt confident in my abilities to provide help on all but the most complicated analyses.

As the fall semester began, I wanted to re-insert myself into the Dunster House community, joining friends from before my absence. Peabody Terrace was adjacent to Dunster House. How convenient, I thought. But, the Dunster House senior tutor recommended that I transfer to Dudley House, a non-residential house located in Harvard Yard, which catered specifically to married and other students who lived off campus. Reluctantly, I transferred to Dudley House. Soon afterwards, I realized that it was, indeed, a better house for young married couples, especially those with children. Our interests no longer coincided with those of the single students in Dunster House.

I was back in the Harvard groove. Now, with a declared concentration in biology, I faced the need to enroll in a handful of biology courses, which I did without enthusiasm. Quite simply, I didn't enjoy biology; I much preferred mathematics. But it was too late to change areas of concentration once again. So I enrolled in the minimum number of biology courses needed for graduation. In addition, I re-enrolled in the dreaded organic chemistry course. Moreover, I picked up where I left off with the glee club and other musical activities but soon realized that they took too much time from my new home life with Jane. So, I discontinued my singing. Meanwhile, Jane enrolled in several Harvard extension courses on this and that subject, hoping to maintain her momentum towards an undergraduate degree.

Despite my job, we had little discretionary money, so early in the semester I took out a $1000 loan from the university to ease our plight. Plus, I took a second job typing an annotated bibliography on the relationship between brain size and intelligence for a famed paleontologist, Tilly Edinger, who worked at Harvard's Museum of Comparative Zoology. I would pick up her handwritten notes and type them onto 3" x 5" index cards. Jane also took a job as an assistant in the Peabody Terrace superintendent's office, which helped us financially even further.

In late November, Jane bore our son, Curtis Dean, at Boston Lying-in Hospital. I drove her to the hospital, hoping to stay with her during the birth. But, when she was admitted, I was sent home and told to await their telephone call. Since we didn't have a telephone, I relied on our neighbor to take the call, which came a day later. We were now young parents; Jane was 20, and I was 21. When we brought Curtis home to the apartment, we soon discovered that neither of us knew how to care for an infant's needs: change diapers, burp him, and so forth. Fortunately, we had bought several books on the topic. I would read the books' instructions out loud while Jane learned the "tricks of the trade." Furthermore, Dudley House and our married-student housing had many other young parents who counseled us on this and that aspect of infant care. We quickly became members of the "gang."

At the time, perhaps the most challenging aspect of parenting our new baby was the need to change Curtis's diapers. Oh, the smell of his baby poop wasn't so bad; in fact it was usually a bit sweet. But dealing with the diapers was something else. In those days, cloth diapers were the norm. In fact, disposable diapers weren't widely available yet. So, we had to make a decision: to buy cloth diapers and wash them ourselves or to enroll in a commercial diaper service. All of our neighbors recommended a commercial service. So, despite our meager income, we enrolled in a local company's program. Once a week, they delivered a stack of clean cloth diapers and took away a load of dirty diapers that had been stashed into a bucket with a tightly fitting lid. Near the end of the week, the dirty diapers usually began to emit a smell like ammonia, despite the lid, so we were always glad when the "diaper man" came to take them away. There were several other diapering challenges that most other parents and babysitters seemed to know: how to fit the diaper tightly enough to keep the mess from dripping down the legs and onto everything surrounding the baby; how to avoid sticking the diapers' safety pin into soft skin—the baby's or ours; how to stand back quickly if the little guy decided to pee (usually straight up into the air) while the diaper was off; how to treat the inevitable diaper rash; and so forth. Sigh. As parents, we were so young and naive. But we learned.

Significantly, Harvard paid all expenses of the child's birth: doctors' bills, hospital fees, everything. And they paid all costs of follow up care with a renowned pediatrician at the best children's hospital in the nation, Boston Children's Hospital. We paid nothing. In fact, the costs of having a child never entered my mind. Looking back, I marvel at this perquisite of being a Harvard student. Free health care for the entire family: wife, baby, and me. No co-pay, no costs to me whatsoever. Privilege, indeed.

Despite the extra burden of helping care for a baby and holding a two part-time jobs, my junior year went smoothly. Without the distractions of singing, my grades improved. Indeed, for the first time, I got more A's than B's. Most importantly, I earned a B in the feared organic chemistry course.

Moreover, thanks to Dudley House financial support, Jane and I were growing up socially. Among other advantages, Dudley provided us with an occasional $10 stipend (worth about $100 in 2024) to host a dinner party for three other Dudley House couples; these round-robin affairs honed our social skills and allowed us to enjoy high-quality home-made dinners and wines that we might not otherwise have been able to afford. As young couples, we all worked resolutely to imbue elegance to these events: fine sherry aperitifs, one or two bottles of French wine (recommended by the nearby liquor shop owner), properly set tableware, semi-formal dinner attire, fresh flowers on the table, and so forth. Usually sometime during the evening, we discussed various rules of etiquette (according to Emily Post and Amy Vanderbilt) for these festive dinners. We were entering a privileged social environment and wanted to get it right.

The academic year seemed to pass by quickly. Soon it was over. During the ensuing summer between my junior and senior years, I took on another job—my third—as an applications programmer with the Center for Population Studies, under the direction of Dr. David Heer. My assigned task was to develop a Monte Carlo simulation of population growth under varying levels of economic prosperity. With my now vastly improved statistics background and computer programming experience, I made good progress on the assignment, but I hadn't completed it by the end of the summer. So, Dr. Heer asked me to remain on the job part time through the next academic year. Gladly. It paid well and didn't take too much time.

With my three jobs, we were now more comfortable financially. Indeed, we could now afford a telephone. Nonetheless, I took out another $1000 loan, figuring that if we didn't need the money, we could easily repay it when repayment came due. As a young couple with a child, we were "getting on our feet," so to speak.

Fate intervened at one point when Tilly Edinger was struck and killed by a garbage truck as she crossed a street near the Museum of Comparative Zoology. Although I still had about one hundred bibliographic entries to type, the museum director chose to terminate the project. With sadness, I gave him the remaining, untyped entries, leaving me with only two jobs. But that was okay; I could certainly use the time for studying. In retrospect, I had learned a few things from Tilly while typing these annotated entries. Most notable was that intelligence (including human) didn't correlate with brain size. Never did, most probably never will.

Academically, my senior year started without fanfare. I took several notoriously difficult courses: cell biology, genetics, two upper-level math courses, and the infamous full-year physics course. I plunged ahead, and ultimately did reasonably well in all of them. As the semester progressed, I had to plan for my future. Foremost in my plans was medical school, so I applied to two of them, Harvard and the University of Colorado as a backup, and was admitted by both schools. Jane also planned for her future by applying to several top-quality Boston-area colleges (Wellesley, Simmons, et cetera) where she could complete her undergraduate studies if we stayed in Boston. For some reason, she was not accepted by any of these prestigious Boston-area schools. Oh well. She could always apply to Boston University or Northeastern University.

Once again, fate intervened into our future plans. Its intervention began when a neighbor in Peabody Terrace, a newly minted M.D. doing his internship at Boston City Hospital, invited me to join him in the emergency room the evening of St. Patrick's Day. Why not? So, I put on my white, stained chemistry lab coat and followed him around as he treated various wounds inflicted by gunshots, broken beer bottles, and other weapons of drunken combat. Late in the evening, a disheveled man came in complaining of abdominal pains. My friend took me aside and explained that this man, Joe, came every night hoping to stay in the hospital long enough to get a free meal. "But, we'll get rid of him." Returning to Joe, he said: "I think that you may have a prostate problem. My colleague here will check your prostate. Now, roll on your side." Then he gave me a latex glove and a tube of petroleum jelly. "Put this jelly on your right index finger and insert it into his rectum. All the way." Whoa. I wasn't prepared for this, but he coaxed me into inserting my finger and probing around. Afterwards, my friend explained: "Joe, my colleague couldn't find anything wrong with you. So you've got to leave." Disappointed, Joe stumbled back out onto the streets of Boston.

When I went home early the next morning, I felt revulsion at that entire experience. I had participated in the abuse of another person, a helpless person at that. And I had broken whatever laws regulate medical practice by non-licensed individuals. Notably, I can't remember my friend's name, which is unusual during the traveling. I attribute this lapse of detail to my revulsion at the entire episode.

After this, I began to lose interest in the medical profession. I had envisioned a career on convergent railroad tracks: medical school, internship, residency, compulsory military service, private practice, big house, fancy car, prestigious country club, and so on. But now, my vision changed; I wanted a less structured future, with some turbulence along the way. So, I applied at the last minute to a Ph.D. program in biology at Stanford University (returning to my western roots), and Jane applied to their undergraduate program. We both were admitted with full financial support. This was a tremendous opportunity for Jane to finish her undergraduate degree at a top-notch university, so I turned down the medical schools, and we accepted admission to Stanford. I was particularly pleased, because I would be working in the laboratory of a well-known evolutionary biologist, Paul Ehrlich, on quantitative models of animal populations. California, here we come!

After graduation, which my brother and mother attended, Jane and I stayed in Cambridge for the summer. Harvard continued to provide free housing, and I still had work to complete on my Monte Carlo simulation. Jane worked in a trendy clothing store on Harvard Square. So, we had sufficient money to establish a savings account. Ho; our first savings account. Besides our job-related income, I received a $1500 prize for my performance in second-semester physics.

And, most significantly, I learned that I would not have to repay any of the loans that I had taken out as a Harvard student if I continued to work in a scientific field (including graduate school) for at least five years. Although I didn't know at the time, the loans proved to be a good choice financially, for they were guaranteed by the National Defense Education Act (NDEA), which had passed following the Soviet Union's launch of the first artificial satellite Sputnik in 1957. Fearing Soviet advancement in the Cold War, Congress passed this act to encourage more students in the United States to pursue careers in science. Among other features, this act provided for a waiver of loan interest or principal payment for five years following graduation if the recipient studied or worked in science-related fields and, at the end of the fifth year, it provided complete forgiveness of the loan. In other words, if I pursued a scientific career for at least five years after graduation (which I intended to do) this was free money. Thus, for all intents and purposes, with the extra loan money that I had borrowed from Harvard during the past several years, Harvard was covering the entire imputed cost of my education. And more.

So, barring any unforeseen complications, all of the loan money that I had deposited in a savings account was now ours to keep. Several thousand dollars! For the first time in our marriage, money ceased to be an issue for us. In our minds, we were rich. Fate was treating us kindly.

Stanford

September arrived, and we drove out to Stanford with a brief stopover in Colorado Springs. We first gazed on the Stanford campus as we drove through the eucalyptus and palm trees to the main quad. What a different world this was: idyllic! Surrounded by such beauty and intoxicating weather, I wondered how anybody could concentrate on scholarly matters. Indeed, how could I take Stanford seriously after graduating from Harvard, with its big-city grime and gruesome winter weather?

Within an hour or so after our arrival, the university had assigned us a furnished two-bedroom apartment in the married graduate-student housing complex, Escondido Village. The location was perfect; we could easily ride bicycles to the main campus. And, there were many other young families who willingly participated in shared child-care whenever neither of us could be home.

Financially, we were secure. I had won a four-year graduate fellowship from the National Institutes of Health, which was enough to pay tuition, rent, car insurance, and other discretionary expenses, such as going out to restaurants once or twice a week, buying a new stereo system, and the occasional bottle of wine. Moreover, Stanford had provided Jane a full scholarship until she completed her degree. We were set comfortably. Nonetheless, I continued to take out NDEA-guaranteed university loans, which I deposited in our savings account, knowing that I wouldn't have to pay them back.

We enjoyed an active social life with the other young parents. This was the "age of Aquarius," with hippies, communes, great rock and roll music, and so forth. And the San Francisco Bay Area was at the epicenter of these new cultural phenomena. Accordingly, we drove up to San Francisco regularly to visit the renowned Haight Ashbury neighborhood with all of its long-haired hippies, North Beach with its topless go-go dancers, and the City's generally marijuana-intoxicated ambience.

One of the highlights of our social life at both Stanford (and, for that matter, Harvard) occurred whenever Mohammad Ali (formerly Cassius Clay) fought to defend or recapture his world heavyweight boxing championship. These momentous events usually occurred about twice every year. "Watch parties" were organized weeks in advance with a handful of couples who prepared delicious food (mainly of the heavy hors d'oeuvres variety), to be enjoyed with copious amounts of beer and wine. The televised spectacle usually began at about 10:00 p.m., with Howard Cossell taunting Ali just before his walk to the ring. Ali: "It's hard to be humble when you're as great as I am." "[I'll] float like a butterfly, sting like a bee." "It's hard to hit what you can't see." Oh, we all loved the show. The memories of these extravaganzas still bring a smile to my face.

Few other boxers commanded such anticipated "watch parties." The main exception was Sugar Ray Leonard, the colorful welterweight champion. One of his most memorable matches, again with Howard Cossell on hand, was the championship fight against Roberto Duran when, in the eighth round, Duran turned to the referee and said "No mas." Duran just stopped boxing; he'd had enough. That singular phrase "no mas" became a well-used part of our vocabulary for the next several decades. Those were heady years in boxing, but they were also the beginning of the sport's twilight as the champions retired and public interest in its brutality waned.

The traveling took me to my early interest in boxing. It began in childhood with my father teaching Curtis and me how to box according to the Marquess of Queensbury rules and the classic routine: left jab, right cross, left uppercut. Left jab, right cross, et cetera. I enjoyed the lessons but I didn't enjoy the prospect of getting hurt—punched in the nose, for example. I was definitely a spectator of this sport, not a participant. And, in that regard, I seldom missed The Friday Night Fights, sponsored by Pabst Blue Ribbon beer. Curtis and I huddled in front of our small (12 inch) black and white television screen to watch our favorite boxers: Rocky Marciano, Sugar Ray Robinson, and the like. We expected them to dominate their opponents, and most of them did. And there were lots of lesser boxers who filled the void between the occasional championship bouts. These boxing matches dominated Monday conversations at school with our classmates who had also watched intently. The older folks (our parents, grown-up neighbors, and so forth) had their favorites as well: Joe Louis, Rocky Graziano, et alia. We had heard of them and seen them box in movie newsreels, but they didn't excite us like the heroes of our era did.

Other sports began to appear on television in those childhood years. Football, for one, grabbed our interest. I remember many cold, snowy Sundays watching the original National Football League teams play each other in boring ground games. Three yards and a pile of dust. The forward pass was not en vogue yet; that didn't catch on until years later when the American Football League came on the scene with quarterbacks like Joe Namath. We had our favorite players: Otto Graham, "Crazy Legs" Hirsch, et cetera. Baseball began to appear on weekends as well. We watched our heroes: Mickey Mantle, Duke Snider, Yogi Berra, and others. There were three New York teams in those days: the Yankees, the Dodgers, and the Giants. Inevitably, the Yankees would play in the World Series and usually win the championship. Reflexively, I disliked the Yankees. Let somebody else win for a change. But that wasn't going to happen. Not with their talent. Ditto for the University of Oklahoma which dominated college football, and for the Montreal Canadiens which dominated the National Hockey League. There was an element of comforting predictability to the dominance of these teams.

Returning to my years at Stanford: at this point, I should add that the Vietnam War raged during my four years there. The San Francisco Bay Area was a hotbed of protest against this increasingly unpopular war. Protests at the University of California, Berkeley grabbed national attention for their acrimony. The anti-war movement was less acrimonious at Stanford, but it was nonetheless a disturbing presence on campus. For most male students, the possibility of being drafted loomed ominously, for that meant dropping out of school for military service, most probably in Vietnam. I had several Stanford classmates who were drafted and several others who burned their draft cards and fled to Canada to avoid induction. Either way, their graduate school career was interrupted, perhaps forever.

Stepping back in time for a moment, like all males my age, I had to register with the Selective Service when I was 18 years old. Initially, I was classified I-A, Available for Military Service. At the time, the Colorado Springs draft board, which controlled my fate in the draft, granted me a deferment because I was a college student. However, when I took my leave of absence from Harvard, the draft board cancelled my deferment, and I was again a prime candidate for the draft. Fortunately, Bill Osburn convinced the draft board that my work studying Chinese nuclear fallout was of greater value to the country than military service. So, I was reclassified to II-A, an occupational deferment. When I returned to Harvard with Jane, I was again classified I-A, but the military was not drafting married men at that time. As the war progressed, married men became subject to the draft, but by then, I was a father, which again excluded me from the draft. A bit later, in 1969, while I was at Stanford, the Selective Service resorted to a lottery based on birthdays to determine who would be drafted. Married with children made no difference. My number was 308; the cutoff was 304, so once again, I avoided the draft. In 1970, I turned 26 years old, the upper age limit for the draft. I no longer had to worry about that potential disruption to my education and family. To celebrate my birthday, I disingenuously burned my I-A draft card over a candle flame at a nice Mexican restaurant near the Stanford campus.

Despite the distractions of raising a child and the war, Jane did quite well academically, which impressed me. She got nearly all A's. With her transfer credits from the University of Denver and a couple of Harvard Extension courses that she had taken at night, she was able to graduate with honors in two years. Her graduation was a very special occasion in my mind, for it closed the gap in her education that I had imposed on Jane by getting her pregnant. "But she was equally responsible for getting pregnant," it might be said. Yes, I agree. But, I had carried the subtle guilt of having the privilege of returning to Harvard to complete my undergraduate degree while she remained at home to care for our child. Now, that wrong was righted. And at a great university, Stanford, nonetheless.

Shortly before Jane's graduation, we decided to have another child. After minimal effort, she became pregnant and delivered our second son, Corey, in August, 1969. Unlike Boston-Lying-In hospital, Stanford University hospital welcomed me into the delivery room, and I watched the entire delivery. This time when we took him home, we knew what to do. We were now experienced parents of two joyful children.

Our joy soon dissipated, however, for Corey's head was outgrowing his overall body size. This continued for a couple of months, leading to a prognosis of hydrocephalus due to a blockage somewhere in the ventricles — the canals — in the brain, causing a buildup of cerebrospinal fluid, thus expanding the skull size. Jane and I were devastated with that possibility. The only solution was to locate the blockage and then remove it surgically. Of course, this posed any number of imaginable bad outcomes. The chief neurosurgeon arranged for a pneumoencephalogram: inject a small bubble of air in the lower spinal column and watch its progression through the brain until it reached the blockage site. Then, he would surgically open the site, relieving the pressure. Several days before this procedure, the doctor made a pre-operative measurement of Corey's head. Whoa. It hadn't grown since the previous week's measurement. So, he delayed the procedure for a week. Again, he measured the head size just before the procedure, and the head still hadn't grown any more. Delay another week. And so it went for about a month; Corey's head had stopped growing, and his body size grew into his now stabilized head size. Ultimately, the doctor declared the problem resolved. Corey simply had a big — but not too big — head. The case was closed, and, of course, we were quite relieved. We now had our young healthy family intact.

As at Harvard, we incurred no costs for the child birth and subsequent neurosurgical and pediatric care. And, as before, money never entered my mind. With no paperwork on my part, Stanford picked up the bills, never informing me of the amounts or the payments. The fates of privilege continued to favor us.

Unlike Jane, I did less well academically at Stanford, mainly because I wasn't entirely committed to a career in biology. I found mathematics and statistics more interesting. Hoping ultimately to reconcile these divergent interests, during the first year I took three graduate-level biology courses: vertebrate morphology, evolutionary biology, and neurobiology. In addition, I took courses in stochastic processes, statistical inference, and linear algebra. I didn't perform particularly well in any of them; in fact, I nearly flunked stochastic processes, barely managing to get a B- in the course. In retrospect, I shudder at that grade, for if it had been any lower (a C+ or lower), I would have been placed on academic probation at best and dismissed from graduate school at worst. That was a close call, to say the least.

Also in the first year, I began my Ph.D. research program in evolutionary biology under the direction of Dr. Paul Ehrlich. He assigned me a research topic that required development of a Monte Carlo simulation of animal populations. This assignment pleased me, for it built upon my Harvard experience with Monte Carlo simulations and, importantly, provided an opportunity to link my interests in biology and statistics. At the same time, he paired me with a senior graduate student to collect butterflies as part of the laboratory's major research program on butterfly behavior. I didn't enjoy running around a hillside catching butterflies in a net. Not at all. But that was how the laboratory members gathered data for their subsequent analyses—statistical and otherwise. So, despite my eagerness to continue working on statistical models of animal populations, I informed Professor Ehrlich that I planned to transfer out of his evolutionary biology program at the end of the first year. I wasn't cut out to be a butterfly chaser.

But, where would I go from there? I contemplated the Statistics Department, but I wasn't confident in my skills as an academic statistician. Not after the near debacle in stochastic processes. I contemplated medical school, but Stanford Medical School required five years for the M.D. degree; I didn't want to prolong my graduate education by another couple of years. No, I should stay in biology. Although I had taken only the single course in neurobiology, that field seemed to be more to my liking than evolutionary biology. So, at the beginning of my second year, I chose to join the neurobiology program directed by Professor Donald Wilson, who had taught several mathematically related topics in the neurobiology course. To supplement my knowledge base, I promptly took three neuroscience courses offered to first-year medical students. These courses provided broad descriptions of human brain anatomy and physiology and introduced me to experimental approaches for measuring brain activity in cats and monkeys. All of that seemed interesting and far more relevant than chasing butterflies. Notably, at the end of the second year, with only a marginal background in biology, I managed to pass the biology department's Ph.D. preliminary qualifying exam, which enabled me to receive an M.A. in biology.

In those days, Wilson and numerous other neurobiologists around the world posited that to understand the human nervous system it was first necessary to understand the nervous systems of simpler organisms, invertebrates such as crayfish, locusts, fruit flies, and the like. With a few notable exceptions, invertebrate neurophysiologists were at the forefront, the "cutting edge," of the neuroscience field in those days. Accordingly, as a thesis topic, I chose to study the cellular basis of muscle control in the crayfish claw. Studying the crayfish seemed less relevant than the medical school approach to the nervous system, but Wilson and another professor in the department, Donald Kennedy, had international reputations in this particular area of research. Consequently, they attracted numerous highly qualified graduate students, postdoctoral fellows, and visiting scholars. Many of them, including Kennedy, had Harvard degrees, so I felt a kinship in this environment. Moreover, the laboratory work, recording electrical activity in single nerve cells, and the statistical analysis of the data appealed to me.

Right from the beginning, Wilson introduced me to neurophysiological recording techniques. He stood behind me as I learned how to make electrodes, insert them via a micromanipulator into a muscle or nerve, stimulate the nerves, and record their electrical activity using an amplifier and oscilloscope. This sure beat chasing butterflies. Within a year, with his help, I had generated the data needed for a publication. I was doing okay.

A curious event complicated this beginning in Wilson's laboratory: Wilson left his wife and four young children for a second-year graduate student in Kennedy's laboratory, Rebecca. I don't know how or when the romance started, but I know that it "blossomed" at a party that Jane and I gave. It was a festive party, to say the least. We had good food, lots of beer and wine, loud music of the era, a strobe light, and on and on. When Wilson arrived, the first thing he did was to sprinkle marijuana seeds in the big pot holding our rubber tree plant. With that symbolic act, the party really began. Rebecca and her husband were there, along with most of our neighbors and members of the Kennedy and Wilson laboratories. Sometime near the end of the party, Rebecca and Wilson disappeared. The next day, I heard rumors that they had both left their spouses that evening and moved together into an apartment near campus. A couple of days later, she moved from Kennedy's laboratory to Wilson's, with an office right next door to his. From that point on, Rebecca became a distraction to me—and to Wilson as well. Indeed, on more than one occasion, while he would be carefully showing me how to insert microelectrodes into a nerve or muscle, she would slip behind him, insert a lit cigarette into his mouth, and massage his neck and shoulders. After a few minutes of these pleasures, they would disappear for the rest of the day. I was left alone to finish the experiment.

Despite this distraction, I was happy with my choice of Wilson as a graduate advisor. Indeed, I was proud to be his student. When he wasn't available, I had easy access to Kennedy and his retinue for advice and companionship.

As a reward to ourselves for my new laboratory and her graduation, Jane and I traded in our Pontiac for a new Volkswagen Beetle. We had enough savings to pay cash, which set the standard for buying all of our future cars: no loans, no monthly payments, all cash up front. The Beetle was quirky to say the least: small interior, funny looks, and definitely underpowered. Indeed, when driving along the magnificent Pacific Coast Highway, I would have to accelerate the little car to maximum speed going downhill simply to have the momentum needed to climb up the next hill in anything but a crawl in low gear. But that was part of the fun of the iconic Beetle.

During my third year, I was awarded a Grass Foundation fellowship, which covered all expenses for me and my family to live in Woods Hole, Massachusetts, where I would have a laboratory in the Marine Biological Laboratory (MBL) for the summer. The Grass Foundation had arranged for us to live in a wonderful cottage in a cluster of cottages owned by the laboratory. Fortunately, a Harvard classmate of mine lent us his Saab station wagon for the entire summer while he was in Bolivia. That car made a good summer much better, for we could travel up and down Cape Cod, visiting various restaurants, lighthouses, beaches, and other quaint attractions (except on weekends when the traffic from Boston clogged all major roads). Our neighbors included my undergraduate advisor at Harvard, Professor E. O. Wilson, as well as three other Grass fellows who became colleagues for life. We all enjoyed going to the beach with our young children, eating unlimited amounts of lobster, and all of the other attractions of Cape Cod.

Unfortunately, our contentment was disrupted less than a month after we had arrived there: I received a phone call from Stanford telling me that my advisor, Don Wilson, had died in a boating accident in Idaho. With the Grass Foundation's help, I flew to Stanford, where I pieced together a plan to continue my thesis under the direction of Donald Kennedy. I would move my lab into his area and formally join his research group. This posed little difficulty, because Kennedy was renowned for his pioneering work on my thesis topic, motor control of the crayfish. Moreover, I knew all of his lab members. So, despite the tragedy, I flew back to finish the summer in Woods Hole, comfortable with what awaited me at Stanford.

My research progressed smoothly. The MBL was an ideal environment for experiments, and the cottage was a quiet place to analyze data with few distractions—except for the occasional raccoon or skunk searching for the remnants of our lobster dinner in an overturned garbage can. After I returned to Stanford, I managed to complete my thesis quickly. Although I was not well prepared academically in the fundamentals of cellular neuroscience, I passed my thesis defense in December, 1970, slightly less than three and a half years after I began, and formally received my Ph.D. at the next formal commencement in early January, 1971.

Shortly before getting my degree, I received two pieces of good news. First, I was awarded a National Institutes of Health post-doctoral fellowship in biostatistics, starting right after my pre-doctoral fellowship terminated when I received my degree. Although officially I became a member of the Statistics Department, which administered the award, Kennedy allowed me to retain my office in his laboratory during this period and appointed me a lecturer in the department in return for my teaching in the neurobiology course. Second, the Helen Hay Whitney Foundation awarded me a three-year postdoctoral fellowship to any laboratory in the world. The foundation would pay all expenses: a generous salary, travel, and a $10,000 stipend each year for my research program to the laboratory I chose to study in. This was a stupendous stroke of good fortune. We could move to Europe, see the world. Accordingly, I arranged to begin a one-to-two year fellowship in the laboratory of Dr. Anders Lundberg, director of the Physiology Institute at the University of Gothenburg, Sweden, starting in July, 1971. That would allow me six months in the statistics department and time to learn rudimentary Swedish. The future looked bright, very bright for us.

The brightness dimmed after a couple of months in the statistics department, however. While preparing to give a departmental seminar on my thesis, I discovered that the computer program that I had written to analyze my data contained an error, a serious error affecting my thesis and the two manuscripts that I had submitted for publication. I told Kennedy about this disaster, and he just slumped in his chair, saying nothing for a while. Finally, he told me not to correct the thesis; "It has already been filed with the library and, besides, nobody reads theses anyway." But I must withdraw the manuscripts before they were published. So, I informed the journal (the *Journal of Neurophysiology*), which promptly took them out of the publication queue. I quickly corrected the computer program, reanalyzed my data, and prepared a revised manuscript which the *Journal* readily accepted for publication. Years later, I tossed my bound thesis, a source of embarrassment, into the trash.

I was quite proud of my affiliation with the statistics department. It was, after all, one of the best departments in the country—if not the world. Whenever the Stanford statistics department hosted the University of California, Berkeley, statistics department faculty members for a seminar, at least half of the leading statisticians in the world would be in the room. They all sat in the auditorium according to a rigid protocol: full professors in the front row, associate professors about a third of the way back, the assistant professors about two-thirds of the way back, and the graduate students in the back rows. I was the only postdoctoral fellow in the audience and sat alone midway between the assistant professors and the graduate students. In addition, there was an acknowledged "peck order" among the faculty members according to presumptive intelligence. All of this formality differed greatly from the casual ambience of the biology department. I still smile when thinking about it.

In retrospect, I wasn't a great statistician, despite my considerable training. In fact, I wasn't a particularly good statistician by Stanford's standards. But I was good enough to earn the respect of my colleagues, who regularly taught me "tricks of the trade." I thought about getting an M.S. in statistics while I was there, but the qualifying exam occurred after our planned departure for Sweden. So, that never happened.

An unusual opportunity arose during that last spring at Stanford: a wine appreciation course. This was not just any wine appreciation course. It was quite remarkable. The instructor was Dr. Peter Ray, a professor of plant physiology in the Stanford biology department. In fact, his office was right across the hall from mine. Peter, as we called him, came with unique credentials to teach about wine. For starters, as a plant physiologist, he understood the biochemistry and physiology of grapes and winemaking. But, he had another incredible advantage: his father, Martin Ray, was one of the premier American winemakers. Indeed, his winery on Mt. Eden, just south of Stanford, produced some of the finest wines in the world. And, as his son, Peter learned to appreciate the nuances of very good wines.

For the first (and perhaps only) time in his career, Peter offered to teach a course for eight advanced graduate students in biology. And, as a postdoctoral fellow, I was asked to be his assistant. The course would not be cheap. We all had to pay $45 (about $365 in 2024) to cover the cost of the wines. Now, Peter had several very strict rules that must be followed. Everyone must take a shower shortly before the class session. And no perfumes. Otherwise, it may prove difficult to appreciate the delicate smells (the "nose" as it's called) of the wine. Apropos smelling the wine: we all had to buy four large fine crystal wine glasses (chosen by Peter) for swirling the wine to appreciate its "nose" before the tasting. "Fine wines deserve fine stemware." And, finally, spouses and significant others were not allowed in the class.

When it came to the wines, Peter concentrated only on French reds and whites from the Bordeaux and Burgundy regions. In his opinion, except for his father's wines, they were unarguably the best in the world. So, each week, I would accompany him to Beltramo's, a high-end wine purveyor in nearby Menlo Park, where he would buy the very best wines in the store (Château Lafite Rothschild, Château Petrus, Domaine de la Romanée-Conti, and the like). Usually, he chose more than one vintage of the same wine. As his assistant, I had to carry the cases of wine to his car and then into the biology building. During the class, we would study these wines, comparing them side by side. Notably, Peter insisted that it took more than a casual sip to understand a wine, so we always poured sizeable amounts in each glass. In fact, after each class, we were all quite inebriated. Jane was incredibly tolerant of these bacchanalian evenings.

At the end of the eight-week course, Peter hosted a party at his father's vineyard. We could all bring our spouses. Moreover, he assigned specific French food courses for us to bring. Accordingly, the spouses (mostly wives) got together to prepare the feast. Jane prepared boeuf bourguignon, other wives prepared boiled potatoes, Caesar salads, a gateau for dessert, and an Exploreteur cheese plate. The highlights of the evening were the rare Martin Ray wines that Peter brought from the winery's cellars. They were stunningly delicious. And, there were a lot of them to enjoy. My favorite was the 1948 Mariage, which was my introduction to well-aged wines. By evening's end, in a drunken stupor, we all drove our cars down the narrow mountain road and then on home. When somebody drove off the road, which happened several times, Peter, who was no more sober than we were, pulled the car out of the ditch using the winery's tractor. Thus ended the course in wine appreciation, a course that prepared me for many happy evenings in the future.

  As summer approached, Jane and I began to prepare for the European adventure. We had Swedish neighbors in student housing who taught us basic Swedish language and etiquette. We gave our Volkswagen Beetle to Jane's mother in Colorado Springs and bought a new Saab that we would pick up in Stockholm and drive to Gothenburg. Another Swedish friend of ours arranged for her sister to pick us up at the airport in Stockholm and drive us to our hotel and then to the Saab dealership to pick up our new car. In early May, we moved from Stanford to Colorado Springs, where we stayed with my mother for a month. During this time, we visited our family members, packed and re-packed our suitcases, studied Swedish, and managed our anxiety about the move. On two occasions, I had to return to Stanford for departmental business, such as picking up a paycheck or completing a teaching or course assignment. Despite these obligations, my mind was on Sweden.

Gothenburg

Finally, the departure day arrived. We flew to Stockholm without any difficulties. I will forever remember my excitement at the view of Bergen, Norway, as the plane landed for a stopover: the red tiled roofs, the blue water in the magnificent fjords, the green fields. When we arrived in Stockholm, we were picked up as scheduled, delivered to our hotel, and, the next morning, to the Saab dealership where we picked up our new car. With a map in hand, off we went, driving to Gothenburg, our new home. Along the way, we discovered that our rudimentary Swedish helped a bit but not enough to carry on a conversation.

In Gothenburg, we drove straight to Professor Lundberg's office in the Physiology Institute at the University of Gothenburg. To our relief, everybody in the institute spoke good fluent English, which greatly eased the inherent difficulties of moving to a foreign country. The office assistant, Brigitta, also eased our arrival by arranging for us to stay in student housing while she looked for an apartment. In a stroke of good fortune, she found a quaint house in a beautiful neighborhood (Landala Egnahem) near the institute. Indeed, it was an easy walk. The house belonged to the president of Husqvarna, who was going to Denmark for a couple of years, and it was furnished magnificently: beautiful antique furniture, crystal glasses, bone china, and so forth. And there was a fenced yard with beautiful rose gardens where the children could play. In our minds, this was perfect. Adding to the sense of perfection, the house was only two blocks from an English-speaking elementary school catering to the British residents in

Gothenburg. The school offered Curtis, who would be in the first grade, a full scholarship. It proved to be excellent educationally. The children learned to read from simplified versions of classic British literature: Shakespeare, Dickens, and the like. None of the simplistic American "Dick and Jane" stories.

Shortly after our arrival, the Swedish government presented us a most unexpected gift: money. On my first day in the institute, Brigitta handed me several forms to fill out, with her help. She then directed me to a downtown governmental office of some sort, where I handed over the forms, signed several other undecipherable documents, and received a stamp in my passport. Several weeks later, we received two sizeable checks—enough to double our fellowship stipend, which was quite generous. I asked Brigitta why we had received these checks, and she explained that they were standard income and child-care stipends. "Should I return them?" "No. You're entitled to them." For the duration of our stay in Sweden, we received these stipends every month. Jane and I could now live very comfortably without worrying about money.

Within our first week in Gothenburg, I discovered that the Swedish government presented us with another unexpected gift: affordable fine wines. For years, the Swedish government controlled the alcoholic beverage industry to regulate consumption and maintain affordable prices. Accordingly, the government would buy French wine by the barrel directly from the wineries, bottle it in Sweden, store it for aging in cellars underneath Stockholm, and finally put it on the market when it was fully aged. In 1962, a great year for French Bordeaux wines, the government used slightly shorter corks to save money. Nine years later, just before we arrived, the government realized that the shorter corks allowed too much oxygen to diffuse into the bottles. Within the next few years, all of these fine wines would probably turn to vinegar due to excessive oxidation. They must be enjoyed before this tragedy happened. So, the government flooded wine stores with bottles of 1962 French Bordeaux wines, including the very finest, at fire-sale prices. After my Stanford wine appreciation course, I knew exactly what a bargain these wines were, so we bought many, many bottles of these premium wines and drank them in excess from the beautiful crystal stemware in our house. My Swedish education had begun.

That first week after our arrival, before formal training began, most of the institute researchers went to Moscow for a scientific meeting. Because we were new to the institute, we were not registered for the conference and, therefore, could not join them. No problem. After hiring a babysitter from a professional agency, we used the opportunity to arrange a tour to Marrakech, Morocco, with a local travel agency. What an adventure that was: visiting the bazaar with its exotic sights and smells, traveling into the nearby Atlas Mountains, hearing the call to prayers, and so forth.

After we had returned from Marrakech and the rest of the institute members had returned from Moscow, the laboratory immediately woke up, so to speak. Because there were five newcomers, in the first week there was a training session on how to use the electronic equipment: amplifiers, stimulators, and so forth. Although I used simple versions of this kind of equipment during my doctoral research, I had no experience with the more sophisticated electronic devices used in the institute. Oh well, I would learn how to use them. In addition, there were several seminars by senior members of the institute, where they described their own projects studying how vertebrates (mainly cats) control their limbs while walking. Again, I had no experience in vertebrate motor control. Moreover, most of the laboratory researchers were medical doctors, M.D.s, so they knew the vertebrate anatomy and physiology quite well. My thesis work on invertebrates seemed trivially naive compared to the complexities of these studies on mammals. Of course, I had read articles on the subject before coming to Sweden, hoping to familiarize myself with the scientific issues and the technical procedures for addressing them. To my dismay, however, I found them devilishly difficult to understand. In short, I realized that I was inadequately prepared for the work in the institute. Nonetheless, here I was; I had to overcome this huge handicap.

For my first project, Professor Lundberg, Anders as most of the institute members called him, assigned me to work with Bill Roberts, an assistant professor on leave from the University of Minnesota, to characterize a technical aspect of nerve stimulation procedures used in the laboratory. Bill was very patient with me as he explained the technical issue we were studying. My shortcomings became quite evident during our first experiment. The initial steps were to fetch a cat, anesthetize it, insert a breathing tube attached to a ventilator, attach blood pressure and temperature monitors, and surgically expose the major hind leg nerves and the lumbar spinal cord. All of this took about six hours. Even with the help of two well-trained technicians, I could not have done any of these procedures, not even fetching the feisty cat which usually sensed what lay in its immediate future. So, I was little more than a spectator as the technicians set up the experiment until about three in the afternoon when the actual recordings began. Bill sat at the controls: electrode insertion, amplifiers, stimulators, and recording devices. I sat looking over the cat to monitor its anesthesia and blood pressure and to record data in a bound lab notebook. As I discovered, experiments generally lasted about 24 hours—non-stop. I certainly wasn't prepared for this. But, I had no choice. Finally, at 7 o'clock the next morning, we concluded the experiment and went home. But only for a couple of hours, for we were expected back in the institute no later than 10 o'clock a.m. to report on the results of the experiment to Anders. After our meeting, we were expected to analyze our results and record them in a written log book. Finally, at about four or five that afternoon, I could go home, exhausted. The next day, I was back in the laboratory for another experiment. Altogether, there were usually three experiments per week. There was no reprieve from this demanding schedule.

After a couple of months, Bill and I had sufficient data to prepare a manuscript for publication. Although I didn't really understand the physiological background of our study yet, I could at least analyze our data statistically. With Bill as the primary author, after some floundering we produced a publishable manuscript, my first in vertebrate physiology. Although my contributions were limited, I took pride in this publication.

Regardless of our accomplishment, Anders wasn't happy with my progress. Indeed, he was quite unhappy. In one meeting, he explained that he had agreed to accept me into his laboratory as a favor to Don Wilson, my deceased thesis advisor. He didn't need to explain the meaning of his comment; he expected much more from me. After all, I still couldn't prepare and dissect a cat without considerable help nor could I competently operate the electronic equipment.

To remedy my shortcomings, he assigned me to work with Elzbieta Jankowska, one of the most respected members of the institute and certainly one of the most reticent. At least she was reticent with me, the cocky Californian. According to Bill, Elzbieta's reticence derived most probably from her childhood in Poland. During World War II, she and her mother fled to Sweden, where Elzbieta grew up and established her career in Gothenburg. Whenever I asked her about her past, Elzbieta just shrugged and said nothing. So, I stopped asking, which was just as well, for I sensed that she disapproved of me in many ways—my American brashness, my incompetence as a researcher, and nearly everything else about me.

With Elzbieta firmly in charge, we began a study of neuron connections in the spinal cord. The procedures were the same as with Bill: technicians prepared the cat, Elzbieta controlled the equipment, and I monitored the cat's health and recorded data. Gradually, after about ten experiments, she allowed me to perform the laminectomies that exposed the spinal cord since I had been practicing that delicate procedure on cat cadavers. But she never allowed (that is, trusted) me to operate the equipment. Under her watchful eyes, she did, however, entrust me to analyze all of the experimental data and to write the first draft of our manuscript describing our results. The published manuscript was well received in the tightknit community of spinal cord researchers, which made me quite proud. As we continued to work together, I began to realize how much Elzbieta was teaching me: teaching me how to be a disciplined neurophysiology researcher. With this realization, I developed a strong appreciation and respect for her; ultimately, as I matured scientifically, we became good friends.

After a successful collaboration with Elzbieta, Anders assigned me to a project with a young Swedish researcher, Sten Grillner. Sten proposed to study an arcane topic, the small, brief after-hyperpolarization at the tail end of a motor nerve action potential. Does it affect the control of leg movements in the cat? I found the project uninspiring from the start, but, then again, I still had a limited understanding of the field. So, we launched a proposed series of experiments, designed entirely by Sten, of course. Unfortunately, late at night during the fourth experiment, the ventilator pump for the cat's breathing broke beyond immediate repair. Sten told me to crawl under the cat, disconnect the ventilator, and breathe in and out of the ventilator tube, keeping the cat alive, while he searched the institute for a spare pump. After about half an hour of searching, he returned empty handed, sat down on a stool, and smoked a cigar while he pondered what to do. Meanwhile, I kept breathing for the cat: in and out, in and out, in and out. After another hour of this, fatigue slowed my breathing, and finally the cat died. The next morning, Anders scolded Sten and me mightily for this failure to complete the experiment. Afterwards, Sten decided to scrap the project. He was glad to get rid of me, and after the cat-ventilation debacle I was equally glad to part ways with him. Of course we remained on cordial speaking terms, but the "love" just wasn't there. Sten, by the way, went on to become a highly respected member of the Karolinska Institute. In retrospect, I am quite proud of having had the opportunity to work with him, albeit briefly.

Despite the intense laboratory schedule, Jane and I had an active social life. Every couple of months, the institute hosted a dinner party with good Swedish food and drinks. Way too many drinks, usually. At these gatherings, we learned the niceties of Swedish etiquette, which everyone observed even when highly inebriated. Also, we enjoyed the company of several couples associated with the institute, Swedish and American, and would go "out on the town" with them most weekends. Our social life extended to Oslo and Stockholm, where good friends from Stanford and Harvard, respectively, were spending the year. On several occasions we spent long weekends in their small apartments. Some weekends, we took the ferry to Denmark, exploring this neighboring country. During one vacation week, we took a tour with the boys to Tunisia. With our supplemental income from the Swedish government, we were able to enjoy the best restaurants wherever we were and, at least in Sweden, the fine 1962 wines. The pleasures of our social life blunted the displeasures of my research experiences in the laboratory.

The highlight of the institute's social activities was its annual Christmas party. It was the subject of animated conversation before and after the event. Jane and I were swept into the excitement as the party drew nearer and nearer. Finally, the day arrived. We were greeted at the front door with a large glass of punch. And then a second glass. And then another. After several more glasses of this delicious beverage, we all sat down waiting for the exquisite Christmas dinner to be served, followed by a long night of dancing and carousing. During the wait, according to Swedish custom, males would take turns raising a glass of Aquavit (Sweden's version of vodka), toast the table, and then everybody would toss down their drink in one gulp. After more than a few rounds of this, but before the dinner was served, I was shamefully inebriated. So inebriated that Jane had to haul me up to my office and "babysit" me for an hour or so before she dragged me home and put me to bed. Consequently, we missed most of the party, the party that everybody had been anticipating for the past year. Lesson learned: beware the punch.

One other monumental social event warrants mention, for I have never forgotten it: the 1971 Nobel Prize ceremony. Every year, Anders received two tickets to the awards ceremony in Stockholm. Magnanimously, he gave them by lottery to two laboratory members. To my surprise and his dismay, I won a coveted ticket. Thus, in December, I rented a tuxedo and took the train to Stockholm to attend the ceremony, which included a gala seven-course meal and copious amounts of the finest French wines. Seating at the dinner tables was assigned according to rigid protocol, with the most distinguished guests sitting closest to the king and royal family. As an American with a Ph.D., I merited a seat fairly close to the royal family — close enough to recognize Princess Christina (whom I knew from Harvard Glee Club days) but not close enough to exchange greetings. Incidentally, the other recipient of Anders' tickets was a

Taiwanese M.D., also a visiting researcher in the laboratory; he was assigned a seat at one of the tables far back in the hall, certainly too far away even to see the king.

As my first year drew to an end, I decided not to continue in Anders' laboratory. I had accomplished quite a lot: two good publications and a much improved approach to research. Moreover, I had earned membership in the informal guild of spinal cord researchers with an excellent pedigree: Sir Charles Sherrington (Nobel prize 1932), Sir John Eccles (Nobel prize 1963), Professor Anders Lundberg. Although I would certainly have benefited from another year of training there, I wanted to experience more of Europe. And, the Helen Hay Whitney Foundation would pick up the bill.

Having decided not to continue for another year in Anders' laboratory, I faced the challenge of finding somewhere else to continue my postdoctoral studies. This became a difficult challenge. Because I was still insecure about my background in neurophysiology, despite the rigorous training in Gothenburg, I gravitated initially towards less demanding topics (at least in my opinion) such as animal behavior. But, I wanted a world-class laboratory. Accordingly, I inquired about studying under Professor Konrad Lorenz, whose research on animal imprinting had become quite popular recently. (The next year, he went on to share the 1973 Nobel Prize for this work). He replied simply: "Sorry, the laboratory is full for the next two years." As an alternative, I inquired about studying biological rhythms (circadian rhythms) with a leading researcher in that field, Jürgen Aschoff. His approach involved a lot of mathematical modeling, which appealed to me. He agreed to take me into his institute, but I would be the only other member besides himself — no students, no technicians — with only a small office furnished with a desk and chair. The institute was isolated: a small Max-Planck Institute located in a small village, Erling-Andechs, located about thirty miles south of

Munich. Despite the appeal of his work, I could do better than that; I needed an active laboratory environment with numerous colleagues I could learn from. So, I kept looking.

Ultimately, I decided upon Professor Josef Dudel, who had recently published several landmark articles on the control of movement in the crayfish claw. I understood his projects and would be returning to a familiar invertebrate preparation. So, I wrote a letter of inquiry to Professor Dudel, whose address was at the Physiology Institute of the University of Heidelberg. He responded promptly offering me a position with my own laboratory setup. And, incidentally, he had just moved to Munich, where he was the new Director of the Physiology Institute of the Technical University of Munich. Now, this was more like it: a famous professor in a sizable laboratory setting at a famous university in a big city. Okay. We're going to Munich.

When I told Anders about my plans, I sensed his disappointment. Initially I thought that this was directed towards me personally. I had certainly not been his best student but I had matured into a respectable student who could have continued his legacy in a spinal cord physiology laboratory anywhere in the world. And now I was walking away from that heritage. As I thought about it, however, I rationalized that his disappointment was directed less at me than towards my choice of Germany and working with Germans. Indeed, I recalled numerous anecdotes about his heroic efforts to move threatened Jews out of Germany to safe havens in Scandinavia during World War II. By choosing Germany, once again I hadn't lived up to Anders' expectations. Or, so I thought.

Munich

In late August, 1972, Jane and I packed all of our belongings into the Saab and drove down to Munich. Along the way, we were detained for a day at the German border (Kiel) until we registered the car in Germany and attached German license plates. That task, by the way, was slow and complicated because few Germans spoke English in those days, and I couldn't speak German. With our car finally showing German registration, we continued the drive to Munich. Once there, we drove to the institute, which was associated with a major hospital, Klinikum Rechts der Isar. The institute occupied the basement, first, and third floors of a house across the street from the main hospital complex.

Professor Dudel — or, Herr Dudel, as he preferred to be called — proved to be a most cordial host. Until we found a suitable apartment, he allowed us to live temporarily in a sizeable apartment located in a university-owned small castle (the Biedersteiner Schloss) located about a mile from the institute. His junior colleague, who spoke fluent English, helped us find a long-term apartment in a quiet residential neighborhood about five miles from the institute. The distance was no problem, because a nearby streetcar line provided reliable transportation back and forth, which allowed Jane use of the car when she needed it. The apartment itself was not special; it was on the top floor of a three story building. The owner of the building, Frau Brunn, lived on the ground floor near the front door to the building. So, we encountered her frequently while coming or going but had limited conversation initially because she didn't speak fluent English. The one thing she did talk about in understandable English was exactly how to pay the rent.

Importantly, she also told us how to set up a regular beer delivery to the building's front doorstep. Yes, once every week or two, the various large breweries in Munich delivered a case of beer (containing 25 half-liter bottles) to our home and picked up the case of empty bottles from the previous delivery. Several of the breweries still used horse-drawn wagons for these deliveries. We tried all of the local brands and settled on Spaten as the best of them all. So, every two weeks, we took delivery of a case of Spaten beer and paid the bill by funds transfer at the nearby bank. Incidentally, we never failed to drink every bottle before the next delivery. This was good beer.

Despite the importance of beer deliveries, as in Sweden our first concern was a school for Curtis, who was entering the second grade. The only English-speaking school was an American school located about twenty miles away on the other side of town. Catering primarily to English-speaking businessmen, its students came from throughout the greater Munich area. So, the school arranged for bus service to transport students to and from the school. Fortunately, the school offered Curtis a full-tuition scholarship, but we had to pay for the bus service, which nearly equaled the tuition. Every day, I walked Curtis to the pickup spot, about two blocks away, and Jane walked him back home at the end of the school day. We were not very impressed with the quality of education offered by the school. Unlike the English school in Gothenburg, the American school had the students read simplistic children's books, hardly comparable to the English classics read in Sweden.

After two years in the American School, the principal told us that Curtis no longer qualified for any financial aid. We couldn't afford the exorbitant tuition, so, reluctantly, we withdrew Curtis and enrolled him in the Munich public school system. At least, he could attend a school located only two blocks from the apartment. The only problem was that Curtis didn't speak German well, and the school didn't have any formal provisions to teach him the language. Because of the language deficit, we decided to hold him back a year, repeating the third grade. Gradually, he became fluent in the language and caught up with his classmates. This was a difficult period in his young life, but he overcame the language hurdle and ultimately received a good education in the Munich public school.

We also sought a kindergarten for Corey. We decided to enroll him in a nearby private kindergarten owned and operated by a married German couple who spoke English. The tuition was very reasonable, and there were no transportation costs. Jane and I took turns walking Corey back and forth. Right away, Corey fit in, learning German from his classmates and his teachers. Importantly, he learned to read German at a young age. I remember many evenings listening to Curtis and Corey both read Asterix and Obelix comic books in German to each other. Despite a few minor setbacks, the boys seemed happy in their new home.

Jane and I had to learn German as well. Unlike Sweden where about half the population spoke English, in Germany a much smaller percentage spoke English, which limited our ability to engage with colleagues, shop in the stores, buy specific grocery items, and so forth. Although Herr Dudel and several staff members could speak English, they seldom spoke it in the institute — only German. Furthermore, most of them had little interest in teaching me the language. But, the machine shop workers took delight in teaching me German — Bavarian, that is — which they often laced with embarrassing crudities and profanities. With their help and a Berlitz German textbook, I learned the language fairly quickly. And, as I learned to speak the workshop Bavarian in the basement, my colleagues upstairs corrected my slang and dialect into proper high-German. Jane, too, learned German by taking an intensive course offered by the State of Bavaria, mainly to help foreign guest workers. Consequently, within a couple of years, the entire family was speaking German together at home.

Shortly after our arrival, Herr Dudel made our lives much more comfortable financially. When we left Sweden, we no longer received the supplemental income from the Swedish government. But, we continued to receive my monthly stipend from the Helen Hay Whitney Foundation, so we had a modest income to pay rent, and so forth. Fortunately, Herr Dudel stepped forward and appointed me as a scientific employee in the institute, which paid a salary comparable to what a German assistant professor earned. All I had to do was get a formal work permit from the Bavarian government, which I did without difficulty. Now, I was a scientific employee of the Technical University of Munich, with its health and other benefits. With two sources of income, once again we had sufficient money for a comfortable life.

With this extra income and a working knowledge of the German language, we were able to enjoy Munich and Southern Bavaria. We drove into the nearby Alps, spend one or two nights in one of guest houses, visit beer halls and wine cellars where we learned the pleasures of German wines. Occasionally, we drove into Austria and on into the South Tirol region of northern Italy. Of course, we explored the city of Munich itself, with its charming architecture and Bavarian culture, concentrating on beer halls and beer gardens, wine cellars, museums, small castles, and ornate churches. On numerous occasions, Jane and I asked Frau Brunn to keep an eye on the boys while we went to an evening concert, either in a castle courtyard, or to the Bavaria State opera. The opera was quite special, for it required the audience members to dress formally. So, I wore a tuxedo, and Jane wore a beautiful gown. Although we had been to several symphony concerts in Gothenburg, they didn't match the elaborate settings and ambience of these musical events in Munich.

Every day, the entire institute would walk across the street to the hospital cafeteria, the Mensa, as they call it in German. With few exceptions, the meals were classic German food: sauerbraten, schnitzel, sausages of one kind or another, and so forth. In a short time, I became quite familiar with German cuisine. Except for the blood sausages, I enjoyed it all. Beer was always available from a large vending machine. For the most part, only a small group of men in gray lab coats drank the beer; they were the body washers from the morgue.

Apropos lab coats: they played a significant role in the Mensa. Everybody wore a lab coat for lunch. I had found a tattered white coat in an institute store room, which suited my purpose. Or, at least I thought so for a while. After a month or two, I noticed that some people would always cut into the front of the line, without any protests. "Who are these people?" I asked. They were the doctors. "Well, I'm a doctor. I have a Ph.D." Yes, but I didn't have the right kind of lab coat. Mine had a collar; the doctors' coats didn't have a collar. I looked into this annoying situation and discovered that I needed proof of my doctorate in order to qualify for a collarless lab coat. So, I ordered a copy of my diploma from Stanford, but that wasn't enough. It had to be translated into German by an official government translator. Okay; I found a translator. Finally, after several months, I received the required approvals and, therefore, acquired a collarless lab coat, which qualified me to cut into the front of the line. Several other institute members were M.D.s with the proper lab coat, including Herr Dudel, and routinely cut in line. So, I simply joined them. Yes, I belonged to an elite group.

After lunch, the entire institute staff—less the two members of the workshop—gathered for afternoon coffee. This was an elaborate affair. The main secretary, Fraülein

Volkmann, was responsible for milling the coffee beans and then making the coffee in an automated drip machine. Only the finest coffee would do, and it must be fresh. Science was never discussed around the table, just mundane chit chat. Or, an occasional joke at my expense. At one point, I asked why the workshop men weren't invited. "Oh, they wouldn't feel comfortable." I suggested that we should at least allow them the opportunity to join us. Herr Dudel reluctantly agreed to my suggestion and instructed Fraülein Volkmann to extend the invitation. They accepted and quickly integrated themselves into the group. Notably, they spoke only the Bavarian dialect, not high German like the others. Everybody seemed to enjoy the Bavarian, which they all understood without difficulty. Only I had troubles keeping up with them at first. The coffee break usually lasted an hour, until mid-afternoon. For the staff members, that left only another hour or so before quitting time. For all intents and purposes, they accomplished very little during the afternoon.

In general, my routine in the laboratory was far more relaxed than in Sweden. Herr Dudel had a laissez faire approach to my activities. I could choose my own research projects. With this freedom, I began my research program by expanding on several studies on the crayfish nervous system derived from my Ph.D. thesis research. Because Herr Dudel used crayfish in his own research, experimental animals were always readily available. And whatever experimental apparatus I needed, Herr Dudel would either buy or, more often, direct me to the two-man machine shop in the basement to have it custom made. Moreover, they built various unique devices, such as electrode holders and so forth, that made experiments easier to perform. With their help, I made rapid progress and within a year, I had sufficient data for two publications. I was quite pleased.

Herr Dudel also arranged for his technical assistant Fraülein Hofnagel, an attractive, impish young woman, to prepare saline solutions and any photographic slides or prints that I might need. The services of Fraülein Hofnagel were a mixed blessing. Often she made mistakes in the solutions, which I would correct after she had gone home for the evening. Her help in the darkroom was also a mixed blessing. Yes, she prepared the slides and prints that I requested. In fact, she "doctored" slides and prints—removing or enhancing parts of the images—using various tricks, which improved the quality of the image. Importantly, to my knowledge, she never created false images. I often wondered if Herr Dudel knew about her tendency to make mistakes in the laboratory and to alter photographic material in the darkroom. I suspect that he did; Herr Dudel always seemed to know everything. Regardless, he certainly seemed to enjoy having her around. We all did.

Fraülein Hofnagel merits a few more words. She enjoyed telling tall tales. Who knows what stories she told other people about her background, but somehow she managed to befriend minor nobility in Munich. Baroness Ulrika for one. (I don't remember ever knowing her last name). Ulrika had a wealthy American friend, Norman, who was an archetypical rich playboy. He drove a Porsche 911 and frequented all of the upper-crust parties. At one of those parties, he met Fraülein Hofnagel—Irmgard by name in this social context. Irmgard saw an opportunity to legitimize her entry into these lofty social circles by marrying Norman. The only problem was that Norman had decidedly homosexual tendencies. No matter, he and Irmgard agreed to get married. After all, that would take the social and legal spotlight off of his homosexuality. And, Irmgard had no problem attracting other men if the need arose.

But wait. Norman had a lover, Reynaldo, who lived in Almuñecar, Spain. Reynaldo was a local entrepreneur who owned several houses and a hotel on prime property along the coast, the Costa del Sol. Coincidentally, Reynaldo had also arranged to marry a woman, namely Irmgard's friend Baroness Ulrika, presumably to conceal his homosexuality. With their interwtined proclivities, the four of them, Irmgard, Reynaldo, Norman, and Ulrika, became good friends.

Unfortunately, fate interfered rather abruptly when Norman accidentally drove his Porsche over the side of a steep cliff near Almuñecar. He died instantly. The question arose: who would inherit his sizeable estate? As Norman's lover, Reynaldo considered it his. But, what about Irmgard, Norman's betrothed? Somehow, Reynaldo had to remove her from consideration. Ah, bribery. Reynaldo offered her one of his houses in the hills above a picturesque bay near Almuñecar, if she disappeared (figuratively). Irmgard accepted the offer, agreeing to forego any claim on the estate in return for the house.

About a year later, Irmgard offered to let us live in her house for a month during the summer. Free! We accepted her offer and spent a delightful time down there. When talking with Irmgard about the wonderful house after our return, she mentioned that she still hadn't received the formal deed to the property. In fact, she had retained a lawyer to enforce her unwritten contract with Reynaldo. When the time came a couple of years later for us to leave Munich for the United States, she still hadn't resolved the issue. In fact, I suspect that she may never get title to the house. But, who knows…

Incidentally, Reynaldo married Ulrika, and together they operated a small hotel on the Costa del Sol. I'm not sure what has happened to them. But, Irmgard went onto a successful career as a photographer, producing beautiful coffee-table books featuring her photographs taken in foreign lands.

One other technical assistant in the institute, Sofia Gräfin Buckhauser, appeared in the traveling now and then.

That's right: *Countess* Buckhauser, of a noble Austrian-Hungarian family. We called her Fraülein Buckhauser, with no reference to her lofty title. Fraülein Buckhauser worked in the laboratory next door to mine, but often came to visit my laboratory. I enjoyed talking with her, mainly because she spoke fluent English and partly because she had such interesting experiences as a countess.

Take her planned wedding, for example. During my last year in the Institute (1975), Fraülein Buckhauser announced during one of our coffee sessions that she planned to get married. The lucky man was Wilhelm von Menor, the son of an Austrian countess. The formal marriage announcement arrived in the mail. It consisted of two pages. On one page, Fraülein Buckhauser's parents announced the pending marriage of their daughter, followed by her lengthy noble pedigree, going back half a dozen or so generations. On the next page, von Menor's parents made a comparable announcement along with his lengthy pedigree. When I read this announcement, I thought "Hooray. I look forward to attending this gala affair." But my enthusiasm was quickly curbed by my colleagues at the institute; they explained that the announcement was not an invitation. And, as a commoner, I could not expect to receive an invitation to an affair of this standing. Too bad.

The marriage required careful planning. First off, von Menor must ask Fraülein Buckhauser's father, Count Buckhauser, for permission to marry his daughter. That seemingly simple task was, in fact, fraught with bothersome details. According to aristocratic protocol, this must occur in the Buckhauser's family castle in Austria. But, to save money on heating and so forth, nobody lived in the castle most of the year. Consequently, the Count had to turn on the heat to warm it up for von Menor's visit. Because the castle was so large and drafty, that took nearly two weeks of constant heating. Then there was the issue with the cars. The Count drove a Volvo, but von Menor drove a Jaguar which ranked above the Volvo in the automotive peck order. According to aristocratic protocol, that won't do; the older Count must have the more prestigious automobile. So, for the visit, von Menor had to rent a Ford, which ranked lower than Volvo on the peck order. With these social issues settled, the marriage was on track.

But, fate threatened to sidetrack the planned marriage. Shortly before the eventful day, Fraülein Buckhauser learned that von Menor had recently fathered a child with one of her close friends. Oh no. That's unacceptable; Fraülein Buckhauser had no intention of mothering that child or, for that matter, ever acknowledging the child's existence. So, as a condition of her marriage with von Menor, she forbade him from ever seeing the child — and that meant never. It must be expunged from their lives. He agreed, so the marriage plans could proceed. And, in fact, they got married without further major glitches. After the wedding, I never saw the Countess again. However, many years later, I learned that von Menor died at age 45. Although I had never met him, I felt a twinge of sorrow.

Back to the laboratory: as my initial experiments wound down, Herr Dudel asked me to help a new doctoral student in the lab, Hanns Hatt, in his thesis research. Herr Dudel had assigned Hanns an interesting project studying synaptic transmission, so I agreed without hesitation. I was older and more experienced in this aspect of neurophysiology research than Hanns, but he was quite well trained. Indeed, speaking only German, we both learned from each other. Our project went smoothly. In general, Hanns, the better experimenter, gathered data, and I analyzed them, sometimes using non-trivial statistical methods. Because of his limited English, I wrote two manuscripts describing our experimental results and my analyses, which were published in a top-notch journal. Significantly, these manuscripts became the backbone of Hanns's Ph.D. thesis. After completing his

Ph.D., Hanns remained in the institute, where we continued our collaboration on synaptic transmission. Ultimately, several years later, after I had returned to the United States, Hanns had established his independent research program on olfaction, earned an M.D., and completed the requirements for a second Ph.D. Ultimately, his formal title was Dr. Dr. Dr. Hanns Hatt.

During one of our long coffee breaks at the institute, Hanns and I made an unusual discovery: axon conduction block. While studying synaptic transmission in crayfish leg muscles, we were recording electrical activity (action potentials) in the nerve terminals innervating these muscles. We had gone to lunch earlier than usual to allow time for an experiment before coffee. As it turned out, this particular experiment was quite productive; we were gathering good data, so we were reluctant to conclude it when it became time for coffee. Nonetheless, for us coffee took precedence, and we simply walked away from the experimental setup without turning anything off. When we returned about an hour later, the preparation was still intact, just as we had left it. However, we noticed that the electrical signals evoked by nerve impulses were quite different in some nerve terminals. We successfully repeated this result many times and became convinced of its reality during prolonged nerve stimulation. Hanns and I puzzled over this observation. When we first told Herr Dudel about this curious result, he immediately explained to us what we had seen: nerve terminal invasion failure. The action potential had ceased to invade all of the nerve terminals, thus altering muscle activation. Ach; why hadn't we thought of that? Hypothetically, this was due to localized buildup of potassium ions, which depolarized the surrounding nerves, rendering them unexcitable. I wrote the manuscript reporting these unique findings and continued to study the underlying physiology of the phenomenon for the next several years.

The Fates of Privilege

During my third year in Munich (1974), Herr Dudel arranged for several members of the institute—himself, Fraülein Hofnagel, Hanns, and me—to visit the Biology Department at the Hebrew University in Jerusalem. The funding for this visit derived from the Volkswagen Foundation as part of its reconciliation payments to the Jews following World War II. For a month, we would collaborate with Israeli colleagues on projects of joint interest. It was never made clear exactly what projects we would work on, but that didn't matter much. This would be an adventure, and I looked forward to the trip.

After arriving in Tel Aviv, we drove to Jerusalem. Occasionally alongside the highway, abandoned military vehicles lay rusting. Our driver explained: "Remnants of past wars." He also explained that our visit coincided with the one-year anniversary of the 1973 Yom Kippur war between Israel and several Arab states such as Egypt and Syria. Entering Jerusalem, we noticed immediately that the Israeli defense forces were on high alert. Indeed, armed policemen roamed the streets and alleys. Moreover, many civilians, both men and women, carried Uzi submachine guns slung casually over their shoulders.

We lived in the St. Andrew's Scottish Hospice located near the walled old city of Jerusalem. Hanns and I had adjoining rooms with balconies overlooking Jaffa gate. We spent many early evenings watching the Orthodox Jews going through the gate en route to the Western Wall for prayers. Although we could take our meals in the Hospice, most of the time I chose to eat at restaurants in the Arab parts of the city, namely East Jerusalem. I liked the Arab food. To get there and back, I had to walk through the mysterious Old City. Despite the general commotion of the markets and stalls with people lurking everywhere, I felt very comfortable in that environment. Hanns usually chose to eat European food in downtown Jerusalem: pastries, schnitzels, and so forth. He didn't care for the Israeli or Arab fare. But he quickly discovered the "club scene," where he enjoyed the city's night life.

The biology department was housed in the Russian Compound, not far from the old city. The building was very picturesque and replete with noteworthy history. Within the laboratories, however, we realized right away the futility of any meaningful research in the building. Fuses blew out with regularity, leaving us not only in the dark but also with no way to power our equipment. Nope; no research would occur during this visit. How disappointing. After all, that's ostensibly why we went there in the first place.

Despite the disappointment, this meant more free time to explore the city, which I enjoyed. Our hosts accommodated us further by arranging for numerous outings throughout the country: the West Bank, Jericho, the Dead Sea, the Negev desert, and on and on. Whenever we traveled outside Jerusalem, at least one armed soldier always accompanied us. During one extended sojourn, our group traveled to the university's marine biology laboratory in Eilat, where we ventured down the Sinai Peninsula for a couple of nights in Dahab. We snorkeled in the spectacular coral reefs in the Gulf of Eilat and toured up and down the Peninsula, which was occupied by the Israelis at the time. The scenery—steep red stone cliffs, Mt. Sinai, the blue waters of the Gulf—was absolutely stunning. No wonder people found closeness to God there.

During these sojourns, I wondered sometimes how comfortable our Israeli colleagues (faculty members, students, drivers, and so forth) were with the notion of hosting citizens of the country that killed six million Jews during World War II and quite possibly would have killed the other six million while they were at it if the Allies hadn't stopped them. We never discussed the matter. But I took every opportunity to point out that I was American, not German.

By and large, I enjoyed Israel. In fact, I found myself thinking that I could live in Jerusalem without hesitation. I liked the people in general and our hosts in particular. Although the facilities of the Russian Compound precluded any meaningful research efforts, the facilities of the Hadassah Medical School located several miles away on Mount Scopus provided state-of-the-art research laboratories and major equipment (freezers and so forth) for several world-class neurophysiologists in the school's physiology department. Surely I could find a research position there. But not now; I was happy in Munich. So I set those thoughts aside for consideration sometime in the future.

Near the conclusion of the institute's visit to Jerusalem, Jane arranged for a babysitter to watch the boys and flew down to join me on the return trip home. We stayed for a week in Israel so Jane could visit various tourist sites. Our flight back to Munich included an optional stop in Athens, so we spent another week exploring that city and its environs. Neither of us was particularly enthralled about Athens or Greece in general. Sure, the Acropolis and other ancient structures were worth visiting once, but they weren't inspiring. Moreover, the traffic with its noise and congestion was overwhelming. By the time we left, we looked forward to our peaceful apartment in Munich.

Shortly after our return, Herr Dudel prompted me to apply for a research grant from the German Research Foundation (the Deutsche Forschungsgemeinschaft). I complied gladly and wrote the application, in German I should add. The day before it was due, I gave it to Herr Dudel to proof read. At 5:00 p.m., as I was preparing to go home, he called me to his office. He held up my grant application and pronounced "Dies ist nur Käse": this is just cheese. He tossed it aside, told me to call Jane telling her that I wouldn't be home for dinner, and launched into a marathon session on how to write a research grant proposal: the structure, the rationale for the proposed research, the specific aims, the methods for accomplishing the aims, likely outcomes, alternative outcomes, and so forth. Importantly, he taught me how to write it myself, without incorporating any of his words or ideas. This proved to be an invaluable lesson in grant writing that benefitted me many times in the future. The application was submitted on time the next day, and I would know the outcome in about nine months. As I think about that session, I realize how very important it was for my career as a professor. Although I didn't realize it at the time, fate had smiled on me in the guise of Herr Dudel during that lesson in grant proposal writing.

I should point out that while we lived in Munich, several noteworthy events occurred. First, and most personal, my father died in December, 1972. I flew back to Colorado Springs to help my brother sort out the estate. He didn't leave a will, and we didn't hire a lawyer. We simply blundered through the probate process: inform insurance companies, pay outstanding debts, file taxes, and so forth. It was all wrapped up in about two weeks. I returned to Munich, quite saddened by the loss. Second, the Vietnam War was winding down, ever so slowly. Although we weren't impacted by the war while in Germany, it still weighed on us as Americans. We welcomed the end, regardless of the outcome. Third, Richard Nixon resigned the presidency. We had listened with interest to the various news reports about the Watergate break-in and the subsequent investigation on the local Armed Forces Radio station, located in Munich. As with the war, we welcomed the end of that unpleasant saga as well. There were other momentous world events, of course, but none that I remember as clearly as these.

And, fourth, fate introduced me to Roger Eckert who was to become quite influential in my life. Roger was a middle-aged (that is, about forty) biology professor at UCLA who was on a one-year's sabbatical in Munich at the Max-Planck Institute of Neurobiology laboratory of Dr. Dieter Lux. As a graduate student at Stanford, I had heard of Roger but had never met him until one fateful afternoon when he came to our institute in Munich to present a seminar. To my surprise, he delivered it in fluent German—German he learned as a child growing up in a German-speaking community in Massachusetts. After his presentation, Roger and I spent a couple of hours talking about Munich, a city he knew well. Several days later, he invited Jane, our boys, and me to join his wife and four boys to a local circus performance. With such a large family, we seldom all met together again, but I met with Roger alone on numerous occasions in Munich, usually when I visited his laboratory at the Max-Planck Institute.

As Roger prepared for his return to Los Angeles, he asked me what my plans were. I told him that I planned to continue working in Munich. He suggested that I might be better off professionally if I were to return to the United States. In addition, he mentioned that a temporary position might become available in the Biology Department (his department) at UCLA and that he would recommend me for it. I paid little attention to that potential opportunity, for I was quite content in Munich.

But, not long after our return from Israel, I received an offer to join the biology department at UCLA as an acting assistant professor. I would replace a professor who would be on a 12-month sabbatical leave in Bonn, Germany. This involved teaching his assigned courses, supervising his graduate students, and maintaining his laboratory. The appointment would extend from April, 1975, for one year, but I could extend it through June, 1976. I had mixed feelings about this opportunity. On the one hand, it presented a good springboard for returning to the United States. On the other hand, as a family, Jane and I enjoyed

Munich. Herr Dudel had offered me an indefinite appointment in the institute, which meant that we could stay as long as we wanted. But, without German citizenship, I had no chance of advancing in the system. Joint United States-German citizenship was not an option in those days; it had to be one or the other, and I wasn't about ready to give up my American citizenship.

Ultimately, Jane and I decided that I should accept the UCLA offer. It meant that I would have to go to Los Angeles alone until the boys' school year came to an end, which was in mid-June. Because my UCLA appointment didn't include the summer term, I would return to Munich in June, work in the laboratory for the summer, and then we would all leave for California in time for the new academic school year in September. We weren't thrilled about this schedule, but it was the best option available. Herr Dudel wasn't thrilled either. He claimed that I would be walking away from a golden opportunity to continue in the institute. In his opinion, California and America in general represented the worst attributes of modern civilization. Sometimes, I had difficulty arguing with him about this assertion, but this time I just ignored him and prepared to leave.

UCLA

Los Angeles was totally different from Munich: vibrant, pulsing with West Coast energy and glamor. And, in my opinion, UCLA was the epicenter of this exciting cultural mecca. On my arrival, I bought a sporty new car, a Volkswagen Scirroco (Jane had the Saab in Munich), found a room in Santa Monica for three months, and settled into my job. Of course, challenge number one was to obtain a good parking spot close to the biology building. Challenge number two was to prepare lectures for courses in general animal physiology, introductory neurobiology, and sensory physiology. That was a tall order for somebody with so little teaching experience. But, I had no family in town, so I could stay up until late in the evening preparing for the next day's lectures. Somehow, I managed to bumble through the classes. For relaxation, I explored UCLA with its beautiful campus and greater Los Angeles, with its beautiful beaches, swanky neighborhoods, and so forth.

Ah yes. And then there was Roger. My office and laboratory were across the hall from his, so I interacted with him regularly. Quickly I discovered what a good-natured flirt he was. No female walking down the hallway, or anywhere else for that matter, could escape his unconcealed flirtatious scrutiny. Most of the females just smiled: "Oh, that's Roger for you."

My life in Los Angeles become much more interesting with Roger as a friend and colleague. Academically, he tutored me in many practical aspects of being a professor and researcher. Personally, he looked after me as well. He introduced me to sushi, for example, and guided me through the various artistic treasures in Los Angeles and, for that matter, the UCLA campus. And, vice versa, I helped him in one way or another. For example, at one point, Roger's attention shifted to a recently widowed woman he had met in Munich. She came to visit him for two weeks. In order to have full time with her, Roger asked me to handle his lectures during her visit. Okay. After all, he had arranged for me to get the UCLA job. So, I doubled my workload to help him in his tryst. After the widow had returned to Munich, Roger gratefully offered me in return one of his girlfriends, an Indian graduate student at the University of California Berkeley. For him, this was a very generous gift. For me, it was not a very practical gift; one that I had no use for.

Shortly after my arrival, Roger announced to me that he was divorcing his wife. In fact, he had already rearranged most of their joint assets in preparation for a settlement and within a few weeks had rented a room in a Pacific Palisades house, not far from where he had lived. With alarming speed, he had moved into his new place and, as it turned out, into the waiting home of his recently divorced landlady. Fortunately, he didn't ask me to cover his teaching duties this time. But he did ask me to look in on his soon-to-be former wife now and then. I wasn't inclined to become involved in that aspect of his personal life. My loyalty to Roger had its limits.

With the assets that he had squirreled away from his dissolved marriage and a sizeable advance royalty on an introductory physiology textbook that he was writing, Roger bought a beautiful house overlooking the ocean in Pacific Palisades. This would become his castle, so he spent a small fortune fixing it up. Indeed, Roger once told me that he had just written a check to a contractor for more money than I earn in a year. Clearly, Roger was doing quite well.

As the spring semester came to an end, I arranged housing for when we returned to Los Angeles in September:

a nice bungalow amidst many grand houses near the beach in Pacific Palisades, not far from Roger's new house. The place was a bargain: it belonged to a UCLA professor who was going on a two-year sabbatical and only wanted to recoup his mortgage expenses—$250 per month.

Before leaving Los Angeles, I competed successfully for a Fulbright scholarship to help pay our summer living expenses in Munich and moving expenses from Munich to Los Angeles. Along with the Helen Hay Whitney moving allowance, we had adequate resources for a very comfortable move.

Back in Munich for the summer, I resumed my experiments with Hanns. We turned our attention to the release of transmitter substance from nerve terminals. These experiments were very productive, resulting in several publications in top-notch journals. All too quickly, the time for our return to Los Angeles came upon us. In general, these had been three very productive years in Herr Dudel's laboratory.

Everything for our return trip was set: airline tickets, shipment of the Saab to Los Angeles, rides to and from the airports, and so forth. We sent the boys ahead to Colorado Springs where they would stay with my mother for a couple of weeks while we cleaned the apartment and packed our belongings. That made life easier for us as we sorted out things to keep and to discard.

There was only one hiccup: Jane decided not to return to America. She was insistent on staying in Munich without me. "What the hell?" That's right: she wasn't going with me for reasons not entirely clear to me. I surmised without proof that she had found a lover, but she refused to discuss her reasons. We had terminated our apartment lease, but she had made other housing arrangements with "friends." With a sad heart, I joined the two boys in the United States without her. A single father! Now what? The boys and I stayed with my mother in Colorado Springs for a couple of weeks to recover from the long flight and then continued onto Los Angeles. I appreciated my mother's comfort during this difficult period in my life.

In Los Angeles, I enrolled the boys in a neighborhood public school: Corey in first grade, and Curtis in fourth grade. That came with unforeseen challenges. First, the boys had German clothes, German accents, and German expressions. This didn't go over well, for the school student body was heavily Jewish. More than once, the boys were taunted "Nazi, Nazi, Nazi." Needless to say, they unlearned the German language and German customs very quickly, becoming quintessential California boys virtually overnight. A second challenge was that Corey couldn't read English: German, yes but English, no. All of the other students had learned to read in kindergarten. The teacher threatened to demote Corey from first grade to kindergarten where he, too, could learn to read English. That wouldn't do. Kindergarten classes were only half-day sessions, but I needed him in a full day of school while I taught a full day of classes at UCLA. So, every morning before school, I sat with Corey for an hour or so teaching him to read English. And, the three of us read to each other before going to bed at night. Our favorites were the English-language versions of Asterix and Obelix comic-book stories, which they knew very well from the German editions. Fortunately, Corey learned quickly, and before long he had caught up with his classmates. With time, we three managed to establish a comfortable routine. Whenever somebody asked about their mother, I said that she was simply on a "mother's vacation." Nothing further.

 Then, after about two months or so, Jane announced that she was coming home: "Meet me at the airport." I had mixed emotions about this. Very mixed. On the one hand, why should I try to resume what appeared to be a broken marriage? On the other hand, the boys needed their mother, or at least so I thought. In the end, I picked her up, and our family was intact again. She found a job working in a downtown Los Angeles art dealership, which kept her busy. But, an uneasy tension lurked beneath the surface of our relationship. She seldom seemed happy. Hoping to relieve the uneasiness on my part, I traded the Saab for an Alfa Romeo Spider—a sexy, muscular convertible sports car. Most of the time, I drove it to work, and Jane drove the Scirroco. I was happy and relieved to have Jane back home with me and the boys but was worried, right or wrong, that some aspect of her European "mother's vacation" had followed her to Los Angeles.

Nevertheless, together Jane and I had a reasonably pleasant life in Los Angeles. We had a wonderful home, nice cars, and satisfying jobs. Evenings, we often drove into Westwood Village (near UCLA), where we would go to record shops, outdoor taverns, and other college-oriented activities. Moreover, occasionally we drove to East Hollywood to visit the country-western nightclubs. This was Los Angeles, after all, and commonly we saw first-class entertainers in person at these venues. But even on these enjoyable occasions, the subtle tension lay under the surface of our relationship due to her initial reluctance to return to America with me. I found it difficult to forget that experience and was always on edge, wary that she might again leave me for some reason or another.

Oh yes: while we were there, we got a dog. Two dogs, actually. The first was a favor to Roger; he asked us to take an old silky terrier belonging to his aging mother, who could no longer take care of it. We agreed but quickly regretted that decision. The dog nipped incessantly, pooped on the floor, and made a general nuisance of itself. Unfortunately—for the dog anyway—after about a month with us, it ran in front of an oncoming car in front of our house, dying immediately. Frankly, Jane and I were relieved, but the boys were heartbroken. To appease the boys, we decided to get another silky terrier, a young puppy with championship lineage, from a breeder in Pasadena. We named her Holly. Immediately, Holly became a dear member of the family.

At work, I managed to get through my assigned courses. I still was not a good teacher—I didn't know the material well—but at least I was slowly improving on the job. In my spare time, I wrote several manuscripts based on experiments done in Munich. And, I audited a UCLA course in electron microscopy taught by a pioneer in the field, Fritiof Sjöstrand. I learned his trade, so to speak, and in subsequent years, electron microscopy became a valuable addition to my tool chest of experimental techniques. Importantly, several months before my UCLA appointment was to end, I wrote an application to the National Institutes of Health (NIH) for a grant to support my research activities. Despite my training with Herr Dudel, this was not an easy task, and even with Roger's counseling it took me about three months, right up to the end of my contractual appointment at UCLA to complete. I would submit it after I had found a permanent position at some university.

But, where would that be? I decided not to apply for a continued appointment at UCLA. Right or wrong, I thought that I could do better; UCLA was not the premier academic institution then that it is now. I applied to the Biology Department at the University of Virginia and the Physiology Department at the University of Wisconsin and received offers from both of them. I chose Wisconsin for two reasons: the appointment would be in the medical school (not a biology department), and Jane had family ties to the Madison area. Moreover, at Wisconsin, I would have access to an NIH Training Grant administered by the Neuroscience Training Program, which provided salary support for graduate student training. I knew that I had chosen well when a well-respected molecular biologist at UCLA said enviously "Congratulations. You're very lucky to get a job at Wisconsin." I didn't know why I was so lucky. Wisconsin was just another Big Ten university as far as I knew. It wouldn't be until I arrived on campus that I realized its world-class preeminence in the life sciences, with several Nobel Prize winners over the years, 64 members of the National Academy of Sciences (UCLA had one), and so forth.

In August, 1976, we packed up our household, shipped it to Madison, and started our journey in our two cars. Along the way, we stopped in Colorado Springs, where we stayed with my mother for a couple of weeks. Unexpectedly, the Alfa Romeo did not perform well at that altitude; its carburetor jets were set for sea level. We decided to sell the crippled car and found a buyer who was visiting from Kansas. The performance issue didn't bother him, for he would be driving it to a lower altitude presently. Now with only one car, the Scirroco, our journey to Madison would be easier. To ease the move even further, my mother agreed to care for the boys for a week while Jane and I, with the dog, drove to Madison to arrange for housing. We found a nice house on a bus line to campus for me and within a couple of blocks of both an elementary and junior high school, for Corey and Curtis, respectively. Now, we were set. After returning to Colorado Springs to pick up the boys, we drove as a family to Madison to start this new phase of our lives.

Lest I forget to mention it: we acquired a pet tortoise while in Munich. This acquisition actually began while Jane and I were on a trip to Bulgaria for a scientific conference. In Sofia, we stayed for several days in a townhouse that had a small garden. On our first day, we encountered a tortoise with a five-inch shell eating in our garden. It seemed to live there, for we saw it every day during our visit. When the time came for us to return to Munich, the tortoise had become our familiar pet. We were fond of it, and we thought that the boys would enjoy taking care of it. So, Jane put it in a piece of hand luggage, along with ample lettuce, and we brought it back to Munich. (It never occurred to us that we might be stealing somebody's pet tortoise; we just assumed that it was wild.) The boys named it "Panzer" and took very good care of it, cleaning up its mess every day before school. (Tortoises make huge messes.) Regularly, they took Panzer out into the garden to explore the outdoors for half a day or so. Although it could easily have run away, the tortoise chose to remain in its new territory, close to the house.

When the boys returned to the United States, they took Panzer with them, safely tucked into one of their small backpacks. After the interlude with my mother in Colorado Springs, where the tortoise lived mainly under the furniture, Panzer came along with us to our new home in Los Angeles. The boys continued to care for Panzer, but they also began to leave it outdoors for longer and longer periods of time. Occasionally, Panzer would disappear for several days and then reappear, to our great relief. Ultimately, when the day came for us to leave Los Angeles for Madison, we couldn't find the tortoise, who was on one of its several-day sojourns. Regrettably, we had to leave our beloved pet Panzer behind.

Madison-I

On the first weekend after our arrival, before I had even gone to my department on campus, we—including Holly—visited Jane's aunt Mabel (her mother's younger sister), who lived in a nursing home in Stoughton, a short distance from Madison. Like Jane's mother, she was born in Stoughton, a predominantly Norwegian community. Indeed, their birth certificates were written in Norwegian. Mabel was a font of information about Madison and Dane County in general. She told us about the lakes, the ethnic traditions of the surrounding towns, and so forth. And, she told us about Jane's Norwegian heritage. After all of our wanderings over the past few years, Jane and I began to feel at home with Mabel as a stabilizing anchor.

During that same first weekend, we bought furniture for the house. Following Mabel's recommendation, we shopped for everything at Frautschi's, Madison's oldest furniture store. Frautschi's was definitely a high-end establishment: top quality merchandise, matched by top prices. Okay, we had money left over from selling the Alfa Romeo, so we splurged on Frautschi's best furniture, which we never regretted. A short time later, we decided to refurbish the kitchen, installing new custom-made cabinets, tile counter tops, and new appliances. And, we decided to repaint the interior, which we did ourselves. Finally, all of these projects were completed. Our new home looked beautiful inside.

Before moving on, I should probably mention that refurbishing the kitchen was not such a pleasant experience as I might have implied. After the workers (the craftsmen, as they preferred to be called) had torn out all of the existing cabinetry and disconnected the appliances and water, leaving a chaotic mess in the kitchen, they disappeared. Gone, nowhere to be found. I called the contractor, their boss, and asked where they were: "Is something wrong? We can't go on living like this." "Oh, Mr. Smith, don't worry. They're okay. This is deer-hunting season. They're up north, but they'll be back when it's over." And, sure enough, they were. The project was finished within a few days after their return.

But, I was still unsettled. The house had an unfinished attic: a good place for a master bedroom, I thought. With youthful ambition, I decided to finish the attic myself, although I had no meaningful experience with framing, wiring, drywall, and so forth. Nonetheless, after reading a "how-to-do-it" book, I installed thick insulation to preserve the rising heat in the winter, framed the walls, pulled two electrical circuits up from the main breaker box in the basement, laid drywall on all surfaces, and painted the entire room. All I needed was a professional carpet installer to finish the job. When it was done, we had a very nice, spacious attic bedroom, which allowed Jane and me to move upstairs and the boys to have their own private bedrooms. Now, I felt settled in our home.

I couldn't say as much about my office and laboratory at work. During my first week at work, I was shown my new laboratory, which also served as my office. It was an empty single dark, clammy room in the basement, right across the hall from the medical school carpentry shop. What a disappointment compared to what I had in all of my previous institutions. But, over the course of a few days, I managed to clean up the room, scrounge various pieces of furniture—mainly a desk, swivel chair, filing cabinet, and reading light—from the campus surplus warehouse, and claim a used typewriter from the departmental office.

By the end of the week, I managed not only to clean up my laboratory but also to give my NIH Grant application, which I had prepared at UCLA, to the departmental staff for typing. After several drafts, it went first to the medical school dean's office and then onto the campus sponsored research office for submission. All of this took nearly a month. As a backup I submitted the same grant proposal to the National Science Foundation (NSF). This was in September; I wouldn't know the outcome of these proposals until next March or April.

As the summer came to a close, we had to enroll Curtis and Corey in Madison's schools. They would be in fifth and second grades, respectively. The fifth through eighth grades were taught in Cherokee middle school, located only three blocks from our house. Second grade was taught in Thoreau elementary school, also only about three blocks from our house but in the opposite direction. The sidewalks were good in both directions, so the boys could walk to and from school safely.

Routinely, I rode the city bus to and from work. There was a direct route to the campus, with bus stops right in front of our house and my laboratory building. About half of the passengers were faculty members, as far as I could tell, mainly because parking in the heart of campus was quite limited and expensive. I didn't mind the bus ride; it gave me time to reflect on the day's activities. But I did mind the need to adhere to the bus schedule; I had to stop in the middle of things to be at the bus stop at the scheduled time. After a few weeks, I bought a bicycle, which I rode to work. That was much more convenient, at least until the first of many snowy winter days arrived.

Meanwhile, I received my physiology teaching assignment: 17 lectures on cellular neuroscience to first-year medical students. This course didn't start until spring semester, so I had time to prepare lectures and write manuscripts describing research done in both Munich and

UCLA. When the teaching began, I realized that I was still poorly prepared for the task. Nonetheless, as at UCLA, I managed to get through the assignment without any major embarrassments. For the most part, the students paid little attention anyway. Their minds were ostensibly on extracurricular activities, probably of a romantic nature. Over the years at Madison, I taught these lectures (which were reduced to 14 along the way) every spring. Finally, after about ten years, I had learned the material well enough to feel comfortable, indeed quite capable, with the subject.

I was also responsible for the laboratory sections that accompanied my lectures. To accommodate all of the students, about 150 of them, I had to repeat the same material three times in a week. Fortunately, the Department provided two experienced assistants to help with this task. In one of the laboratories, I had to demonstrate the leg reflexes and several aspects of cardiac pharmacology in an anesthetized dog. One of my assistants wheeled the dog into the laboratory room, and then I anesthetized the dog, dissected the hind leg nerves, opened the chest, and exposed the heart. All the while, I had to keep an eye on the dog's anesthesia level, blood pressure, and body temperature. At the conclusion, I injected a lethal dose of pentobarbital into the dog's leg vein. As I pointed out the dying sympathetic surge, the students and I watched the unfortunate creature die. All of this disturbed me greatly. And it disturbed many of the students as well. After three years of this, I asked the department chair if we had a videotape of this experiment. In fact, we did. With my fervent pleading, the department faculty agreed reluctantly that I could simply show the video rather than use a real dog. What a relief! A few years later, most major medical schools had made the same decision to discontinue teaching with live dogs. Following the discontinuance of live-dog demonstrations, only an endocrinology exercise used live animals, white rats, noninvasively. The rats didn't evoke much sympathy among the students or the faculty, and those laboratories continued without objection for many years in most medical school curricula, including Wisconsin's.

While preparing my lectures on the visual system for the first year medical students, I had a startling epiphany, one that altered my viewpoint of reality and truth. That cryptic statement warrants explanation. It traces back to a classic series of experiments on frog vision that I studied in graduate school: "What the Frog's Eye Tells the Frog's Brain" by Jerome Lettvin et alia. In that study, the authors demonstrated that a frog can see a dark spot the size of a fly moving through its visual field but not if the spot lies stationary. By inference, a frog can see and presumably catch a moving fly but not a nearby stationary fly (for example, a dead fly). Of course, the frog's retinal cells detect the stationary black spot, but in the neuronal pathway to the brain, its nervous system filters out that aspect of its visual field, an aspect that we perceive as real. Thus, the frog simply can't see the immobile flies; they don't exist as far as the frog is concerned. Presumably, this filtering process somehow protects the frog's ability to propagate the species.

Now, if the frog's visual system filters out dead flies (which we can see), I surmised that the human's visual system may also filter out some aspects of the world around us. For example, unlike honeybees, we can't perceive ultraviolet light emitted by certain flowers. That color doesn't exist in nature as far as we're concerned. What else can't we perceive? It might be claimed that modern electronic detectors scanning ultraviolet, infrared, and the other wavelengths, surely capture everything around us. Perhaps. But maybe not if we don't know what to look for. Stated bluntly, who knows what's out there that we cannot perceive in our wildest imagination?

About the time when I was preparing these lectures for the first time, the use of LSD as a conscious expanding drug had become popular. "Dropping acid," in the vernacular. Vivid reports by credible users (for example, Aldous Huxley), described an exotic world full of various colors, images, and relationships beyond our normal perception. Are these simply hallucinations of a mind unhinged, or has LSD chemically turned off some naturally occurring filters in our nervous system, revealing aspects of the world normally unknown to us? Notably, LSD blocks filtering activity in the thalamus, a major gateway for sensory information en route to the cerebral cortex, the center of our consciousness. Stated differently, has the LSD somehow added extraneous, made-up information to our visual system or has it simply removed filters that block existing information?

I strongly suspect that LSD and perhaps other psychedelic drugs in fact remove some filters, revealing aspects of the environment that have been filtered out during human evolution. Of course, we cannot perceive what these aspects might be, any more than the frog can perceive the presence of immobile flies in its presence. Would I ever take LSD to explore this expanded world first hand? No. I fear a bad trip. So, I continued then and now only to ponder this expansion theoretically and look for other manifestations of extra sensory information.

In addition to teaching, the university expected me to establish an independent research program. And, that required money. Fortunately, both my NSF and NIH grant applications were successful. Because they were identical, I turned down the NSF and activated the NIH award. That provided about forty percent of my salary, a technician's salary, various pieces of equipment, and supplies needed to set up my laboratory and get started on my research. But, I could always have used more money.

Okay, I knew where to turn. The university routinely provided start-up funds to new faculty members. In fact, my chair had promised me a start-up package when I accepted the job. When I asked how much, he said that it would be "adequate." That was in August, 1976; it was now April, 1977, and I still hadn't received my start-up award. I asked my chair for the money; he said he didn't have it, go ask the dean. So, I asked the dean. He replied: "You already have an NIH grant. Why do you come to me asking for more money?" I told him that it was a matter of principle: "The university promised me a start-up package." The dean offered me $2500 and told me to leave. $2500! That was just enough to buy the newly introduced Hewlett Packard pocket calculator, which I did with my start-up money. This was much less than I had expected, but I was not inclined to argue with the dean this early in my career. However, I promised to myself that if I ever were in a position to influence the start-up award process, I would see to it that the new faculty members were treated much better. That promise would later alter the trajectory of my academic career. But for now, I had to concentrate on building my nascent research program.

The pocket calculator, by the way, was a major advancement technically. As recently as my years in college, we relied on hand calculations, slide rules, or books of tables for arithmetic operations. Hand calculations were slow, slide rules were imprecise, and large printed tables were often cumbersome and incomplete. Mechanical calculators had become available for routine addition and subtraction but they lacked many of the capabilities needed for scientific operations (square roots, log functions, exponentials, and so forth). Then, in the 1970s, both Texas Instruments and Hewlett Packard introduced electronic pocket calculators that provided the capabilities needed for scientific calculations. And now, thanks to the dean, I had one.

In this context of technical advances, I should mention memories of preparing grants and manuscripts during the early years of my career at Wisconsin. These were hand written, usually on a yellow pad of paper. A draft version was then typed. Inevitably, this version, and several after that, were further refined by "cut and paste" editing. Eventually, a satisfactory version was ready for the final typing, which usually involved multiple copies: the original and several carbon copies. Xerox copy machines were available but not widely used yet, mainly because of the high cost to copy a page.

Looking ahead, in 1981, the first IBM personal computer went on the market. I promptly bought one. By 1982, I was writing my manuscripts and grant proposals on my computer using word processing software and printing them with a dot matrix printer. No longer did I have to cut and paste paper documents for a typist; I could do it all electronically on the computer. Furthermore, I began to perform many of my arithmetic data analyses using first-generation spreadsheet software. An exciting new era in world history had just begun.

The only thing missing was a graphics program that automated the tedious process of photographing hand-drawn charts and figures, printing them, and then re-assembling them into a figure needed for a grant proposal or a manuscript. Computer-graphics software was slower in coming to the marketplace. But when Microsoft PowerPoint and several alternative graphics packages arrived in about 1990, it was, indeed, a major breakthrough. Now, using these digital tools, I could easily prepare not only manuscripts but also figures and even slides for speaking presentations.

The traveling took me to memories about that first NIH grant. Soon after the award, I learned that the NIH had considered 87 basic neuroscience grant applications in that session but made only one award: mine. Word of my success got around in the neuroscience community both on and off campus. I encountered few congratulations but overt jealousy among several prestigious colleagues whose application had been unsuccessful. One National Academy of Science member asserted that: "I can't believe that NIH awarded your grant but not mine." Years later, I would hear pejorative comments about my success from younger colleagues who were having difficulties getting an NIH grant: "It was much easier in your days. It's much more difficult to get a grant these days." I simply ignored these comments. In fact, getting an NIH grant was quite difficult in "my days." I feel no sympathy for these individuals.

With grant money in hand, I began my research career at Wisconsin. For starters, I planned to concentrate solely on the specific aims of my NIH grant on nerve terminal invasion failure in crayfish. Following the advice of my colleagues at UCLA (mainly Roger), I had completed half of the grant's specific aims before submitting the proposal to NIH. Now, although the award was for three years, I hoped to complete the remaining specific aims within a year or so, which would allow time to develop new approaches before the renewal application was due. My UCLA colleagues also counseled me to hire a technician before considering graduate students; technicians work full-time on the project, without the burden of formal coursework. So, I hired a technician, Millie, a young woman who lived several houses up the street from me. Although she had no formal training as a scientific laboratory technician, she knew basic skills from her studies as a dental hygienist. That would suffice. I could teach her the rest. She learned fast, and in the long run, proved to be very productive.

After a year or so, I took on my first graduate student, Lane. He was a Caltech graduate and clearly very smart. He had applied to the Neuroscience Training Program's Ph.D. program rather than the Department of Physiology. That benefitted me financially, for the program's

NIH Training Grant supported Lane for four years. He worked day and night in the laboratory on his own project studying mechanisms of transmitter release in the crayfish and ultimately produced two papers, the core of his thesis, which the prestigious *Journal of Physiology* accepted with no recommended revisions: "as is." That was an admirable, rare accomplishment.

My own experiments went well. Within a year, I had sufficient data for several manuscripts which I submitted, successfully, to major journals in my field. During its peer review, one of the reviewers suggested that I incorporate electron microscopy into the revision. Okay. From my UCLA training, I knew basic electron microscopy, so I would train Millie in the technique. Better yet, I arranged for her to learn from the staff electron microscopist in the Anatomy Department, Edward. She learned quickly, and within several months, with Edward's help, she had generated the electron microscopy data suggested by the reviewer. This marked a significant expansion of my research expertise.

My progress slowed marginally, however, when Millie decided to pursue a Ph.D. under my direction through the Neurosciences Training Program. Halfheartedly, I encouraged her in this endeavor. On the one hand, I harbored doubts about her innate intellectual curiosity; did she have the capacity to develop an independent research career? On the other hand, I admired Millie's enthusiasm for laboratory work; no doubt she would generate sufficient data to produce a meaningful thesis. Moreover, she would be supported by the Training Grant, thus freeing up her salary for other uses in my research budget. So, she embarked on this new phase in her career. After two years of course work, she returned to my laboratory as a graduate student to work on her thesis project.

On several occasions, the traveling took me to memories of an influential colleague at the University of Wisconsin, Peter Lipton. When I arrived, Peter was an assistant professor in the Department of Physiology. I didn't meet him during my job interview (he was out of town), and that's probably just as well. I'll explain why presently. But first, a few words about Peter. He was an only child of a caring mother after his father died in a plane crash. She moved Peter from their home in New York City to London where he learned "English" ways. Proper accent, an appreciation of cricket, and many other things English. After receiving college degrees from Oxford and the University of Edinburgh, Peter moved back to the United States, where he did his doctoral and postgraduate studies. In 1972, he took the job at the University of Wisconsin. With his elite background, Peter quickly became the intellectual star of the department. And, as I learned, he deserved that acknowledgement.

Outside of work, Peter and his wife (also English) became our good friends. Not intimate or, for that matter even particularly close, but we enjoyed each other's company. At work, Peter clearly kept his distance from me, although our laboratories were next to each other. Why the distance? Quite simply, Peter didn't respect my research. He thought I really didn't know what I was doing. And, he was right on many occasions. As I began probing into the cellular mechanisms of axon conduction block, for example, my research became more and more complicated from a theoretical perspective, requiring analyses of ion movements across the cell membranes, diffusion through small extracellular spaces, and so forth. Peter knew all about these topics, certainly more than I did. He flaunted his superior knowledge by suggesting seriously that he should read every manuscript I wrote before sending it to a publisher. I took him up on that offer, and sure enough, he routinely found conceptual errors that I had to correct. At one point, he said bluntly that he would never have voted for me to join the department if he had been present during my job interview. Okay, okay. I brushed off that insult. But, I was glad that he hadn't been present during my interview.

Ironically, despite Peter's erudite intelligence, he had serious difficulties obtaining grant money. Time and time again, his grant applications were turned down by Federal granting agencies (NIH, NSF, and so forth). I read several of his unsuccessful applications and could not imagine why the reviewers turned them down. Nonetheless, ultimately he used personal money to cover his laboratory expenses; that was the primary source of his research support. Meanwhile, I had little difficulty obtaining grant support. Indeed, I was quite successful. This irked Peter immensely. In fact, I suspect that my success in this regard provoked his disdain for my research efforts. Nevertheless, despite these rough edges in our relationship, I enjoyed and admired Peter as a colleague and friend. I'm not sure, though, that the feelings were entirely mutual.

During that first year, another assistant professor in the department, Peter, and I decided to drive to Toronto for the Society for Neuroscience annual meeting. This would be a ten-hour adventure that the three of us looked forward to. The trip became a bit more interesting when Elzbieta wrote that she would be in Madison about then and would like to visit the campus. I invited her to stay with Jane and me and arranged for her to visit some of the more senior vertebrate neurophysiology faculty members. She seemed quite happy with this invitation. Moreover, I invited her to ride along with us to Toronto for the meeting. Even better. So, the four of us drove up there with only one complication: Elzbieta's crossing from the United States into Canada. We had to wait for several hours while she arranged for a last-minute visa and so forth. But, finally, everything was settled, and off we went to complete our journey.

On our drive back, it was just the three of us, for Elzbieta flew from Toronto directly back to Sweden. En route, we discussed the meeting: What had we seen and heard? What new information had we learned? What aspect of neurophysiology was under-represented? The answer to that last question was "aging." Hmm. We might be able to get in on the ground floor of this field and, importantly, attract significant grant money. So, we decided to submit jointly a grant proposal to NIH to study aging in the nervous system. Both of my colleagues quickly backed out of that decision, but I struck out alone, studying the available literature on aging. Drawing from my expertise at the neuromuscular junction, I wrote a proposal to study synaptic transmission in aged rats. The proposal was successful, and I now had a lucrative second NIH grant.

My entry into the field of aging brought professional and personal dividends. Because the field was so new, I emerged quickly as a prominent expert. Initially, my experiments were essentially descriptive: how do various nervous system parameters change with age? It was hardly the "cutting-edge" kind of work that would command any attention in a rigorous area of research. But in aged rats, the results were groundbreaking. Within a couple of years, I had documented most of the age-related changes and began to probe more deeply into their physiological consequences in the old rats. I was now adding rigor to the field. I received invitations to present my studies at numerous forums, both nationally and internationally. Indeed, I presented a featured lecture at an annual meeting of the American Association for the Advancement of Science and other distinguished venues. These included invited lectures in a handful of countries behind the Iron Curtain (the Soviet Union, Czechoslovakia, Hungary, and so forth), Western Europe, the Middle East, Australia, and on and on. Moreover, I was called upon to serve on several NIH study sections and review panels for various organizations, such as the Alzheimer's Foundation and the newly established

Howard Hughes Medical Institute. And the University of Wisconsin awarded me its prestigious A. I. Romnes professorship. In their public announcement of the Romnes award, the university cited me as "the world's best neurophysiologist in the field of aging." Put simply, I was on a roll.

Despite my successes as a physiologist, I began to sense uneasiness with my treatment of animals in the laboratory, specifically aged rats. I had already confronted this unease when I objected to using live dogs in the medical school classroom. But it gradually encompassed my treatment of other animals as well. With the aged rats, I routinely anesthetized them with an injection of chloral hydrate before commencing any experimental procedure. Of course, the rats didn't like the needle prick, but the anesthesia set in very quickly, ostensibly limiting their discomfort. Initially, I administered the anesthesia, but as my uneasiness grew, I handed the task over to my technician.

Even my handling of the lower invertebrates, mainly crayfish, began to disturb me. Ever since my graduate school days and postdoctoral studies in Munich, crayfish were kept in a tank with running water. I would reach into the tank and retrieve an animal as it desperately tried to free itself by grabbing me with its claws. Gripping it firmly, I would cut off a claw or walking leg for experimental use and then toss the wounded animal back into the tank for use in a subsequent experiment. When I returned to harvest another claw or leg from the same animal, it would frantically wave its claw in defense. I could easily reach around the defensive claw, grip the animal, and clip off the other claw or another walking leg. At that point, I would toss the live, wounded animal into the toilet and flush it away. That's how I learned to handle the crayfish, without giving any thought to the animals' pain or suffering.

However, as an assistant professor using many crayfish, I began to pay more and more attention to the wounded animals' defensive posture when they saw me approaching from several feet away to take another limb. I surmised that they had experienced pain and recognized me as the inflictor of that pain; they were sentient. What was I to do? There was no standard anesthetic for invertebrates, and I required crayfish limbs for my experiments. So, once again, I assigned the task of cutting off the limb to my technician. He didn't seem to mind. But, I became more and more disturbed by the use of live animals in my research program. Something had to change.

Accordingly, I decided to shift my research gradually in more biochemical directions. Two colleagues that I knew well in the Biochemistry Department used animal tissue (mainly mouse livers), but at least the animals were properly anesthetized and the tissue was shared among several researchers. Ideally, I could discontinue my use of crayfish and piggy-back onto somebody else's mouse or rat dissection. Furthermore, I rationalized that neurophysiology was drifting in a biochemical direction, and I didn't want to be left behind. Fortunately, the University of Wisconsin's Biochemistry Department, arguably the foremost in the world, provided an ideal training environment to make this research shift. To take advantage of its expertise, I applied successfully for an NIH Research Career Development Award (RCDA). This magnificent award provided my full salary for five years, thus allowing me the time and resources to develop skills as a biochemist. I arranged to study with Henry Lardy and Wallace "Mo" Cleland, two very distinguished professors who agreed to mentor me during this period. Notably, although the grant paid all of my salary, my department chair refused to release me from my teaching or other departmental obligations. That was okay. I could manage. As I learned biochemistry, I gradually nudged my research program in that direction. I felt not only relieved but also stronger professionally. I could speak and understand the language of the biochemist. And, I fit into the elite biochemical crowd on campus.

Hypocritically, as I developed these opinions about animal sentience, I took up deer hunting. Before casting judgment on my hypocrisy, let me explain. One day while reminiscing about Munich, I thought about several particularly memorable meals of saddle of venison. They had been delicious, so Jane and I decided to prepare it ourselves. No local butcher shop sold venison; I would have to get it myself, and that meant shooting a deer. But I had never been deer hunting before. My physiology colleague, Larry, offered to help me in that regard. An avid hunter of anything that moved, Larry lent me a rifle, ammunition, and a pair of hip waders. I bought the other necessary accoutrements, blaze orange hat, hunting knife, and so forth, and off we went early in the morning on the first day of the ten-day Wisconsin deer hunting season. He took me to his favorite spot, a stand of trees in the middle of a swamp in public hunting grounds about fifty miles from Madison. I climbed into the tree that he assigned to me, as he hiked off to his favorite tree about half a mile away. To make a long story short, I didn't see a male deer until the last morning of the season. One shot at a long distance was all it took. Larry heard the bang, rushed over to my tree, and taught me how to track down and field dress the animal. What do you know? I had successfully procured a saddle of venison, which Jane prepared deliciously.

    I continued to hunt deer successfully for another nine seasons. I took Corey with me on two occasions, and he successfully shot a deer both times. The last time I went hunting, a young buck wandered directly under my tree without knowing I was there. I shot it and quickly climbed out of the tree to field dress it. So quickly, in fact, that I saw the deer up close as it died. Although I had seen anesthetized dogs and cats die in the laboratory, I wasn't prepared for what I saw in this deer: the forlorn look in the eyes of this wild animal as it gasped for its final breaths. That look, that experience of watching death settle in, expunged any further desire to hunt. Never again. Never again!

During the traveling, I encountered fleetingly memorable people from my time at Madison: strangers who came to Madison for a day or two and then disappeared. Edwin Land was one of these people. For background: Land made his fame and fortune by developing the Polaroid camera, first as a black and white model in 1948 and then as a color model in 1972. By the time I began working at the University of Wisconsin in 1976, the Polaroid camera had become a standard laboratory feature. The invention of instant photography alone would have secured Land a place in history. But, he made another seminal contribution: the so-called retinix theory of color. For neurophysiologists, this theory posed many puzzling challenges to explain. But they accepted it as a thought-provoking alternative to the widely accepted Helmholz trichromatic theory of color perception.

The physiology department invited Mr. Land (who dropped out of Harvard before earning a B.A.) to give a seminar on his retinix theory of color vision: to "explain himself," so to speak. Three departmental colleagues and I were tasked with taking him to dinner after his lecture at a cozy Italian restaurant. As the dinner progressed, Mr. Land drank more and more of the house Chianti. At one point, while pouring another glass, he said that "Anything worth doing is worth doing in excess." And with that sage, memorable comment, he downed another glass of wine.

I have long remembered that evening because of Mr. Land's comment. And, as I became older, I began to think that he was right, for I could easily justify doing things that I enjoyed. Of course, limitations apply, but the principle stands: anything worth doing is worth doing in excess. Incidentally, as I remember, none of us in the audience understood exactly what Mr. Land was saying about color vision. I guess that we were too ingrained in the standard dogma.

And then there was Kary Mullis, winner of the 1992 Nobel Prize for his invention of the polymerase chain reaction (PCR). This was a huge breakthrough scientifically, for it greatly expanded the horizons of recombinant biotechnology. Overnight, Mullis became a hero in academic circles. Accordingly, shortly after he won the well-deserved Nobel Prize, the university's Biochemistry Department invited Dr. Mullis to give a seminar on the theoretical and practical aspects of the technique.

With great enthusiasm, all of the university's top biochemistry researchers and many others, including me, crowded into the packed lecture hall. Significantly, the crowd included Howard Temin who had won the 1975 Nobel Prize for the discovery of reverse transcriptase, a critical element of the PCR. Mullis began his talk with an explanation of how he came up with the concept of PCR: it appeared to him as a vision on his car windshield one evening as he was driving from Berkeley to Marin County to meet his girlfriend. Those were his first and last words about PCR, for he then announced that he was no longer a biochemist and had no further interest in the topic. "I'm a poet now." What the hell? The audience sat stunned. Despite this announcement, a couple of intrepid graduate students asked questions about the biochemical basis of PCR, but Mullis refused to answer them. "I'm a poet now." And so the widely anticipated lecture came to an abrupt halt. No more questions were asked, the disappointed audience slowly left the room, and Mullis returned to the sanctuary of his hotel room. And that was that for the great Kary Mullis. He was now a poet.

Memories of my brief interactions with famous people like Edwin Land and Kary Mullis were generally pleasant. One minor exception to this generalization persists in my memories: a comment by Jay Goldberg, a renowned professor of neurophysiology at the University of Chicago. I met him when I had been invited to present a seminar on my research to his department. After my formal presentation, during the public question and answer session, he asked a particularly penetrating question about the scientific foundation of my work. I fumbled for an answer, and finally said that "it was just common sense." Uh oh. Wrong answer. He soundly berated me for even suggesting that common sense had any meaning in rigorous scientific debate. I had never thought about that before but, after licking my wounds during the reception in my honor, I concluded that he was right. I retreated back to Madison in shame. Professor Goldberg certainly meant no harm, but his stinging comment stuck with me for the remainder of my scientific career. There is no such thing as common sense in science—or any other academic discipline, for that matter.

In this context of wrong answers, I should mention a similarly humiliating experience at the University of Texas at Austin when I was a finalist for the dean of arts and sciences position. During the final interview with the search committee, one of the most distinguished committee members, Professor Steven Weinberg, who had recently won the 1979 Nobel Prize in Physics, posed a hypothetical question: "Should you ever hire a faculty member who is not expected to do research?" Hmm. I couldn't imagine that there was anything new left to discover in human gross anatomy. And hadn't Millie been hired to teach gross anatomy with no expectation to do research? Likewise, I remembered being told that "we" know everything there is to be known about trigonometry. So I answered "Yes; some disciplines have few opportunities for further research, such as human anatomy and trigonometry, yet they must be taught at a university level." Oops, did it again. Professor Weinberg quickly corrected me: "Wrong! At a credible research university, every faculty member is expected to do research, no matter what they teach." I could sense instantly that my candidacy for the position had ended. That evening and during the flight back to Madison, I thought about Professor Weinberg's assertion and concluded that he was right. I had learned another enduring lesson the hard way.

A curious episode occurred in 1978, two years after I arrived in Madison. It began with a telephone call from my mother, who was in Colorado Springs. "I have been diagnosed with metastatic cancer." What? Yes, she had cancerous growth in the lymph nodes in her left neck and the muscle tissue of her left shoulder region. Stunned, I drove immediately to Colorado Springs to help her through this crisis. I felt as if I were going to help my mother set her affairs in order before the cancer took its toll.

I had two mundane issues to address as soon as I arrived. First, I queried her doctor about his diagnosis. Oh, that annoyed him; how dare I question his authority? Furthermore, he insisted that she owed him several hundred dollars. No matter. I had plenty to do besides quarrel with him over the diagnosis or the money. In fact, I suspected that he was right. So, I paid him on the spot. Second, I responded to a cranky letter from a local lawyer, claiming that her $800 bill was months overdue. Again, I dipped into my shallow pocket to clear that debt.

My mother was not prepared to yield to this pernicious disease without a fight on her terms. According to her doctor, the medical solution was to remove the cancerous tissue: the lymph nodes and surrounding musculature. But, my mother explained, that was totally unacceptable, because she rested her violin on that specific tissue when playing. So, she had decided to explore alternative, non-surgical treatments for cancer. Notably, they included taking laetrile, a putative anti-cancer agent derived from apricot pits.

At the time, laetrile was quite a controversial anti-cancer drug. Some people claimed it worked, and others claimed it didn't. Among the latter group was my Ph.D. Advisor, Donald Kennedy, who was now commissioner of the Food and Drug Administration (FDA). In that capacity, he declared publicly that laetrile was a hoax and denied FDA approval for its use in the United States. Thus, to gain access to this potential wonder drug, my mother had to travel to Mexico, Tijuana to be exact. So, she resigned her job teaching music in the schools and moved to San Diego (just across the border from Tijuana) several months after telling me about her diagnosis.

Because laetrile wasn't FDA approved, my mother's insurance wouldn't pick up the bills for her treatments. That was unfortunate, for the drug, the travel, the housing, et cetera were very expensive. To cover these costs, my mother sold her house, the one where she and I had grown up. After completing her treatment, she returned from San Diego and moved into a small rental house in a seedy neighborhood on the north side of Colorado Springs. Several months later, she bought a modest house in a far more desirable neighborhood.

Then, there was a more unsettling issue about money. While she was in San Diego, my mother joined a cult-like church that espoused preparation for the forthcoming apocalypse. That included, among other things, free love and, much more expensively, the purchase of myriad survivalist supplies: a tent, sleeping bag, camping clothes, utensils, a big Swiss Army knife, and so forth. Plus, it required assignment of all its members' assets to the church. On that count, my mother was spared financial ruin because she didn't have much left after the laetrile bills. Nonetheless, I persuaded her to hang onto her money and to leave this church, which she did reluctantly. (She gave me all of the camping supplies, which I appreciated.)

This saga came to a happy ending six months later when her doctor pronounced her cancer free. Whoa! Had the laetrile worked? Had the pathologist misdiagnosed the cancer in the first place? Had the cancer gone into spontaneous remission? Who knows? But, my mother was now at ease, healthy, and ready to begin her life as a retiree. Fate had toyed with my mother during this episode but spared her from a far worse outcome.

During these early years in Madison, as I was developing my career, Jane floundered. Oh, as a mother of two boys, she had her hands full at first. She was a good mother. But, they were growing older and less reliant on her constant attention. In search of a career, Jane spent a year earning a teaching certificate from the University of Wisconsin, hoping to become a teacher in the local school district. She succeeded, first as a substitute teacher and then, after a year, as a full-time mathematics teacher at the nearby middle school where Curtis was a student. Nonetheless, she became disenchanted with the job. The problem was twofold: she didn't enjoy mathematics; and, she didn't enjoy working with young, rebellious teenagers. So, she quit after a year. A short while later she decided to go to law school. Why not? She took the Law School Admissions Test, did well, and applied successfully to the University of Wisconsin law school. After seven years in Madison, at age 36 she entered law school.

I should point out that just prior to Jane's matriculation into law school, two meaningful events occurred in my career. First, I was promoted to Associate Processor and awarded tenure. That, of course, was a big deal. But, I had anticipated this accomplishment based on my successful NIH grants, two Ph.D. recipients and several more in the "pipeline." I wasn't blasé about my promotion, but it was eclipsed in part by the second meaningful event: I received a job offer as Associate Professor of Psychobiology (with tenure) at the University of California, Irvine. Jane and I both went out there twice to visit the campus and look for housing. The entire setup seemed idyllic: beautiful weather and scenery, modern university, good colleagues. On a second trip, we looked for houses with a real estate agent. We were sorely tempted to accept the offer. However, there was one glitch: Jane had just been admitted to the University of Wisconsin's law school. She couldn't transfer to The University of California, Irvine because it didn't have a law school. The nearest major university law school was at UCLA, over an hour's drive away from Irvine in the best of traffic conditions. I had disrupted her education once (when she got pregnant) and couldn't confront doing it again. So, I turned down the UC Irvine job, and we stayed in Madison. On many cold days afterwards, I questioned the wisdom of that decision.

Jane did quite well in law school. She was elected to the Law Review and offered summer clerkships with premier law offices in town. She was on her way to a career as a lawyer. Of course, law school claimed much of Jane's time and attention. But, we knew that would happen. What we didn't know was that she would become involved romantically with a lawyer for whom she had clerked: Dave. Stated more bluntly, she was having an affair with Dave, which claimed even more of her time and attention. She did little to conceal the relationship. The boys knew about it, and this troubled them, especially Curtis. Of course, it troubled me, too. Although I claimed little moral authority to speak on the matter, I did claim a need to put an end to this, for not only her career but also the family's stability and happiness. But, my complaints to her fell on deaf ears. Things went from bad to worse as Jane spent more and more time with

Dave, away from home, culminating with her missing Christmas Eve with us.

A couple of troubled months later, midway through Jane's third and final year in law school, I made arrangements to move out of the house, hoping that this would prompt her to terminate the affair and I could move back in. Well, it didn't work out that way. I moved into a small apartment close to campus, but Dave promptly took my place, moving into the house with Jane. The boys instantly disliked Dave, who, conversely, instantly disliked them. Indeed, years later, the boys told me about an incident when Dave threatened Corey with a gun. Dave shot the gun through the upstairs floor in anger and then ordered Corey to clean up the mess downstairs: patch the bullet hole in the ceiling, clean up plaster bits and dust, and so forth.

With Dave in the house, the boys wanted to get out. I couldn't accommodate them in my small apartment, and I didn't have the money to buy a larger house. The best I could offer was a caring shoulder to lean against when they came to visit. As the boys grew older, Jane began to limit her participation as a parent. For example, she wrote me a note stating that she would not contribute to their college expenses. Nor would she contribute to their music lessons or any other "extracurricular" activities. Okay; I'll cover those expenses. For their part, the boys left home at the first opportunity. Living under the same roof as Dave had become intolerable. Curtis moved to Stockholm, Sweden, on a hastily arranged senior-year abroad program, and two years later, Corey moved to Oslo, Norway, on a similar, but not so hastily arranged program. Both boys learned the local language quickly and, thus, had little difficulty in school. Jumping ahead in time, each of them returned for their high-school graduation in Madison and enrolled at the University of Wisconsin, opting to live in the freshman dormitories and then local housing. I was glad to have them back in town.

Indeed, they comforted me whenever they came for a visit, either in my apartment or laboratory.

Inevitably, Jane and I agreed to get a divorce, formalizing our separation. Thus, with the help of our lawyers, we launched our divorce proceedings, which limped along for nearly two years. In the settlement, I gave her my interest in the house and half of our meager savings in return for foregoing any child support obligations for Corey. (Curtis was now 18 years old, so he didn't qualify for support). Sadly our marriage of nearly twenty years had come to an end. After the court hearing, I seldom saw Jane again. Retrospectively, I have occasionally wondered if we could have salvaged our marriage one way or another. Perhaps, but it would have required tolerance and forgiveness far exceeding our capabilities at the time.

The divorce disturbed me profoundly. Primarily, I had a sense of failure. Since that fateful moment when Jane announced her pregnancy, we had worked diligently together to complete our college educations, to ensure our children's wellbeing, and to keep our family intact. And, despite some hiccups, we had managed to maintain our marriage. Now, by leaving Jane I had given up. The boys would live in a broken home. Because of my own background of growing up in a broken home, I had hoped never to inflict that fate on my own children. Oh sure: it might be said that Jane had laid the groundwork for this breakup by not returning with me and the boys to Los Angeles. Perhaps. But we had made it past that difficult hurdle. I could go on writing about my painful feelings following the divorce, but they border on the pathos common to many divorcees. There's nothing new to be learned from them. I simply had to move forward with my life and career.

Madison-II

I made an interesting discovery following the divorce. Word gets around quickly, especially to unmarried women looking for a mate. For example, a couple of female friends from high school got in touch with me, referring directly to my single status and asking me to join them for one occasion or another. Likewise, several female colleagues at work quickly showed a new interest in me. Of course, I was flattered by their attentions, but none of them interested me.

Well, wait. There was one exception: my former technician and now graduate student Millie, who also was divorced. Like the several others females, she became more attentive after my divorce. Because we had been working together closely in the lab during the day, we had many occasions to talk about our lives and so forth. She became a good friend, and I developed a fondness for her. I enjoyed her company. We would have lunch together down by the lake, play racket ball occasionally, and sit together at department seminars. Topping this off, Millie was fluent in German (her major in college), so we would often speak German together. But, as long as she remained my graduate student, a romantic relationship was off limits. I respected that taboo. Because of our closeness, however, I felt obliged to relinquish my role as chair of her final oral exam for the Ph.D. degree. Technically that was unnecessary—we had not crossed the nepotism line—but prudently, it was the right thing to do. Or, at least, so I thought.

My relationship with Millie careened out of my control over the first few weeks after she received her Ph.D.

degree in 1984. She became more attentive to me in public, which embarrassed me. But that embarrassment paled compared to what was to follow. Several months earlier, I had arranged for her to spend two years as a postdoctoral fellow with one of the best neuroscientists in the country: Uel "Jack" McMahan at Stanford University. This was a coveted position that would surely launch her career as a reputable neuroscientist. Under McMahan's guidance, she wrote an application for an NIH postdoctoral fellowship to pay her salary and some research expenses while in his laboratory. I wasn't surprised when she got the award; McMahan had a very successful "track record" of training postdoctoral scholars. Everything was set: the travel date, her housing with other postdoctoral fellows in the lab, a reasonable salary provided by NIH.

But then, the unexpected happened: Millie refused to leave Madison. She wouldn't go to Stanford. Instead, she wanted to stay in my laboratory and perform the research documented in the postdoctoral grant application. "But that was written for McMahan's lab, not mine. It's beyond my expertise," I protested. She was resolute. The next day, she asked NIH to transfer the fellowship to my laboratory, which they did without question. McMahan was perplexed, to say the least. Anyway, here she was, still in my laboratory, with what I began to suspect were romantic notions about our relationship. In a sense, I felt stuck with her. Oh well, I thought, "I could do worse."

Without going into the myriad details, against my better judgment Millie and I began to socialize publically: going to restaurants, movies, departmental parties, and so forth together. And, we went to scientific conferences together. Not surprisingly, this relationship caused some friction in my laboratory, as Millie assumed an ex officio role of "queen bee," the dominant researcher, the boss's girlfriend. Fortunately, she managed to get along well with most (but not all) members of the laboratory and, equally importantly, with members of the neuroscience community on campus.

Initially, I was uncomfortable with the relationship and what I imagined was the image it projected: "Smith is sleeping with his postdoc, ha-ha," and the like. But gradually, our colleagues accepted us as a "couple." We began to travel to scientific meetings as a couple, where we developed common friends from various foreign countries. Those friendships led to invitations to more and more national and international conferences. Gradually, we visited laboratories in most Eastern and Western European countries, plus Israel.

Our trips into and out of Eastern Europe during the Cold War always entailed the potential for high drama. Most countries banned importing Western news media, such as *The New York Times* or *Time* magazine. They were routinely confiscated at the border. Furthermore, the repressive governments discouraged conversations between Western foreigners and the "locals." Indeed, we were required to stay at hotels designated specifically for Westerners.

Leaving the East Bloc countries was no less stressful. Government police agents thoroughly inspected all railroad cars for both smuggled goods and also people. For example, at one crossing from Czechoslovakia to West Germany in 1984, our train stopped on the Czechoslovakian side of the border while policemen searched with dogs under every seat, among the overhead bins, and so forth. Meanwhile, on the next track, police searched a train of cars loaded with coal for any people trying to escape the country by hiding under the coal; systematically they thrust long rods of steel into the coal. Most likely, nobody hidden within the coal could escape these vicious probes without serious injury or death. At the time, I wondered at the demented government leadership that would impose such cruelties on its citizens.

And, of course, the crossing between East and West Germany was a constant sore spot. Western newspapers periodically reported on some potential East German defector's death while trying to climb the Berlin Wall or evade the watchful border guards. Writers and movie producers, like John LeCarré, made a good living telling stories about these dangerous attempts to escape the East Bloc.

The scientific conferences in Eastern Europe were always less interesting scientifically than culturally. The science in these countries —Czechoslovakia, East Germany, Hungary, the Soviet Union, et cetera— was usually less rigorous than in the Western countries. Sure, they had some distinguished professors, but by and large, the Communist economies limited their access to foreign markets for chemicals and routine research supplies. For example, when I visited Prague, a distinguished Czechoslovakian colleague literally begged me to send him a supply of potassium chloride from Sigma Chemical. He would have to wait up to a year for approval of an order for such a routine laboratory chemical in the Czechoslovakian system. Incidentally, several years later I met this colleague at a West German conference. At the opening breakfast, bananas were served; he scoffed down several of them on the spot and stuffed his pockets with several more. "We haven't had access to bananas in years," he explained.

Another example: at a prestigious scientific conference in Budapest, the opening reception at an elegant conference center outside the city featured a wonderful selection of caviar, pâté, quail eggs, and other delicacies served on fine crystal plates. It was a delicious feast. In addition, it featured fine Hungarian wines served in beautiful crystal wine glasses. At the end of the evening, all of the guests boarded large buses for the ride back to our hotels in the center of the city. The buses were packed, so most of us had to stand. As the bus lurched forward, all of the standees bumped into each other to keep their balance. This bumping was accompanied by the unmistakable sound of breaking glass. I noticed a large group of nearby East Germans looking dejectedly into their satchels at what must have been their sizable stashes of purloined crystal plates and glasses. I heard several of them bemoaning that it had all been shattered. I was ashamed of my professional colleagues.

The traveling took me to memories of several other similarly distressing events behind the "iron curtain." One last example proved most heartrending for a young Czechoslovakian professor who was the keynote speaker at a world conference on synaptic physiology in Prague. Like most researchers in those days, he delivered his lecture using celluloid slides. While he was showing his first of many slides, the projector's bulb burned out. After a flurry of activity, the correct replacement bulb could not be found anywhere. But no worry. A similarly sized brighter bulb was found. So into the projector it went. Sure enough, the bulb was brighter—and hotter. So much hotter that within seconds, his slide began to melt. As one slide melted, the professor moved quickly onto the next slide, just to watch it quickly melt as well. And so it went; we in the audience watched every slide melt, paying little attention to what the speaker was saying. Needless to say, we all found this misfortune very sad but somewhat amusing.

Of course, this kind of projection tragedy is not limited to melting celluloid slides in Eastern Europe. A more modern Western counterpart occurred with some regularity during the early days of Microsoft PowerPoint slides, when numerous catastrophes arose due to the incompatibility of Apple- and PC-based operating systems. For example, I remember a widely anticipated lecture by a celebrated Nobel Prize winner at a large Washington, D.C. conference about twenty-five years ago. He prepared his slides using an Apple computer, but the conference organizers provided only PCs for projection purposes. None of his slides came out right; text was misaligned, figures were jumbled, and on and on. The speaker had to proceed without them. What a disappointment for him, I'm sure, and certainly for the audience.

Well, enough of the misfortunes of others. Back in Madison in my own laboratory, Millie developed expertise in not only electron microscopy but also several biochemical techniques, such as Western blots, needed to solve certain problems in my research program. In that regard, she became a valued collaborator in my aging studies. My career benefitted, but I could tell that her career as an independent researcher stalled. We continued to publish numerous papers together, but I was always the lead author. Often, I wasn't convinced that she understood fully the scientific basis of our studies. Although Millie won a competitive two-year research grant on her own accord, she had little interest in developing her own program. In fact, she acted more as a technician than an investigator and seemed quite content with that. I puzzled what lay in her professional future.

Ultimately fate intervened twice, solving the puzzle. The first intervention occurred when the Anatomy Department asked Millie if she would like to help them teach gross anatomy to first-year medical students. They would teach her the subject during the summer school course, and then she would join the department as a full-time instructor for the fall semester. She would return to research in my laboratory the following spring. I endorsed this transition in Millie's career, for it provided an alternative career trajectory for her. The second intervention occurred shortly after her return to the laboratory when Millie was diagnosed with a health condition that called for surgery. The surgical procedure kept Millie inactive and out of the laboratory for another couple of months. After this prolonged gap in her research career, Millie realized that she didn't want to return to research and was much happier teaching gross anatomy. The Anatomy Department offered her a full-time appointment as an instructor, with no expectation of research. She was quite pleased to be out of research, and I was relieved to have her pursuing a more satisfying profession.

Now that Millie was no longer working for me, we could formalize our relationship publicly in Madison. In a major step, we took out a mortgage as "cohabitants" and bought a house together near campus—a fixer-upper. For several months, we spent every spare moment sanding, painting, remodeling the kitchen, refinishing the wood floors, and so forth. Ultimately, we had a very nice, quaint house about a mile from campus. As a housewarming gift, my mother bought us a beautiful old upright piano, which we both enjoyed playing. The house had a third-story room that I turned into my office, my sanctuary. Up there, I spent many late hours preparing lectures, analyzing experimental data, and reading journal articles. In short, we now had a home.

My career continued to prosper. At the conclusion of my Research Career Development Award in 1983, I applied successfully for full professorship, which was awarded in spring 1984. That major accomplishment brought me great pleasure; I had "made it" to the apex academically.

This promotion opened a door: a few weeks after I was promoted to full professor, I received a telephone call from Robert M. ("Bob") Bock, Dean of the Graduate School, asking me if I would like to serve as an associate dean, a position available only to full professors. I would join three other associate deans, each responsible for one of the four academic "quadrants" of the university: life sciences, physical sciences, social sciences, and humanities. Because of the university's pre-eminence in the life sciences, I would be considered the senior member of the group. This was a very good job, indeed a coveted job on campus. In those days, the dean of the graduate school was also the university's chief research officer and, in that capacity, controlled the enormous Wisconsin Alumni Research Foundation (WARF) funds supporting the university's research efforts. I would chair the life sciences' sub-committee of the overall campus research committee, which distributed more than $14 million in WARF research funds annually to the faculty members. Moreover, I would have oversight of two primate centers, the Biotron (controlled environment research building), the Molecular Biology Laboratory, the High-voltage Electron Microscope facility, and myriad other centers, institutes, research facilities, and so forth.

My appointment would be half-time, with an allowance to pay for a graduate student to help keep my research program intact. Before accepting the offer, I needed time to think. On the one hand, my research program was running smoothly, and I didn't want to risk losing ground to my competitors. On the other hand, this would be an ideal entry into higher administration—a new dimension of university service. Enough thinking: Yes, I would accept the position if the allowance would be raised to an amount needed for a postdoctoral fellow, about twenty percent more than for a graduate student. Bob agreed, and so I stepped onto the "other side," from a faculty member's perspective the side of the university's administration.

As I learned very quickly, the University of Wisconsin's graduate school was highly respected internationally, as was Bob Bock, who had been its now legendary dean for more than twenty years. Bob and his staff members spent many hours teaching me the fundamentals of graduate school and research administration. Of course, I learned the technical aspects of the job. But, I also received quite practical advice, more along the lines of the "art" of research administration. For example: don't offer to pay the full amount for something such as a piece of equipment or a faculty member's startup funds, for then it becomes a free good with no value; share the cost with the college dean and department chair. And, importantly: always be reasonable; as the graduate school states in its bulletin, "Ultimately we are all reasonable people." Or, as the graduate school old-timers said informally, "We reserve the right to be consistently inconsistent."

I developed a routine: spend the mornings in my graduate school office and afternoons in my laboratory. Of course, I had to remain flexible in my schedule, but, as Bob taught me, I always told my assistant where I would be and how to get in touch with me at any given time. Bob taught me a related rule of thumb: always be predictable. I thrived in this new environment, helping graduate students and faculty members accomplish their goals.

As associate dean of the graduate school, I encountered real academic power now and then. By that, I mean very successful senior faculty members—certainly more senior than I, a freshly appointed full professor. For example, on one occasion I had just overturned the human oncology department's decision to admit a young woman into its Ph.D. Program. Her undergraduate grades failed to meet the graduate school's minimum standards. A few days later, without warning, a very stern-looking man in a pressed white lab coat walked into my office: a distinguished professor of cancer research, long-time member of the National Academy of Sciences, winner of various prestigious prizes, and so forth. "I want you to admit this young woman." I explained why I had rejected her. He replied crisply "Young man, this is not a debatable matter. I'm a much better judge of academic potential than you are. I'm telling you to admit her. If I'm proven wrong after one year, I'll come in person to ask for her dismissal from graduate school." The stern look in his eyes warned me not to quarrel with him. So, I meekly relented. When I told

Bob Bock about this encounter, he smiled and said: "Don't get into a pissing match with a skunk." The point was well taken. Notably, a year later, the professor again entered my office unannounced and told me that he was wrong and that I was to "kick the young woman out of graduate school immediately." I did just that without question.

All the while as the associate dean, my career as a faculty member continued unabated. I kept up my teaching, which now included introductory physiology to as many as 608 students each summer and my expanding research program. My laboratory increased in size, as I generated more and more grant support and took on more graduate students and postdoctoral fellows. I was happy in my professional life.

That happiness waned in my personal life, however, for Millie struggled to get along with Curtis and Corey. She seemed jealous of my attentions to them. Nonetheless, she prepared dinner for them on a regular basis. These occasions pleased me, although I sensed serious tension between them. Curtis, in particular, drew her ire with an occasional remark that somehow insulted her. Corey was younger and, by nature, more amicable, but even then, I sensed tension. Stated bluntly, Millie didn't like Curtis and Corey, and the feelings were mutual: they didn't like her. This animosity became deeply ingrained and persisted without letup as they grew older.

Once again fate intervened most unpredictably. This time it involved son Curtis, who had enrolled in 1984 at the University of Wisconsin-Madison as a freshman. Since I paid about three-fourths of his college expenses, Curtis needed to earn more money. Thus, he took a job as an assistant in the laboratory of an eminent cell biology professor who had immigrated from China to the United States many years earlier. Curtis and the professor spent many hours talking about China, which they both seemed to enjoy.

Near the end of his first semester, Curtis declared a major in engineering. Accordingly, in his second semester, he took introductory calculus to satisfy the engineering requirements and, piqued by his conversations with his boss, three Chinese-related courses to satisfy the general education requirements. At the end of the semester, Curtis received his grades: three A's and one F. The A's were in the Chinese-related courses, and the F was in calculus, which did not bode well for success in engineering. Consequently, he changed his major to Chinese and continued to take as many Chinese-related courses as the curriculum would allow.

Fate's intervention extended to the conclusion of the spring semester (1985). Using money that he had saved from his work in the laboratory, Curtis went to Taipei, where he arranged to teach English as a second language for the summer. And once again fate intervened: he found a girlfriend, a Taiwanese woman. He was smitten when he returned for the start of the fall semester. Indeed, after one semester, to my chagrin, he took a leave of absence for the spring semester and returned to Taipei. About a year later, in summer 1987, Curtis returned with his girlfriend, Shu-fen Chiu, or Alexia, as Curtis called her, and moved into an apartment shared with another young couple. He said that they planned to get married. I counseled him not to get married until after graduation from college, adding that "if you get married, you are declaring that you're able to support yourself and your wife." My not-so-subtle admonitions fell on deaf ears; love prevailed. I was never quite sure if they had married formally in Taipei, but it didn't matter much, for they married shortly afterwards in a simple ceremony at Jane's house in rural Wisconsin. (Millie and I weren't invited). Now that he was married Curtis took it upon himself to pay most of his college expenses, although I made ad hoc contributions now and then to help them financially. I was immensely proud of him as he matured into adulthood. And, somehow, with that maturity, his relationship with Millie became a bit less hostile.

Alexia tried to enter the university as a graduate student, but the graduate school admissions staff claimed that her undergraduate program in Taipei was not equivalent to a bachelor's degree in the United States. Rather than take the required two years of coursework to complete the undergraduate requirements, Alexia (probably at Curtis's urging) stubbornly insisted that the University of Wisconsin was wrong in its assessment. But, of course, that got her nowhere. As associate dean of the graduate school, I wanted to intervene, but the ethical conflict of interest precluded my involvement in any way. Ultimately, she decided not to pursue graduate studies in the United States. At least not at this time in her life

Surprisingly, Millie took Alexia under her wing and arranged for a position as a technician with a neurophysiology professor whose laboratory was down the hall from mine. The job was not ideal in Alexia's opinion, but at least she was earning badly needed money. More importantly, through her interactions at work, she was learning about America, its culture, its people. She worked in the lab for about a year. I'm not sure why she quit—her salary funding was secure—but I suspect that she found coping with the professor's notoriously brusque personality simply too frustrating.

For Millie and me, life moved on. In summer, 1985, we began a fruitful collaboration with my old friend and colleague Hanns Hatt, who was now assistant professor in the Physiology Institute of the Technical University of Munich under the direction of my former postdoctoral advisor Herr Dudel. Since I left the institute ten years earlier, it had moved into the Biederheimer Schloss, which the university had converted into part of its medical school campus. This collaboration extended for five summers, from

1985 to 1989. Each summer, Millie and I would spend one month at the institute studying electric currents passing through single ion channels in isolated spinal-cord motoneurons using the newly developed patch-clamp technique. During that month, we would record currents and store them using a tape recorder. I would then analyze the tapes and write manuscripts back in Madison. Ultimately, we published six papers based on our work. That's reasonably productive, but the main outcome of our collaboration was the opportunity to spend time in Munich with good friends.

Seemingly each weekend during our visits, Herr Dudel would dedicate his Sundays to driving us around Bavaria looking at the many churches and other historic sites. He knew them all and didn't hesitate to share his knowledge about the history of each building. Millie managed to soak this up, asking questions about this and that, but I have vivid memories of fighting off numbing sleep sitting in the back of his car as he mumbled in barely audible German explaining some aspect of local history while we drove across the countryside. When we weren't with Herr Dudel, we were often with Hanns and other friends roaming the various beer halls and beer gardens in greater Munich. I enjoyed those activities much more than studying churches. Our circle of friends was expanding, and we felt quite at home there.

During that first summer, unhappiness struck in an unexpected way. Coincidentally, Roger also arranged to be in Germany, beginning a one-year sabbatical in Göttingen at the Max Planck Institute. Just before leaving Los Angeles in late May, he discovered a mole under his belt buckle. His dermatologist recommended removing it before his trip to Germany, but Roger decided to delay the removal until the end of the summer. That proved to be a bad decision, for the mole turned out to be a malignant melanoma.

The dermatologist removed the mole, so Roger returned to Germany for the remainder of his sabbatical. But, in the fall, Roger flew back to Los Angeles with significant back pains caused by cancer in his spine. It was too late to control the metastasis from the melanoma, so his health deteriorated quickly. In December, I visited him in Los Angeles for the last time. It was not a pleasant visit. Bedridden, Roger expressed anger, anger at himself for delaying treatment and anger at fate for having inflicted this terrible disease on him at such a young age. He died on June 16, 1986, at the age of 52 years. With his death, I lost a very dear friend.

Another fateful event occurred in the closing days of 1985: Millie and I decided to get married. In the traveling, I can't remember who broached the subject first. But I do remember that she questioned my motive, asserting that I was motivated strictly by the tax benefits of marriage. Stung by that assertion, I was reminded of the Tina Turner song popular at the time, "What's Love Got to Do with It?" Indeed, was love involved? Regardless of the answer to that question, we tied the knot before a justice of the peace in Madison on December 28, 1985, with only her parents and, at my strong insistence, Corey present. Curtis was in Taiwan, so he couldn't conveniently attend. Afterwards Millie's parents treated Millie and me to a nice dinner. Notably, despite my objections, Millie refused to invite Corey to the dinner. That was it. No further celebration, no honeymoon. From that time onward, we were a married couple with whatever tax benefits might accrue.

Africa

While in Madison, Millie and I developed an interest in African safaris. It all began in 1989 when our wealthy neighbors told us about their recent luxurious "Hemingway-style" safari in Kenya. We listened attentively, for we both wanted to see African wildlife—elephants, lions, rhinos, et cetera—in their natural habitat. We couldn't afford $10,000 per person as our neighbors had spent, so Millie and I decided to arrange our own "Hemingway-style" safari. I asked a colleague who studied primate behavior in Africa what country would be best for a first safari. Without hesitation, he replied "Kenya." Accordingly, we wrote numerous travel agents in the United States and in Kenya asking for quotes on a luxury safari comparable to our neighbors', with a maximum of 12 participants. Most of them quoted prices ranging from $5,000 to $25,000 per person for 14 days, more than we could possibly afford. However, one agency, Rhino Travel in Nairobi, quoted a price of $2,500 per person. We could afford that, so we made the appropriate arrangements for a Kenyan safari in February, 1990.

When we flew into Nairobi, our guides (husband and wife) for the safari met us at the airport and took us to the historic Norfolk Hotel where we spent the night recovering from the long flight. Early the next morning, they picked us up in the company's Land Cruiser for the journey into "the bush." We were the only passengers. "Where are the other guests?" I asked. "You are the only ones who requested these dates, so it's just the two of you." So, there we were: two of us, our two guides, and ten staff members waiting on us, including the bartender in his red waistcoat and white gloves. We stayed in beautiful two-person tents with en suite toilets and showers and ate meals cooked on outdoor wood fires. By night, we looked up at the Southern Cross amidst the myriad stars in the southern sky. By day, we traveled the surrounding countryside searching for wildlife. Within a few days, we had seen the "Big Five," elephant, rhino, lion, leopard, and Cape buffalo, plus many other species that I had only seen as a child in the Colorado Springs zoo or picture books. In short, the trip was spectacular.

At the end of the safari, I asked our guide if we could do this kind of trip on our own, without a local guide. No, not in Kenya. The roads are too rough, and the political instability along the Somalia border is too dangerous. But, he added, we certainly could do a safari alone in South Africa or Namibia. Right then, we decided that we would arrange our own unguided safari as soon as possible. That turned out to be in summer, 1993, in the waning days of apartheid in South Africa. With few advanced plans, we flew to Capetown, intending to spend several nights there before driving into Namibia, through the Kalahari Desert to game parks in northern Namibia. While we were checking out of the hotel in Capetown, a stranger at the desk suggested that if we really wanted to see animals, we should go straight up to Kruger National Park, skipping Namibia.

He convinced us. So, we changed plans on the spot. At the stranger's suggestion, we drove from Capetown up the Garden Route to Port Elizabeth, flew to Skukuza, the largest of several camps in Kruger National Park, rented a car, and arranged for lodging up there. In Skukuza, we made reservations for the next ten days at camps throughout the park. (There was no internet or telephone service in the park, so all arrangements were made using short-wave radio). At each camp, we stayed in one-room huts with cone-shaped thatched roofs ("rondavels") and grilled local meat (usually kudu or some other wild animal) over a charcoal fire, called a "braai" by the South Africans. Topping this off, we drank copious amounts of South African red wine. The ambiance was peaceful, very peaceful, as the other guests staying in the camp did the same thing: grill meat on the braai, drink wine, and enjoy the night skies and sounds.

By day, we drove slowly along the paved and dirt roads looking for wild animals. We saw a lot on our own and learned how to observe the animals without disturbing them. Most interesting was the animals' disinterest in our vehicle (a Toyota sports utility vehicle). Even when we had our windows open and talked quietly, they would wander past the car, ignoring our presence. It was as if our vehicle were a large, inanimate rock. Of course, we were under no illusions about what might happen if we got out of the car, but this experience in the car amazed us. Elephants were a bit less inattentive, though. Although they usually ignored us, occasionally an elephant would charge towards the car — a faux charge — warning us that we had come too close, no matter what we were. Importantly, in Kenya, our guide had taught us how to protect ourselves when watching elephants, rhinos, or Cape buffalos from a vehicle: always park the car ahead of the animals so we could easily drive forward out of danger if they were to charge us. That proved to be very useful advice. The entire experience in Kruger was memorably delightful. We were hooked. We had to do this again.

The next time, we arranged to stay several nights at a "wilderness camp" in the park. These camps were isolated in the bush, far from the main camps and other people. The lodging was a bit more primitive: a small A-framed hut with two single beds and communal showers and toilets. In the early mornings and late afternoons, we and the other guests (usually no more than two to four) went on foot safaris accompanied by two guides carrying rifles. On these foot walks, we often unexpectedly encountered large animals quite nearby: elephants, rhinos, lions, Cape buffalo, and so forth. The guides, who had no intention of shooting these beautiful creatures except in the direst emergency, "negotiated" with any threatening animal, extricating us from harm's way. I was amazed at their skills.

By the way, the guides had learned to "negotiate" with wild animals during their training to become certified by the Field Guides Association of Southern Africa (FGASA). The negotiations usually involve talking calmly to the beast, assuring it that the humans intend no harm and backing away slowly to safety. Of course, the animals don't understand the words spoken, but they get the gist of what is being said. Naturally, the negotiations are more nuanced in reality, for each encounter is unique. But the principles are the same, and they work. I witnessed numerous instances with guides in Africa and have personally utilized the technique successfully on several potentially very dangerous encounters with grizzly bears and moose in the United States. The only threatening animals that defy my attempts at rapprochement are wasps and hornets. I don't like them, and they don't like me.

At every opportunity, we arranged another trip to South Africa. Usually we went straight to Kruger National Park, but on several occasions we visited Capetown or Pretoria as well to meet professional colleagues. One summer, we drove to a wilderness camp over the border in Mozambique where we spent several days, and another summer we flew into Namibia where we spent a week driving through the wild countryside. Over the years, we went to South Africa so often that I lost count of the number of visits: at least a dozen. Sure, I could look through my old passports and count the trips, but I simply haven't had the desire to look them up. My memories don't require such granularity.

One last topic concerning our visits to South Africa warrants comment: apartheid. We first visited the country in

1993, a year after the country voted to end apartheid but a year before its formal termination. During our first several visits to Kruger National Park, apartheid and its slowly disappearing remnants were manifest in the camps: white South Africans managed the park and served as armed safari guides while black South Africans meticulously kept the grounds and ablution facilities spotlessly clean, changed the sheets, cleaned out the braais, and so forth. Undeniably, Kruger was a white man's paradise. Over time, however, with the demise of apartheid, the park's management was turned over to black South Africans, with hardly a white park employee in sight, except for a few older safari guides. I must admit that the quality of service declined during the initial several years of this transition. But, after about five years, the staff had developed sufficient expertise to restore the park to a semblance of its order and cleanliness during the apartheid days. Notably, however, most of the guests were white South Africans; Kruger National Park was still their paradise. Quite simply, very few black South Africans could afford to visit the park. And that had not changed as recently as my last visit to South Africa in 2017.

Madison-III

Inevitably, times changed in Madison. After I had been in the graduate school for five years, the university appointed Donna Shalala as its chancellor. Soon afterward, in 1989, she replaced Bob Bock with a new dean, John Wiley, who had been associate dean in the School of Engineering. The timing was awkward for me. He was to begin on July 1, when I would be in the midst of a visit to Munich. I worried about not being there during his first two weeks in office but ultimately decided that usually little happens during midsummer and that I would probably not be missed. Well, I got that wrong. A week or two after I boarded the plane, a troublesome brouhaha over the campus's breeding of genetically modified dairy cattle erupted. Right from the start, John walked straight into the mess. "Where's my associate dean when I need him?" I'm told he asked. When I returned a couple of weeks later, I apologized to John for my absence and immediately took over the problem. John accepted my apology and welcomed me back. From then on, I got along well with John, mainly because he left me alone.

Bob Bock didn't fare as well. Within less than a year afterwards, he drowned in a pond on his farm. I would miss Bob, of course. He had made a huge impact on my career.

But I learned new, different aspects of university administration from both Donna and John. Most importantly, I suppose, was that the chancellor is always the chancellor—the boss, ever-powerful; Donna had a firm grip on the campus administration and didn't relinquish it despite any university rules and policies, or, for that matter, Federal investigations. She also taught me to analyze thoroughly a situation that called for a decision, make the decision forcefully, and leave no opening for debate. At first, I was uncomfortable with that heavy-handed approach to administration, but as time wore on, I realized its benefits for both parties. In retrospect, she was a good mentor.

Another change occurred as well. After seven years as associate dean, I informed John that I would return to the faculty in July, 1991. Why then? The main reason was that I began to sense that my research program was beginning to lag. I had thought that I was keeping up with the research in my field while serving part-time as an administrator, but I began to realize that, in fact, I had not kept pace with the progress made by my competitors. The visits to Munich were part of the problem. Although they were productive, they focused mainly on Hanns's research career, not mine. Consequently, my programs began to suffer from lack of focus, from "mission creep," so to speak. Another important reason was that the powers of recombinant DNA technology had overtaken my field of expertise, and I needed to learn how to take advantage of them or, quite simply, drop off the map research-wise.

John made the transition back to the faculty easy, offering me a one-semester sabbatical plus $50,000 for discretionary use in my laboratory. My continued teaching obligations precluded a regular sabbatical, so John switched the salary funds to a discretionary fund, which I used to take a series of five one- or two-week courses in molecular biology techniques offered by New England Biolabs in Gaithersburg, Maryland. These courses were just what I needed, for they taught me the scientific principles and the practical hands-on laboratory skills of recombinant DNA technology. Naively, I thought that I was ready to incorporate them into my research programs on synaptic transmission and aging.

I say naively, because I soon discovered complicated technical nuances unique to my scientific preparations. Neither the crayfish nor the rat was a suitable experimental model, so I switched to isolated chick motoneurons, which Millie learned to prepare. They proved to be much easier to work with. Fortunately, I had three new graduate students eager to learn these molecular biology techniques. So, with occasional help from various faculty members on campus, we launched our studies of neurotransmission at the molecular level in cultured motoneurons. Specifically, we began by characterizing the glutamate neurotransmitter receptors on these cells, for these receptors mediated motor nerve activity to the periphery (that is, the muscles).

I should mention one other invaluable source of technical help: my son Corey. He was now an undergraduate at the University of Wisconsin, working as a student assistant in a highly regarded biochemistry laboratory. Corey came to our lab on numerous occasions to give us tips on how to make certain procedures work more effectively. I was proud of him, to say the least.

With these new techniques in hand, I successfully renewed my NIH grant to study synaptic transmission. However, my aging grant didn't do so well. Despite my seminal contributions, the field of aging had advanced away from descriptive studies to more focused studies on the etiology of Alzheimer's disease. I continued to receive speaking invitations at conferences and even an offer to become Senior Vice President for Research for the Alzheimer's Association (which I turned down), but I realized that the exciting work was certainly not coming out of my laboratory any more. The reviewers of my NIH aging grant renewal proposal realized that as well, and after nearly eleven years, my grant was not renewed. That aspect of my research program came to an end. I had mixed feelings about this. On the one hand, I was disappointed, of course. On the other hand, I was relieved, for now I could concentrate fully on my core research on synaptic transmission in isolated motoneurons.

The next four years passed by with only a few noteworthy events. My research progressed with just an occasional glitch now and then, and I taught with more and more satisfaction. Curtis and Corey had, by now, graduated and moved to Hawaii and Denver, respectively, to attend graduate school. I was very proud of them. Millie and I continued to travel abroad at every opportunity. Our favorite destination was South Africa, but we ventured into exotic places in South and Central America, the South Pacific islands, China, and on and on. There were increasingly fewer corners of the Earth that we hadn't visited.

During this time period after Millie and I began living together, I resumed downhill skiing. Although I had skied regularly as a teenager in Colorado, I hadn't skied very often since then. But, now Millie and I became avid skiers. Every winter, we would spend at least four weeks at one resort or another. The best Western resorts: Aspen, Vail, Snowbird, Sun Valley, and so forth. In addition, we spent a week each winter in Steamboat Springs, where Millie's parents owned a slope-side condo. Moreover, we attended the annual meetings of the Winter Conference on Brain Research, held at one major American ski resort or another. We attended several similar meetings of the European Conference on Brain Research, held at French and Swiss ski resorts. Millie and I skied a lot and became reasonably good at the sport. Good enough to ski black diamond slopes without hesitation but not good enough to ski effortlessly among the trees in deep powder snow.

In summary, life was good in Madison. Until I noticed an itch, that is. In 1994, I began to look at my older distinguished colleagues as they trudged gloomily across the street through dirty snow in sub-freezing temperatures to get a cup of coffee at McDonald's. Did I want to look like them in years to come? Absolutely not. And, with that resounding answer, I began to explore other job opportunities. A couple of them caught my attention: Dean of Agriculture at Cornell University and Senior Vice President for Research at the University of Hawaii's flagship campus at Manoa. I applied and became a finalist for both positions. I visited Cornell first in December. The weather in upstate New York was miserable, just like Madison: sub-zero wind chill and blinding snow. My interview went well, and the provost indicated that I would be getting an offer. Then, a week later, I visited Honolulu. It was beautiful: sunny skies, warm trade winds, blue waters, and all of the other attractions that Hawaii has to offer. The job intrigued me, as well. Shortly after I returned to Madison, I received an offer from the President of the University of Hawaii, Ken Mortimer. Suddenly I had mixed feelings about these positions. The University of Hawaii certainly wasn't a major research institution. Would I regret stepping down professionally? Maybe. Cornell was comparable to the University of Wisconsin, but the weather was no improvement on Madison. Simply staying at the University of Wisconsin also played in my mind; maybe ask for a modest retention package and stay put. I could do worse, for sure. But the weather...it was abominable. After long hours of deliberation, I chose the University of Hawaii. With that decision, the itch went away.

In December, 1994, therefore, I informed my departmental chair that I would be leaving the university for a position at the University of Hawaii. He took the news well, expressing sadness that I was leaving the University of Wisconsin but wishing me success and happiness. As a goodwill gesture, he allowed me to take a nine-month unpaid leave of absence, just in case the Hawaii job didn't meet my expectations and I wanted to return to Wisconsin. I was quite grateful for that "safety net." Next, I informed

NIH of my move, and it allowed me to transfer my grants to the University of Hawaii. Significantly, both my departmental chair and the NIH allowed me take all of the equipment in my laboratory to Hawaii. Naively, I hoped to be able to set up a laboratory in Hawaii and continue working part-time on my research program.

Then came the most difficult announcement: I told members of my laboratory of the pending move and, because of my administrative obligations, that I couldn't take them with me. They sat in stunned silence. Fortunately, three of them were within about one year of finishing their Ph.D. requirements; I could continue as their advisor while they finished. Two other doctoral candidates weren't so far along, so I helped arrange positions for them under a different advisor. Likewise, the two postdoctoral fellows gravitated to new laboratories with little difficulty. As my final days in Madison approached, one of my doctoral students still seemed stunned. I worried about her, but then again, she only had a year or less to go before she completed her degree requirements. She would make it, I assured myself.

Before leaving Madison, I should tell about one more object of the traveling: the boat. Or, more accurately, the boats. In Madison, which is situated among five different lakes of various sizes, Millie and I owned two boats over the years. The first was a small outboard motor boat that belonged to her family, who lived on a lake in eastern Wisconsin. Although it was "seaworthy," it needed several major repairs (new seats and so forth), so Millie's family (father, brothers, and sisters) allowed us to bring it to Madison where we could use it after we got it fixed up. The boat was light enough to be hauled with our BMW, so we took it to various lakes near Madison and even some up in northern Wisconsin. Notably, I had no previous experience with boats, so Millie always drove it. At most, I would hop out to guide the boat off and onto its trailer.

That little boat was quite enjoyable in the smaller lakes around Madison, but it was not so enjoyable in the biggest of Madison's lakes, Lake Mendota, where the large waves tossed it around mercilessly. We needed a bigger boat to feel at ease on that lake. So, we gave the little boat back to Millie's family and bought our own larger boat—a powerful inboard-outboard SeaRay. Ah, this was much better on Lake Mendota. We rented a slip located in a sheltered cove on the lake, so all we had to do was back it out of the slip and navigate it out through the narrow channel to the main body of the lake. Then, Millie would hit the gas, and off we went. It was an exhilarating feeling. On Sundays, we would take a high-speed cruise around the perimeter of the lake and then drop the anchor in the middle of the lake where we would read the morning newspapers, eat delicious morning buns, and drink several cups of strong coffee. I enjoyed these lazy mornings on the water, especially on hot days. All I had to do was sit and enjoy myself while Millie handled the navigation and driving.

Unfortunately, Millie's surgery disrupted this pleasant routine. During her approximately three-month recovery, she could not go out on the boat because the pounding of the waves against the boat might re-open her incisions. But I wanted to continue using the boat. So, we decided that I could go out alone, despite my inexperience at driving a boat. On my own, I learned quickly and, within a week or two, was confidently going out by myself for solo cruises. Ho, I knew how to drive a boat. And I enjoyed the freedom and solitude on the water.

We planned on taking the boat with us to Hawaii. In fact, we bought a big car, a used Range Rover, to pull the boat to and from our house to a nearby marina in Honolulu. We were excited about using it to explore the near-shore reefs. But, bad news. As we were preparing to move our furnishings, including the boat, from Madison to Honolulu, we realized that we needed more money to help allay the expenses of the new house. Our only quick source of cash was the boat; we would have to sell the boat, which we did.

A common saying is that "the happiest days in a boat owner's life are the day he bought it and the day he sold it." Not for me. It saddened me to lose this "friend," and it annoyed me that we had bought such a large car for pulling a boat that we now did not have. (Large cars in Honolulu are quite difficult to drive in the narrow streets and parking spaces.) Oh well, so it goes.

Hawaii-I

Like my move from Munich to Los Angeles, the move from Madison to Honolulu occurred in stages. Initially, in early 1995, I flew to Honolulu, staying in the president's house, to meet my staff and other colleagues and to attend the board of regents meeting at Windward Community College on the so-called windward side of the island. Right away, various deans, directors, and faculty members peppered me with requests for my support (that translates to money) and warned me of conspiracies on campus to undermine the university's research efforts and other dire threats to my new role as senior vice president for research. I was glad to escape the chaos when I returned to Madison to prepare my laboratory for the move.

When I returned to Honolulu a short time later, my first order of business was to find a place to stay. Fortunately, one of my Harvard professors now on the Hawaii faculty arranged for me to live in the house of a retired architect, Alan Jay, who had moved into the home of his new wife. This was an idyllic place located not far from campus. I would be alone in this house for several months because Millie would not be able to join me in Hawaii full-time until June, when she had finished her teaching obligations for the spring semester.

During Wisconsin's spring break, however, the University of Hawaii paid for Millie to join me for a week in Honolulu to search for permanent housing. We had a good real estate agent who began to show us the available housing near campus. But, unfortunately, our search hit a snag early in the week when Millie's sister called with the bad news that their father was near death. Millie promptly flew back to Wisconsin to be at his side. He died shortly after she arrived.

Meanwhile, I resumed the search alone, hoping to find a house that she would enjoy. Ultimately, I settled on a nice house with a view of the ocean, a swimming pool, and other niceties. The only problem was money: it cost $725,000, which was well beyond our means. (My annual salary as senior vice president was $111,000). Money? No problem. I discovered that bankers could find any number of ways to make such a house affordable. In our case, it was an adjustable rate mortgage, with low affordable payments during the first five years. After that, the rate would presumably rise substantially—but "we'll deal with that when the time comes." Importantly, we had a beautiful house which we could move into when Millie moved to Hawaii in the summer.

The first few months in Hawaii were chaotic as I settled into my new job. Fortunately, I had a very competent, experienced office assistant who helped guide me through the myriad thorny issues. I quickly realized how little I knew about executive-level administration. But, with her help, I began my ascent up the learning curve. Also, I had a competent associate vice president, but she resigned within a few weeks after my arrival. Oh well, with Millie still in Madison, I had plenty of time to absorb more and more of the work.

The biggest chore, the reason I was hired, involved rebuilding the university's research administration. As I learned, the university contracted for an unaffiliated privately operated foundation, the Research Corporation of the University of Hawaii (RCUH) to manage the university's grants and contracts. The university submitted and received the grants on behalf of the principal investigator, who was responsible for the actual research. But it "service ordered" (that is, assigned) the financial and personnel management (buy supplies, hire staff, and so forth) of the grants to RCUH. In that way, university researchers could sidestep restrictive state procurement and hiring policies. The problem was that both the university's research administrators and the RCUH administrators assumed that the other was monitoring compliance with Federal regulations. Wrong. As federally mandated auditors took a close look at the arrangement, they found that things had slipped through the cracks, in violation of Federal laws. Indeed, they identified three "material weaknesses," in auditor's terms. These weaknesses were so glaring that the Federal government stopped all funding to the university for a period of three days. That may not sound like such a long time, but for a university it wreaks havoc on normal cash flow. Predictably, heads rolled. The university's vice president for research, then in his eleventh year on the job, was fired. And that's where I came into the scene.

In the aftermath of this debacle, it was my job to fix this situation. My experience as associate dean of the graduate school at the University of Wisconsin taught me what a well-running research administration should look like. But, I had no experience in the nuts and bolts of the operation. Thus, I relied on help from various members of the university and RCUH communities to disassemble and then rebuild the research administrative structure. The most difficult step was to re-negotiate a new contract between the university and RCUH. These were hard-core negotiations: again, new to me. I relied on the help of a member of my staff, Martin, who seemed to know what he was doing. Indeed he did know what he was doing; he went "toe to toe" with the formidable RCUH executive director. After several months of rancorous negotiations, they finally agreed to a suitable contract. All in all, it took about a year of hard effort to complete the new research administrative structure. I am proud that it has withstood the test of time, with no significant compliance issues during the past thirty years.

These efforts to rebuild the research infrastructure introduced me to the realities of Hawaiian social structure. Early on during meetings with research administrators at various levels of the hierarchy, I found myself to be the only white person, called a *haole* (pronounced "how-lee") in the Hawaiian language, in a room of AJAs, Americans of Japanese Ancestry. Enokawa, Nakamura, Masumoto, Ishii, et alia. That's odd, I thought. Why are there so many AJAs in these administrative positions? Out of curiosity, I began reading books about Hawaiian culture: for example, *Shoal of Time*, by Gavin Daws, *Hawaii*, by James Michener, and others. Moreover, Ken Mortimer, whose wife was a local AJA, explained various aspects of the different ethnic backgrounds in Hawaii. From these and other sources, I learned that since the white missionaries settled in Hawaii about 150 years ago, whites have traditionally run the large businesses and university executive offices, AJAs have dominated the state governmental and university administrative positions, the Chinese have run the financial institutions, and the Filipinos have taken care of the landscaping. The Native Hawaiians have worked primarily in service industries such as tourism and transportation. Simple as that, this stereotypical social structure seemed to be unquestioned by the local population. Indeed, several popular songs by Hawaiian musicians spoof these stereotypes.

Because I was working so closely with AJAs, in particular, I supplemented my reading by asking questions about their culture from various AJA colleagues. Gradually, I developed a reasonably good understanding and appreciation of their history in the Islands and their role in Hawaiian society. Along the way, I also developed a much better understanding of the Chinese, Filipino, and, significantly, Native Hawaiian cultures. Each made a unique contribution to the overall social milieu. As I learned more about the state's culture, I began to feel my roots take hold in the Hawaiian soil.

In addition to rebuilding the research infrastructure, my job required me to visit my constituency on not only Oahu but also the neighbor islands (that is, Maui, Molokai, Kauai, and the Big Island). Thus, I visited various research projects throughout the state. This included the world-famous telescopes atop Mauna Kea; in fact, they reported to me indirectly. The State of Hawaii owned the land up there, but it delegated management of this resource to the university: more specifically, to its Institute for Astronomy, which reported to me. I was, in effect, the landlord for these telescopes. In addition, I visited many agricultural sites: large and small farming operations, food processing plants, and the like. Through these visits, my understanding of Hawaiian culture expanded in both breadth and depth.

In addition, I also traveled throughout the state for monthly Board of Regents' meetings held on each of the University System's campuses. The highlights of neighbor island visits were the quarterly RCUH Board of Directors' meetings when they were held on a neighbor island. The RCUH Board was comprised mainly of AJAs, so they usually stayed at a top-scale Japanese hotel and ate at fine Japanese restaurants, places not generally frequented by haoles. My Hawaiian roots were growing deeper.

With all of this travel, my office work began to pile up. I needed help. Fortunately, while at a reception for oceanographers, one of the professors, Ed Laws, offered to help me. Ed had rudimentary administrative experience from serving as chair of the Oceanography Department for several years, so he "knew the ropes," so to speak, but only if they didn't have any complicating knots in them. No matter. I could take care of those more difficult situations. Although I didn't know him beforehand, I learned in that initial conversation that Ed had graduated in my class at Harvard. With that background, I was inclined to accept his offer. I felt that I could trust him. So, I appointed him half-time at first, with the understanding that we could increase the percentage if his appointment worked out satisfactorily. Ed lived up to my hopes and expectations, and soon I increased his appointment to full-time.

In early June, 1995, at the conclusion of her teaching obligations at the University of Wisconsin, Millie moved to Honolulu permanently. As part of my recruitment package, the University of Hawaii had appointed her as an assistant professor in the anatomy department, where she would teach in the gross anatomy course for first-year medical students—the same as at Wisconsin. Right off the bat, difficulties arose. The senior (and only other) professor in the course, Martha Morgan, took an instant dislike to Millie and vice versa. On the one hand, Millie was young, perky, and well-liked by the students. On the other hand, Martha was middle-aged, overweight, and not particularly liked by the students. Moreover, as a spousal accommodation, Millie had been imposed on the anatomy department without any consultation with Martha. This really irritated Martha, who seldom had a pleasant word to say to Millie. So, although Millie enjoyed working with the students, she loathed having anything to do with Martha. Nonetheless, with her excellent training in Wisconsin, Millie became an outstanding teacher in Hawaii, which, of course, irked Martha even more. Indeed, within a year or two, Millie routinely won the school's "Best Teacher" award, which disturbed Martha even further.

At home, however, Millie began to show signs of unhappiness. The acrimony with Martha took its toll, for sure. But other causes of unhappiness emerged. She began to resent the attention that I received as the new senior vice president for research. Furthermore, she had no patience for me when I would come home with difficult problems at work. "That's your problem" was her usual answer. I suppose, in hindsight, that my job threatened her hegemony as my wife. A deeper cause concerned me. This was Millie's first time living anywhere but in Wisconsin. She wasn't overtly homesick, but I began to sense a repressed longing to return to the comforting environment of family and friends in Wisconsin or, stated more bluntly, with white people from the Midwest. I had no solution to her unhappiness in Hawaii.

All was not doom and gloom for Millie, however. Within a few months, her hairdresser, Mary, introduced Millie to open-water ocean swimming. Having grown up on a lake in Wisconsin, Millie knew how to swim well, and she and Mary soon became close swimming partners. They would go out several times a week and both days on the weekend at Kaimana Beach, joining a larger group of excellent haole swimmers. Excellent, indeed; the group of about ten swimmers included several former Navy Seals, a local lifeguard, an Olympic water polo player, and a swimming coach at a local high school. After about six months or so, I joined her on the weekend mornings. Although I didn't know how to swim at first, a young couple (former NCAA champions from the University of Wisconsin) gave me swimming lessons. Gradually, I became comfortable in the ocean and began to accompany Millie and her group during the long Saturday and Sunday open-ocean swims beyond the reef, the breaking waves, into the wonderfully calming deep waters with their soothing swells. I felt secure out there, knowing that Millie and two or three of her friends constantly kept an eye on me. As I got better, we began to enter local open-ocean swim races, where Millie often won first place in her age group and I nearly always came in last. My poor performance didn't matter to anybody; we were accepted into this predominantly haole community of open-ocean swimmers. We were both very happy in this environment.

When I say that I usually came in last, I mean dead last. For some reason, I couldn't kick effectively, which slowed me down considerably. To illustrate this embarrassing point, I remember one race—a one-mile open-ocean race in Waimea Bay on Oahu's North Shore—when I was nearing the finish line far behind the rest of the pack. Ho! There were two other swimmers near me. Maybe I could beat them. As I got closer to them, I realized that one swimmer was a very pregnant woman and the other was a dog, a golden retriever. Predictably, they both crossed the finish line before me. But I enjoyed the race, and most of the other swimmers seemed to enjoy having me in the group. At least, they knew that the race was over when I crossed the finish line.

At work, a fateful change loomed on the horizon. Carol Eastman, the executive vice chancellor (the de facto chancellor), began to slow down in her work. Often, she would come in late in the morning and leave early that afternoon. She was not keeping up with her workload. Frustrated, our boss Ken Mortimer told me to take over the administration of two major units in her portfolio, the medical school and the college of tropical agriculture. I took on the extra work without any objections. From my experiences as associate dean of the graduate school at the University of Wisconsin, I knew how both units worked administratively, and I got along with their deans and faculty members. But that didn't solve the problem. Carol was still falling farther and farther behind in her work, which was then passed onto me to handle. To make a long story short, skipping gruesome detail, Carol was dying from cancer. In October, 1997, she passed away.

Fate had intervened tragically in Carol's life but now intervened providentially in mine. After Carol's death, Ken appointed me interim executive vice chancellor and then a couple of months later promoted me to the permanent position, removing the interim status. My promotion from interim to permanent executive vice chancellor came with no fanfare whatsoever. Ken preferred not to conduct a national search for the permanent position, although several in-house candidates expressed an interest in the job. Accordingly, he convinced the board that the extensive vetting of my credentials and so forth when I had been hired as senior vice president for research less than two years earlier sufficed for my appointment as permanent executive vice chancellor. At the time, I didn't know anything about these machinations on my behalf; I was too preoccupied with the workload Carol had left behind when she died.

Ken told me about my promotion late one afternoon while he was sitting in the dimly lit office of his trusted vice president for administration. As I walked past the office, Ken called me in and said: "Well, I guess you're it. Don't fuck this up!" And that was that. He had nothing more to say about the matter. Nor did anybody else. There were no formal celebrations, gala ceremonies, or elaborate press releases. In fact, for many of the so-called teaching faculty members and deans, I was an unwelcome substitute for Carol. I thought to myself: "But I didn't ask for this job; it was thrust upon me when she died." Oh, who cares? At most, I simply had to reprint my business cards without the "Interim" title on them. So it goes.

Importantly, Ken and the faculty union leadership formally acknowledged that as executive vice chancellor, I was de facto the chancellor of the Manoa campus—an acknowledgement promised to Carol when she was hired but never granted to her. This was an important acknowledgement because of the ambiguities inherent to the "vice chancellor" title. In practice, all campus vice presidents, deans, directors, and so forth now reported directly to me, with one exception: the athletic director. As an avid sports fan, Ken insisted on retaining that reporting line, although I now controlled the athletic department's budget. Some of the position titles caused confusion. For example, the accreditation association, the Western Association of Schools and Colleges (WASC), asked why the president of the university system also had the title chancellor of the Manoa campus when the executive vice chancellor had those acknowledged duties, or, for that matter, why did two vice presidents for academic affairs report to an executive vice chancellor? The best answer was "Just because." These were atavistic titles that the campus and the state legislature had become comfortable with over many years. Ultimately, under pressure from WASC, these ambiguous titles were all "sorted out" by the board in 2001.

Regardless of the ambiguous titles, I was now the chief academic and chief operating officer of the Manoa campus as well as senior vice president of the University of Hawaii System. Accordingly, I moved into Carol's office, adjacent to Ken's presidential office, and inherited her assistant, Yuki. Although Yuki lacked the professional demeanor of my former assistant, she proved to be quite knowledgeable about university procedures. I enjoyed working with her. In addition, this new position required me to work closely with Ken's executive assistant Edith Imato. On several occasions, I had interacted professionally with her in my previous position, but now I had to meet with her for an hour or so every morning, usually over a cup of strong coffee.

With Yuki's and Edith's help, I became familiar with the campus issues that required my attention. And there were many thorny challenges. For starters, the board of regents expected a new strategic plan within the next several months. Usually, development of a strategic plan required more than a year to allow all constituencies (faculty, administrators, legislators, students, members of the public, et cetera) to vet the plan. I asked the board for an extension of the deadline, but they refused, pointing out that Carol had been working on a plan for at least a year. So, I looked at her draft; it was a shambles. Reluctantly, I wrote my own version of the plan that she had begun, asking the faculty senate, deans, and directors for their comments. None of these groups provided any feedback; they had already provided that to Carol. I was on my own. Ultimately, yielding to board pressure, I submitted my plan to Ken for his perusal. He approved it and forwarded it to the board, meeting their imposed deadline. The Manoa campus now had a new strategic plan on paper but not in the minds and hearts of the faculty.

But that wasn't the worst of the challenges. Shortly before Carol died, the state reduced the university's appropriation by $28 million. The Manoa campus alone had to cut its budget by $14 million within the current fiscal year. The system promptly ordered a hiring freeze and stopped all unnecessary expenditures such as travel, library purchases, and non-emergency campus maintenance and repairs. These actions slowed the flow of cash, but more workable solutions must be found. For Manoa, that became Carol's and my problem to solve. Despite our pleas, none of the deans or directors provided any guidance on potential budget cuts. They became quite protective of their own units with little regard for the overall campus financial difficulties. Nor did the faculty senate provide any help in making decisions. For them, this was an administrative problem.

Thus, to identify where we could make these cuts, Carol and I both established independent faculty committees to review the so-called academic units that reported to her and the so-called research units that reported to me. The committees could agree on only one potential cut: the medical school. Shut it down. By now, the school reported to me, so I had to confront that unsettling conclusion. I call it unsettling, because I could not imagine that the board of regents would ever close the state's only medical school. Nonetheless, I spent many hours explaining medical school financing to the board members, preparing them for a vote on its closure. Well, political pressure, mainly from the local hospitals, intervened on behalf of the medical school, effectively quelling the discussion of its closure.

With Carol's death, I was on my own to solve the campus budget crisis. And I had little time to spare. For example, the chemistry department claimed that they had insufficient faculty members to offer all of the courses required for the B.S. degree, and, likewise, the medical school claimed that it had insufficient resources to offer the M.D. degree next year.

My office staff and I mulled over potential solutions. None was good. But, one solution emerged less bad than the others. The campus budget officer reckoned that we should impose a four percent budget cut for each of the next three years, for a total of twelve percent. That would generate sufficient savings in the first year to offset the reduced state allocations, with money leftover for reallocation to restore the neediest programs, such as chemistry, the medical school, the library, and so forth, and then to rebuild other programs as money became available in years two and three. This came to be known as the 4/4/4 plan. Without any guidance from the faculty or the deans and directors about how the four percent cuts should be levied, we saw no options other than making them across-the-board. Only the library and buildings and grounds would be excluded. When I told Ken about our plan, he simply muttered: "Across the board cuts are very unpopular. You're not going to have many friends when this is over with." At the time, I suspected that his grim prognosis was correct, but I didn't see any workable alternative solutions to the financial crisis. So, I announced the plan. Immediately, the campus, ranging from the deans to the faculty senate, protested my decision. Ken was right; I had few friends, indeed.

The campus limped through the first year of the 4/4/4 plan. The chemistry and medical school budgets were repaired, and numerous other programs received a welcome allocation to restore services. The second round of four percent cuts evoked no less rancor, but it accomplished its goal: meet the state funding shortfall and generate money for re-allocation to needy programs. Resigned to the plan, the faculty senate agreed to help me decide how to re-allocate money during this second iteration. Their participation helped me immensely, for it took the burdensome decision-making off my shoulders. I still didn't have many friends on campus, but at least I received a smile now and then.

During this tumultuous period, another calamity struck the campus: in early 2001, the faculty went on strike. They demanded more pay. Fortunately, as an administrator, I didn't—couldn't legally—participate in the labor negotiations; they were between the state and the faculty union. So, I was spared the faculty's enmity on this particular issue. The strike went on for 13 days, when it ended ostensibly in the faculty's favor. The strike was over, and the faculty members resumed their teaching. But I confronted a major challenge collateral to the strike: how to make up for nearly two weeks of lost teaching days to retain accreditation. The university was obligated to provide 42 teaching hours per three-credit course per semester, usually spread over fourteen weeks. The strike deprived the university of two weeks in this calculus. After considerable debate among my staff members, I decided to mandate makeup classes compressed into Saturdays and Sundays of two successive weekends. Thankfully, the faculty members and students greeted this proposal with few objections, and the semester came to a successful conclusion.

How many more things could go wrong? At Manoa, there seemed to be an endless supply. Lawsuits, botched intellectual property agreements, a lost NSF center grant, and on and on. Among this long list of difficulties, one item stands out: accreditation.

On my watch as executive vice chancellor, the university's accreditation by WASC was up for reaffirmation (WASC's code word for renewal). For the university, this is a big deal, for it entails a lot of tedious work by not only administrators but also faculty members. Usually, this stretches out for about two years prior to a site visit by WASC. Carol had just begun the renewal efforts, meeting with various groups on campus to engage them in the process. Unfortunately, when she died, faculty interest in the reaffirmation process went with her; everybody working on the renewal simply stopped. I had to start from the beginning, with a little less than two years to pull together a convincing case for reaffirmation. The timing was bad; much of this work had to be completed during the first year of the 4/4/4 plan when I had few friends. Begrudgingly, the faculty senate helped me pull together the appropriate faculty committees needed to prepare program analyses, write reports, and so forth. But, my meetings with them often verged on open hostility. My problems were compounded in the most unexpected way: my usually trustworthy vice president for academic affairs (VPAA), who was responsible for many aspects of the accreditation report, froze like a deer in bright headlights midway through his assignments. He simply could not continue. So, sadly, I had to replace him as VPAA, bringing in an energetic young department chair to get the process back on track.

To make a much longer story short, we completed the accreditation report and the WASC site visit. The results contained good news and bad news. Good news: the university's accreditation was reaffirmed for another three years—not the usual ten. Thus, in three years we would have to go through an abbreviated review that addressed several key questions. That meant more work, but the university could handle it. Bad news: in its final report, in the last paragraph, WASC mentioned that the university had come "perilously close" to failing its reaffirmation. That statement startled the university's faculty, board of regents members, and state legislators. I asked the WASC executive director why they had included this inflammatory comment when, in fact, they had granted us the reaffirmation. The director laughed and said that it was simply meant as a nudge to keep us on track for the next review. Okay. But, he was the only person laughing. The rest of the university community began assigning blame for this "perilous" shortcoming that threatened the university's integrity, and, of course, many fingers pointed at me. I had little choice other than to thicken my skin and catch the flak. After several months, the hubbub died down, mainly because we had to begin preparations for the next review.

On several occasions, I encountered power as I had as associate dean at the University of Wisconsin. Only here, the stakes were much higher. In the most blatant case, the governor of Hawaii called me with a singular demand: to close the university's lab school, a tuition-free K-12 school operated by the college of education to train teachers and test new curricular materials. In the normal course of events, I was accustomed to inquiries and even demands from members of the public. That's part of the job at a public institution. But this call was different. It was from the state's duly elected chief executive officer, the governor. The conversation was short and to the point: "Smith, I want you to close the lab school. It is an elitist institution that disagrees with the core values of this state." After a short pause, I answered: "With all due respect, Governor, I don't have the authority to close the school unilaterally. Only the board of regents has the authority to close it, and according to their policy, this is an academic issue that would require consultation with the faculty senate. I'm sure that the senate would hesitate to flout the principles of academic freedom in this case."

The governor wasn't easily dissuaded. "Perhaps you don't realize that the State Constitution, which was ratified by the people, authorizes me to appoint members of the board of regents, who, in turn, appoint your boss, President Mortimer. So I have the authority to order the lab school's closure. Now do it promptly." With trepidation, I replied: "I understand. But I cannot act beyond the limits of my authority." Ho! I had defied the governor. Common wisdom would posit that I would soon be looking for another job and that the school would be closed.

But that didn't happen. In response to the governor's demand, I appointed a committee comprised of members of the faculty, members of the general public, and several students. Its charge was to assess the lab school's performance, with the unspoken mandate to recommend either continuation of the school or closure. A priori, I strongly suspected that the outcome would be to continue the school as is. Make no changes: that's the nature of academic committee decisions. Sure enough. The committee strongly endorsed the school and recommended that it continue to operate as usual. I had done my part, hoping to satisfy the governor. Well, whether satisfied or not, the governor backed off and never contacted me again about the lab school. I had survived this encounter with a very powerful individual.

I could recount several other stressful encounters with power. For example, the chairman of the board of regents insisted that I fire the newly appointed dean of engineering, a National Academy of Engineering member, because he didn't respond to pressure from local politicians to seek earmarked appropriations. He insisted that his faculty members obtain research funding from competitive Federal grants. I agreed wholeheartedly with the dean but had to do something to appease the regent. So, again, I solved the problem by appointing a faculty committee to review the dean's performance after only about two years on the job instead of the usual five years. The committee responded as I expected, recommending that the dean continue for another five years. And, so he did.

A related example was the demand by a member of the board of regents to fire the long-time director of the Institute of Astronomy because he had re-directed money earmarked by the state legislature for telescope operations atop Haleakala (located on Maui, where the regent lived) to Mauna Kea operations on the Big Island. According to the director, the money was put to better use on Mauna Kea. I was caught in the middle of a monumental battle between the director and the regent, who saw this as a racist conflict between haoles (the director and me) and the local Hawaiian community (primarily AJAs). After reading the appropriation statute and, more importantly, the legislative notes, I realized that the regent had the law on his side in this quarrel. But the director defiantly stood by his decision, no matter what the legislature intended by the appropriation. The tremendous pressure from the regent and several Maui state legislators to correct this injustice shifted from the director to me; "Do your job. Fix this!" Ultimately, I relented and fired the director to resolve the conflict. Of course, this angered the director, whose only comment to me was "You're a miserable failure as a vice president for research." The regent never said "thanks."

Shortly after becoming executive vice chancellor, fate smiled on me in an unexpected way: Yuki encouraged me to go to the athletic center gym before work to maintain my health. I hesitated at first, because I had never enjoyed working out in a gym. To encourage me, though, Millie accompanied me to the gym, lifted a few weights, and then walked over to the neighboring campus pool to swim. Reluctantly, I began to workout daily lifting weights and so forth, starting at 6 a.m.

Soon, I noticed that Edith also worked out every morning but then disappeared after about half an hour. I asked her where she went, and she replied "running." "How far?" "About six miles this morning, longer on weekends." Hmm. I had run very short distances (for example 100 yards) in high school but never a distance that long. Nevertheless, the idea of long-distance running intrigued me. So, coached by Edith, I began running, first 400 yards, then 800 yards, and longer and longer until I was running six miles at her side every weekday morning. In less than a year, she coaxed me to run competitively in races ranging from 5 kilometers (3.1 miles) to 26.2 miles, the Honolulu Marathon. To prepare for these long races, on Sunday morning I ran longer and longer distances (up to 22 miles) with Edith and a group of her friends. On Saturday mornings, I still went swimming in the ocean with Millie, but I remained a mediocre swimmer. In contrast, I became a respectable runner, often winning an age-group medal in the local races. Swimming and running brought me closer to "ordinary" Hawaiians—if open ocean swimmers and marathon runners can be called "ordinary." As I made new friends in the swimming and running communities, I felt my roots spreading out even further into the local culture, and I liked that.

In the winter we continued to ski for about a month at various resorts in the West. Sun Valley became our favorite destination, and we seldom went anywhere else. We often skied with major donors to the university who lived in nearby Ketchum, Idaho. They became good friends and allowed us to store our ski equipment in their garage, sparing us the nuisance of hauling it back and forth to Hawaii.

In addition to these athletic activities, Millie and I enjoyed Hawaii as a place to live. Now and then we spent long weekends on the neighbor islands, where we explored the natural beauties of Hawaii. Even the university offered numerous pleasant events that I was obligated ex officio to attend, such as gala dinner parties featuring Hawaiian-style entertainment: luaus, hula dancing, slack-key guitar music. Moreover, we entertained friends and visitors to Hawaii (mainly relatives) in our beautiful house with its view of the ocean, swimming pool, and tiki torches on the surrounding deck.

Apropos the house: Despite its beauty, after about three years there, we sold our house out of frustration with several structural issues, such as leaks in the swimming pool and window frames, which were proving very difficult to fix, and moved into a rented house close to the beach on Diamond Head. That place offered even more opportunities to enjoy the beauties of Hawaii. We looked onto the beach and could hear the waves caress the shore. And, within less than five minutes, we could walk to the beach, where we could swim or simply enjoy strolling in the warm water. Furthermore, because this was a rental property, we didn't have to care for the yard. Nor did we have a swimming pool to care for. I enjoyed not having these chores.

Yes, on balance, I was truly happy with our lifestyle in Hawaii.

I can't say the same for Millie. Although she enjoyed swimming both in the open ocean and the university's pool and regularly won the medical school's best teacher of the year award, she became more and more discontent with Hawaii. I didn't know the root causes of her unhappiness, but I suspected that I played a significant role. My work schedule interfered with our home life. Regularly I had to attend receptions and other social occasions that kept me at work until about 7 p.m. Frequent several-day trips to the neighbor islands further restricted my time at home. Likewise, my running schedule interfered with our home life. Every morning (except Saturday), I would get up alone at 4:30, eat breakfast, and leave the house by 5:30 in order to meet my running colleagues for a 6 a.m. run. While training for a marathon, these runs could last for up to four hours, meaning that I wouldn't get home until about noon. Exhausted, after lunch I would then take a one- or two-hour nap to recover.

But, more insidiously, during these long runs, I developed close relationships, bonding so to speak, with several runners, including Edith. Since Millie had no interest in discussing my work problems, I had turned more and more to Edith in particular for her listening ear and comforting solace during our long runs. Millie noticed my attention to "the other woman," and, of course, this bothered her greatly. To appease Millie in this matter, I cut back the number of times that I ran with Edith, but I couldn't cut back the time we spent together at work. In my own defense, I also reasoned that the root cause of Millie's unhappiness was that she missed Wisconsin and its Midwestern culture. After all, she had never lived out of the state before. And, she often made derogatory comments about the "locals" in Hawaii. Regardless of the causes of her growing discontent with me, we never questioned the strength of our marriage. This period in our lives would simply be a recognizable low point in our relationship.

In fall, 2000, fate intervened once again. It all started in a strange sequence of events. To meet its operating budget deficit, the university proposed a substantial tuition increase (three to four percent for each of the next five years). Naturally, the students opposed this. So, when the board of regents met to vote on the increase, over one hundred mostly Native Hawaiian students and interested "outsiders" signed up to testify against the proposal. They packed the hall. We, the members of the administration, heard disturbing rumors of their plans to disrupt the meeting. So, Gary, the vice president for administration, arranged to have the Honolulu police department standby in case of trouble. The police claimed that they needed to be on campus to respond quickly to any disturbance. Without telling the president or the board members, Gary complied with their request: "But keep a low profile." So the Honolulu police billeted in the shadows of the medical school's parking lot several hundred yards from the site of the board of regents' meeting.

Unfortunately, the profile wasn't low enough. About an hour into the board's meeting, an excited student ran into the hall and announced the presence of police with their dogs on campus. That drove the crowd into a fury. They yelled at the board members and the president: "What's the matter, don't you trust us?" "Who do you think we are? A bunch of thugs?" Stunned, Ken looked for Gary to get an explanation. But, as fate would have it, Gary was nowhere to be seen, for he had just stepped out of the hall for a bathroom break. The angry crowd started to surge forward toward the board members. Hastily, the campus police formed a cordon protecting the board members and led them and the administration members (including me) down the cordon out of the hall into a separate room for safety. The board members, especially the older ones, were visibly terrified.

After a few minutes, Gary entered the room and quickly realized what had happened. Ken told him to order the Honolulu police to leave the campus immediately, which they did reluctantly. Nonetheless, after the campus police had restored calm in the meeting hall, the board members and the administrators returned through a protective campus police cordon to complete their business. First, Ken informed the restless crowd that the Honolulu police had been sent home. Second, the board, still quite jittery, reversed their pre-planned commitment to Ken that they would approve the motion for a tuition increase and, instead, appeased the crowd by rejecting the motion. Ken was deeply disappointed, for he now lacked a plan for repairing the university's fractured budget. Fate had struck him with a harsh, unexpected blow.

The next evening at a lavish dinner party in a Waikiki hotel, Ken whispered in my ear: "I resigned this morning." Yes, he had told the board that he would step down as soon as it could identify a successor. His reason was straightforward: the board had expressed "no confidence" in his leadership when they rejected the tuition increase. I didn't agree with his reasoning but couldn't fault Ken for this fateful decision; during his tenure as president, he had taken a verbal hammering from all constituencies: the faculty members, the deans, the board members, state legislators, and the governor. Surprised by his announcement, the board asked him to reconsider, but he remained resolute. Enough was enough. No mas.

So, the search for a successor began, led by the board chair. After several months, they chose Evan Dobelle, the seasoned president of Trinity College in Hartford, Connecticut, as the new university of Hawaii system president effective on July 1, 2001. As the University of Hawaii board of regents prepared for his arrival, it made several housekeeping changes. Most notable was the sorting out of position titles: for example, changing my title from Executive Vice Chancellor to Chancellor of the Manoa campus. And, while they were at it, they corrected the titles of various other administrators at Manoa from Vice President to Vice Chancellor. These may seem like minor emendations, but they made the accreditors (WASC) happy, for they clarified the reporting lines.

The transition from Ken to Evan became a tumultuous affair. For me, the timing could not have been worse, because Millie and I had arranged for a two-week vacation trip to South Africa spanning the last week of June and the first week of July, exactly when Evan took over as president and, therefore, became my new boss. Hoping to minimize the impact of my absence during his first week on the job, in April, I flew to Hartford to meet him. He pleasantly greeted me and told me that I shouldn't worry about not being present during his first days on the job and that I should enjoy my trip to South Africa. Remembering the debacle when I was in Munich during John Wiley's first week on the job as graduate school dean at Wisconsin, I still worried about my pending absence but, once again, decided not to change my plans.

My stress level rose shortly afterwards, indeed the entire campus's stress level rose, when Evan dispatched two of his Trinity College staff members to scrutinize the University of Hawaii before his arrival, looking for potential academic and operational trouble spots and surveying possible candidates for his staff. Word got around that they were preparing a "hit list" of politically undesirable members of the administration—those who would go. I wasn't sure if I would be on that list or not. The 4/4/4 plan was still fresh in many minds. My anxiety level rose further due to the planned South Africa trip. Oh well, I decided not to worry any more about all of this. Besides, I had been asked by the board to prepare a job description for a new system position, vice president for academic affairs. Maybe that was intended for me in the new administration.

As soon as Evan took over the presidency on July 1, my anxieties proved to be well founded. As planned, Millie and I were in South Africa, spending two enjoyable weeks on a safari. Alas, when I returned to my office on a Sunday afternoon, the enjoyment quickly dissipated. The vice president for research was packing the contents of his office (my former office when I held that position); he had been told on Friday to vacate by Monday because "the new chancellor would be moving in." And that wouldn't be me. It would be Dwayne Newby, a former dean of social sciences. Something was amiss! The next morning, when I entered my office, Yuki asked me "Now that Dwayne Newby is running Manoa, what should I do?" Uh oh. While I was in South Africa, I had been replaced by Newby as chancellor. Evan never spoke to me about this, but Newby explained that I would return immediately to the faculty as a 12-month researcher, no longer a member of the administration. To help me with this transition, he would provide me with a one semester paid leave of absence and $5000 in one-time travel money. I asked for start-up funds to re-establish a research program. Newby asked how much? I thought fast. "$140,000 per year for three years," I answered brazenly. To my surprise, he agreed to the amount: $420,000 spread over three years. To my further surprise, he agreed to continue paying me the same salary that I had been earning as executive vice chancellor, plus a $280 per month supplement that I had been receiving for the use of my automobile for official business. Certainly, I could not complain about this transition package. Thus came a sharp turn in the course of my career.

All I needed now was an office and laboratory space. Several years earlier, I had given away the office and laboratory space assigned to me by the medical school and the equipment that I had brought from Wisconsin. I would be starting from scratch. First things first: an office. The medical school dean, who controlled space in their building, was out of town for a couple of weeks. Nobody else had authority to make this kind of space assignment. So, I approached the dean of the school of ocean and earth sciences and technology (SOEST) whose school had benefitted from the 4/4/4 plan's re-allocations. He readily offered me a nice office. Furthermore, he convinced me to transfer my tenure from the medical school to SOEST; I would become a professor of oceanography. I knew nothing about oceanography, but, I thought that I could certainly learn enough to teach the subject at an elementary level. Besides, oceanography was recognized as one of the best departments on campus.

On my last day as executive vice chancellor, the vice presidents, deans, directors, and other senior staff members held a farewell dinner for me at Willows, a Hawaiian restaurant not far from campus. Besides the wonderful food, one aspect of the event was noteworthy. Following the dinner, Ed Laws (who was now interim vice chancellor for research) suggested that I might enjoy meetings of the Harvard Club of Hawaii. I had not heard of the club before, so out of curiosity I attended the next meeting in Honolulu. Although the meeting itself was of little interest, a positive opportunity arose when one of the members asked me if I would be interested in interviewing local applicants to Harvard on behalf of the admissions committee. Why not? Now I had time, so I volunteered. Within a few months, I began interviewing applicants and have continued to this day, about 24 years later.

(Astute readers might protest that interviewing Harvard applicants while working for another university constitutes a conflict of interest. I cannot dispute this assertion. But I did it anyway, rationalizing that the applicants for Harvard would have negligible interest in applying to the universities where I worked. I can only beg forgiveness for this ethical lapse.)

Hawaii-II

Without the pressures of administrative work, I no longer had rigid time restrictions on my morning runs. I still woke up at about 4:30 a.m. to join my running partners at 6:00 a.m., but now I could run as long as I wanted to. Consequently, my weekday runs extended from about six miles to nine or ten miles. For whatever reason, I also lost weight—15 pounds or so within several months. With better conditioning and less weight, I became a faster runner. Indeed, I received a Mid-Pacific Road Runners Club Runner of the Year award for my age group in 2004 and qualified for the 2005 and 2006 Boston Marathons. Furthermore, in long-distance swimming, I continued to compete in numerous open-ocean races, including the Waikiki Roughwater Swim. In fact, I actually won third-place awards in several swimming races. For the first time in my life, at about age 60, I felt like an accomplished athlete. I felt good.

Likewise, without the pressures of administrative work, I had time to take on an interesting consulting job with the Oceanic Institute, a small research institute located about 20 miles west of Honolulu. One of their main research projects was to increase the growth rate of farmed shrimp. The institute director thought that my scientific research skills qualified me to introduce recombinant DNA techniques into the shrimp farming industry. He offered me $20,000 in three installments for three reports on my recommendations. Not bad money.

Right off the bat, I should answer the obvious question: Why would the institute director think that I had any knowledge about shrimp farming? Well, in fact, I did have a fundamental knowledge of shrimp farming and marine aquaculture in general. Let me explain.

When I first joined the university as its chief research officer, I became ex officio chair of the advisory committee for a large United States Department of Agriculture (USDA) grant awarded to the Oceanic Institute that supported small aquaculture businesses in the Pacific islands, ranging from Hawaii to Taiwan. Most of these businesses involved aquaculture farming of one marine species or another: shrimp, sponges, oysters (for their pearls), and various fish species. At first, I knew nothing about any of this. But, the grant's program director, a renowned aquaculture specialist at the institute, slowly but surely brought me up to speed, at least to the basic level.

As advisory committee chair, I was expecting to visit each grant recipient once every two years. The program director would accompany me and arrange all aspects of the trip which would take more than two weeks. Whoa. That's a long time for me to be away from my office and Millie. Too bad. The time came for my first round of visits, and off we went. The itinerary took us on the Continental Airlines "island hopper" from Honolulu to Guam, with intermediate stops in the Marshall Islands (Majoro and Kwajalein) and Micronesia (Kosrae, Pohnpei, and Chuuk). In Majoro, Kosrae, Pohnpei, and Guam, we stayed several nights and visited aquaculture farms here and there. The entire setting was beautiful: the blue ocean, the coral reefs, the quaint lodging. We spent several nights in Guam, visiting the aquaculture research facilities of the University of Guam as well as the rest of the island. I didn't care much for Guam; it was less beautiful than the smaller islands we had seen. And, it was dominated by a large United States Air Force base and hordes of tourists.

From Guam, we continued to Kaohsiung, in southern Taiwan, where we visited huge aquaculture facilities for farming shrimp. The Taiwanese had this farming down to a science. I was amazed at the scope of these operations. After a few days, we flew to Taipei where I visited Curtis and Alexia. That was a special treat. Finally, the time came to return to Honolulu, via Guam. I had enjoyed the trip, but I was glad to get home.

Two years later, the program director and I made the same trip again. This time, we visited the same facilities and the same people. I felt welcome. (Why not? I represented the grant that provided them a considerable amount of money). And, I had a much better understanding of aquaculture. I looked forward to the next scheduled trip (my third), but by then I was no longer in the university's administration and, therefore, no longer on the grant's advisory board. Oh well, my several years of service on the board had been long enough to convince the Oceanic Institute director that I knew what I was talking about when it came to shrimp farming.

With this fundamental background in aquaculture, I began my consulting job at the Oceanic Institute. Initially, I spent three or four mornings each week researching the topic of shrimp diets in the institute's library. My first report was little more than a brief survey of the existing literature on the topic. Although the institute researchers all knew this material better than I did, the director paid me a first tranche of $3000. My second report was a detailed set of experiments designed to determine the rate-limiting step in farmed shrimp growth. I reasoned that unless that critical step was known, I couldn't know where to intervene at the molecular level. I wasn't sure that my proposed experiments were entirely doable in practice, but at least they seemed reasonable in theory. I could work out farming details with the institute staff. The director paid me a second tranche ($6000) for the report but said that he preferred to sever our agreement. In other words, the institute researchers weren't happy with my reports. I wasn't surprised and didn't argue.

How could I? And that ended my career as a consultant on shrimp farming.

I was not disappointed or, for that matter, embarrassed at this outcome. My future didn't include shrimp farming; it never did and never would. I did learn from this experience, however, that I should concentrate on my academic strengths and not areas where I had limited expertise.

With this in mind, I began to ponder what my research could concentrate on. The more I thought about the possibilities, the more inclined I became to re-establish a neurophysiology program (play from strength), instead of something in oceanography, where I had little expertise. But, there was no point in trying to resume my research program on synaptic transmission, picking up where I had left off when I came to Hawaii. The field had advanced too far for me to catch up. I needed something new, a unique preparation such as archaea or some other microorganism. No, too boring.

But then the epiphany: I would study the electrophysiological properties of stem cells. The scientific community had been excited about stem cells for the past several years because of their capability to differentiate into any other cell type in the body, and there were many unanswered questions about them, leaving plenty of room for me to step into the field. That kind of research program could best be set-up in the medical school where I would have colleagues with similar interests. Fortunately, the dean had now returned from vacation and readily agreed to provide me with adequate laboratory space and an office in the biomedical sciences building, although I would remain formally a SOEST faculty member.

So, I began the chore of establishing the laboratory. This required the help of the buildings and grounds department: remodeling cabinetry, installing telephone and internet lines, laying carpet in my office, and so forth. Amazingly, the buildings and grounds crew gave my project top priority; they remembered that I had spared them from any budget reductions in the 4/4/4 plan. I was reminded of the old saying: "Be good to your camel and your camel will be good to you." Within a few weeks, I had a beautiful new laboratory and office. And, with the start-up money, I bought new office furniture and state-of-the-art equipment. The laboratory and office became my castle.

The first step in my scientific transition was to learn how to culture cells. I had no experience in this, so I enrolled in several workshops here and there to learn the technique. Initially, I learned how to harvest and culture embryonic mouse fibroblasts which were used as a nutritive carpet on which to grow stem cells. Finally, after a couple of months of training, I took the first bold step of establishing a culture of mouse fibroblasts in my lab. Everything worked! For the next several months, I perfected my techniques of culturing fibroblasts.

With my confidence buoyed, I took the bold step of establishing a culture of mouse embryonic stem cells obtained from a starter supply that I had bought from a commercial vendor. Again everything worked, and I built up a supply of them for storage in liquid nitrogen. My laboratory was up and running. What a good feeling; I was on my way towards resuscitating my research career.

The next challenge was to direct the stem cells to differentiate into neurons by adding various growth factors to their culture medium. This was not a trivial undertaking, for many of the cells "had a mind of their own." Importantly, I had to ascertain which stem cells had differentiated into neurons and which had taken a different pathway. The standard method for making this determination was immunocytochemistry: stain the cells with neuron-specific antibodies and then identify the neuronal cells under the microscope. I had no experience in this technique, but it didn't seem to be too difficult, so I decided to learn it on my own. With help from various textbooks, everything came into place.

The final step was to analyze the ionic currents flowing across the neuronal cell membranes using patch-clamp procedures. I was familiar with the technique from my previous work in Munich, so with state-of-the-art recording equipment, this proved to be an easy task.

With lots of money available for the best equipment and endless supplies, my research progressed smoothly for the next year or so. I became proficient in culturing embryonic mouse stem cells and directing their differentiation into neurons. Indeed, I began to feel confident in my newfound skills.

About that time, several laboratories around the world purportedly cultured human embryonic stem cells. Hmm. Human cells seemed far more interesting than mouse cells; I'll give them a try. I obtained a starter culture of human embryonic stem cells from a laboratory in Wisconsin and began to culture them, hoping to direct their differentiation into nerve cells. This proved to be a very difficult procedure because these cells differentiate into many different cell types very quickly in culture. To isolate the undifferentiated cells, whose differentiation I could control, I needed a much better (code for "expensive") microscope and several other pieces of optical equipment. No problem. I could afford the best.

My interest in human embryonic stem cells faltered when I made a startling observation: I detected a cluster of these cells that were contracting and relaxing rhythmically, just like a heart might beat. Whoa! Surely these cells hadn't been in culture long enough to differentiate into a heart or, for that matter, a sentient progenitor nervous system. No way, I assured myself. Nonetheless, I paused my work on human cells indefinitely while I pondered this phenomenon.

Over the next month or so, I learned that several other laboratories had made similar observations of beating cells but had dismissed them as abnormalities induced by the culture conditions. I wasn't reassured, so I discontinued my work on human embryonic stem cells. Somebody else can do that. Not I.

During this first year of my renascence as a laboratory researcher, fate intervened in my life in two eventful ways. First, fate had other plans for our living arrangements. Specifically, our landlord announced that he was planning to sell our house. Oh no! Maybe we could buy it. Impossible, for the asking price was nearly $3 million. So, once again, we had to find a new place to live. This time, we settled on a nice house located in the mountainous rain forest above Honolulu; on the top of Round Top Drive, to be exact. The place was certainly adequate, although it had a couple of quirks. First, the house had no access to a public water supply, so our water came from rain water drainage off of our roof; it was stored in a large 10,000-gallon underground tank next to the house and pumped into the house plumbing system. We were a bit uncomfortable drinking this water, so I recurrently hauled a 10-gallon carboy of double-distilled water from my laboratory to use for coffee, cooking, and dishwashing. Second, the house had no public sewage system. Instead, it had a septic system with a drainage field off to the side of the lot. Despite these quirks, we enjoyed the house and its beautiful surroundings. This was Hawaii at its rural best.

Second, fate had other plans for my administrative expertise. It began one afternoon when a senior physiology professor and good friend, Martin Raynor, asked me to take his place as principal investigator on a large (about $6 million) NIH research grant to improve research infrastructure throughout the state. Curious, of course, I asked why. As Martin explained it, he had been spending the money to offset medical school revenue shortfalls and not on the grant's specific aims. This really angered NIH. In fact, they intended to cancel the grant if the university didn't appoint another, more "responsible" (Martin's word, not mine) principal investigator. And soon.

At first, I didn't see any reason to take on this headache. So, I said no. Martin asked me again and again during the next two weeks as NIH applied pressure. I continued to say no. Until one Saturday afternoon, that is, when the new chancellor (Newby's successor) called me to his office, where he asked me to take the job. I explained disingenuously that I would no longer be able to accept any more consulting work and would, therefore, require a pay raise to compensate for this lost income. Furthermore, as principal investigator of such a large grant, I wouldn't have time to write my own grant applications. Thus, I would need institutional support to compensate for this lost opportunity to apply for Federal grant support. The chancellor didn't quibble. He offered me a $25,000 pay raise and $100,000 per year to support my research program, on top of the $420,000 in start-up funds that I received when I stepped down from the administration. I had to conceal my stunned smile as I accepted his terms. From then on, I was principal investigator of the largest grant that I ever had. Until two years later, that is, when NIH renewed the grant for $14 million. Fortunately, I attracted good staff members to help me administer the grant. Fate had been good to me. Very good.

After a year or so into my new research program, two colleagues joined me—one in the lab and one virtually. Unexpectedly, Millie announced her intention to join the lab full-time, working on Western blots to characterize the differentiated mouse embryonic stem cells. Somehow, she convinced her department chair to relieve her from her teaching obligations. I never really understood what had motivated her decision to quit teaching. But, I'm sure that

Martha was quite pleased to see her go. I was happy to have her in the laboratory, because her Western blots added a new dimension of rigor to my experiments.

And then, Ron Kalil, a good friend at the University of Wisconsin, asked to collaborate with me on one of his projects: characterizing stem cells as they differentiated into neurons in the intact embryonic mouse brain. That interested me. So Ron began sending me embryonic mouse brain stem cells that I then cultured in my laboratory. The goal of my efforts was to identify populations of these cells that had differentiated in situ into neurons using immunocytochemistry and then to characterize their electrophysiological properties using patch clamp techniques. Together, we characterized the cells and ion-channel types, which resulted in a publication a couple of years later. This proved to be the only paper from my new laboratory, and I was very proud of it.

To improve the efficiency in these types of long-distance collaborations, Ron and I wanted to develop a procedure for analyzing the immunocytochemistry results together in real time. Ideally, he could control my microscope in Honolulu, and vice versa, I could control his microscope in Madison. To our knowledge, there were only a few setups like this in the country, so we knew that the project was feasible. But, to accomplish it, we needed a super-fast internet connection to link our microscopes. At the University of Wisconsin, Ron had that capability, but I needed a much faster connection than that available to me at the University of Hawaii. No problem. I wrote a section of a multi-institutional grant to NIH for the money ($10 million) to bring ultra-high-speed internet to the campus and to upgrade every laboratory in the biomedical sciences building, with a dedicated line to the microscope in my laboratory. Ron and I were on the cusp of achieving our goal.

But, fate brought my progress in the laboratory to an abrupt stop when disaster struck: on the evening of October 30, 2004, a flash flood swept down the Manoa valley and across parts of the campus, flooding the biomedical sciences building. Flood waters didn't reach my laboratory on the fifth floor, but they completely destroyed the basement-level electrical power supply to the building. Restoring the building's electrical infrastructure would require at least six months. In the meantime, large diesel-fueled generators provided electricity for critical equipment such as freezers and refrigerators. But they didn't provide sufficient electricity to operate elevators, well-lit hallways, laboratory lighting, or for that matter any routine laboratory equipment. Furthermore, they spewed black diesel-fuel residue which coated many plastic surfaces in the lab and probably the lining of our lungs. Along with the other occupants of the building, I retreated to home, thus abandoning my beautiful office and experimental research program for an indefinite duration.

As the waiting time for restoration of the electrical service to the building dragged on, month after month, both Millie and I became antsy. As always, she wanted to leave Hawaii for the mainland, and, with my laboratory shut down indefinitely, I began reluctantly to look for other job opportunities.

Lo, fate stepped in again when Texas Tech offered us both positions: Millie would teach anatomy as a tenured associate professor in the department of biology, and I would be vice president for research, with a tenured professorship in the department of biology. These were not coveted positions; the university was not particularly good academically, and Lubbock, Texas, was not a very appealing place to live. But, the university offered to pay us generously and to move our possessions from Hawaii to Lubbock. I might have been a bit more enthusiastic if I had been offered a medical school appointment. However, Texas Tech didn't have a medical school. Well, wait: technical correction. There was a Texas Tech medical school located on the same campus, but it was a separate state entity with its own independent legal, administrative, and faculty structure. At best, they could offer me an adjunct faculty position, which I accepted. None of this was ideal, but in 2005 we decided to move from Hawaii back to the mainland to take these new jobs. At the time, Millie was quite elated, but I was profoundly despondent at leaving my home, my paradise.

Fortunately, the University of Hawaii treated us well as we departed for Texas Tech. After ten years working at the university, we both vested in the state retirement system. Furthermore, the university granted us each a one-year unpaid leave of absence, conveying us the right to return during that year if the Texas Tech job didn't work out. I accepted that offer immediately, thus extending my official time as a university employee to eleven years, which, in turn, increased my eventual pension payout by 10 percent. Soured on Hawaii, Millie rejected the leave of absence; she just wanted out. At the end of my eleventh year, I retired officially from the university at age 62, thus activating my State of Hawaii pension and health coverage. Despite these generous benefits, though, for me, paradise was lost.

Before leaving the memories of my years in Hawaii, I should mention that in early 2003, fate had a very personal sadness in store for me. On January 31, my mother died. This was not unexpected, for her health had been deteriorating due to a variety of maladies for the previous several years. Every now and then during this time, I would fly from Honolulu to Colorado Springs to see her. She seemed to enjoy the visits, and I enjoyed spending time with her. I would stay with my brother Curtis, and I enjoyed spending time with him as well. He and I had always been very close.

To ease the burden of my visits on Curtis and his wife, Millie and I bought a condo in a condominium development across the street from his house. With the help of a very handy handyman, we fixed it up to our liking. It became our "home away from home."

In late 2002, I knew that my mother was approaching the end of her life, for she had been refusing to eat regularly. As a result, she lost weight and took on a cadaverous appearance. I hardly recognized her when she died. The coroner's report stated that the cause of death was that she "no longer had the will to live." I suppose that means that she died of "natural causes." After her cremation and a memorial service held at the Unitarian church, Curtis and I sprinkled her ashes in the Garden of the Gods behind the house where she and we grew up while I read "Ashes to ashes, dust to dust" from the Book of Common Prayer. Our parents were both dead now. May they rest in peace.

Like our father, my mother didn't leave a will or any other directive for managing her estate. So, Curtis and I plunged ahead with filling out legal forms, selling her house, distributing various assets (for example, violin, piano, sheet music, and paintings), and so forth. A major task was to file income tax returns for the past five years. Although she had no appreciable assets after we had paid her bills, Federal income tax had been withheld from her Social Security payments, so I still had to gather together her financial records and complete the tax returns. That tedious chore took several days. But when it was done, we could essentially "close the books" on her estate, with only memories remaining.

The traveling returned repeatedly to fond thoughts of my deceased mother. She had been so supportive and influential in my upbringing: right up to when I left Colorado Springs for Harvard. I remember a remark she made when I reminisced that my two boys had "flown the coop": gone to college, got married, fathered children, et cetera. She remarked reflectively that: "Those twenty years when I was a mother of young children were an interesting part of my life." At the time, I thought that was a curious thing to say, but as I grew older, I began to appreciate what she was saying.

It was in her 70s and 80s that my mother's physical condition began to deteriorate. Not her mental condition, though. She remained sharp as a tack. I think, anyway. The uncertainty about that point arises because she developed Parkinson's disease at about age 80 and had difficulty talking as the disease progressed slowly. Consequently, if she failed to respond to a simple question, I never knew if she couldn't formulate the answer mentally or couldn't articulate it due to the disease. Despite this limitation, I enjoyed talking with her whenever I visited Colorado Springs.

From about age 80 and older, my mother's ability to live alone diminished rapidly. The turning point occurred when she nearly burned down her house by leaving a kitchen towel on the open flame of a stovetop burner. That potentially life-threatening event compelled my brother and me to insist that she move into an assisted living facility (code name for nursing home) for her own safety. Okay. No arguments from her. Medicare paid for two six-month stints, but then she had to pay the costs from her own assets, namely a line of credit on her house. This income would pay her bills through January 31, 2003. After that date, she would be broke, meaning that Curtis and I would have to pay her bills. Fatefully, she died on that same day.

During those latter years in the nursing home, I spent many hours sitting next to my mother as she lay propped up in the hospital bed. At first, I proposed reading the Bible to her. Okay. Although she wasn't particularly religious, she would appreciate that. So, I began by reading the New Testament, starting at the beginning, Matthew 1:1. She yawned and said: "No. Start at the beginning." I backed up to the Old Testament and began reading the Book of Genesis. Although she couldn't smile by then, I sensed that she enjoyed the Old Testament, especially the "begats." Admittedly, I did too.

In her final days, my mother mentioned that she had one special regret. What's that? She regretted never having written a book about her method for teaching violin. Well, we can fix that. I sat by her side with pencil and paper transcribing her method as she told me the details. Although I often had difficulty understanding her because of the Parkinson's disease, I managed to get it all down to her satisfaction. It all boiled down to one handwritten page that I still have somewhere in my belongings.

Although I seldom think about her in my old age, I miss my mother. She had been very influential in my life.

Lubbock-I

After arriving in Lubbock in early September, we found a very nice house about a thirty-minute drive from Lubbock with a magnificent view overlooking a canyon (Ransom Canyon) and a lake. The only problem was that it would not be available until mid-December. Okay, it's worth the wait. So, we settled into an apartment on the south side of town. While we were there, Hurricane Katrina struck New Orleans, forcing many families from their homes. Some of these dislocated, traumatized people ended up living in our apartment complex, not knowing when they could return to New Orleans. I felt very sorry for them. Indeed, after my recent experience with flooding in Honolulu, I empathized with them as they coped with their losses.

Again, I brought my laboratory equipment and supplies with me, reckoning that I could resume my research program at some time in the future. Texas Tech had offered me a cramped two-room laboratory in the biology building where I managed to store everything. There was certainly insufficient room for setting up the microscopes, electrophysiology recording equipment, refrigerators, freezers, and so forth in an arrangement suitable for my research program. I needed much more space. Oh well. I would deal with that issue later.

Fortunately, the biology department assigned me a very nice office adjoining the laboratory. But, I gave that to Millie, who had been assigned a small room that resembled a broom closet more than an office. She moved in with glee. I set up a makeshift office comprised of nothing more than a desk and swivel chair in my crowded laboratory. No problem, because I would spend most of my time in the vice president for research office.

From the beginning, Millie liked Lubbock, our new home, and her job. Although there was no ocean nearby, in her mind Lubbock and the surrounding cotton fields marked an improvement over Hawaii. I was much less enthralled. After all, I had given up a beautiful laboratory (at least when the building was intact), plenty of discretionary money to support my research, and a multitude of running and swimming friends. Begrudgingly, I settled into our new home.

Lubbock itself depressed me at the beginning. In 1970, a powerful tornado struck the city, destroying many of the downtown buildings. Only a few of them had been restored. Furthermore, Lubbock's roots in the Old South were manifest in an old downtown building where two public drinking fountains proclaimed either "Whites only" or "Negroes only." That grated on my nerves, to say the least.

Despite my initial depression, Lubbock slowly "grew on me." That is, the depression lifted as I began to adapt to this very different environment. I developed an interest in the cotton industry: the farming, the picking, the bailing, and the pressing for cottonseed oil. I even became fascinated by the oil pumping industry in the surrounding countryside: the pump jacks scattered amidst the cotton fields; the large tank trucks emptying the associated storage tanks and hauling the oil to wherever it went; and so forth. I even began to enjoy the vastness of the land—the caprock (the *llano estacado*)—as it stretched flat as a pancake as far as the eye could see in any direction.

Not everything was different, however, for I continued my early morning long-distance runs, joined by a group of Texas Tech faculty members. We all got along well as we ran through the streets neighboring the Texas Tech campus. Often, I would simply run behind our house in

Ransom Canyon along the dirt roads that stretched into the cotton fields, pausing occasionally at a pump jack for companionship along the way.

Speaking of companions, not long after our arrival in Lubbock, Millie and I decided to get a dog. Our rationale was simple: why not? Millie wanted not one but two mini-dachshunds, remembering the two little dachshunds that joyously chased our car with ears flopping as we drove up to our house in the mountains above Honolulu. Although I had a German shepherd in mind, I agreed to get the little dogs. So, one Saturday morning, we drove to a breeder in Austin to pick up two young black females, which we named Gabriela (Gabi) and Gretchen (Gretl). Oh, they were cute little puppies with only one objectionable flaw: they barked at the slightest provocation. Indeed, they could make any encounter with other people or dogs unpleasant with their incessant yapping. Nonetheless, we enjoyed them, watching them play with each other, having them snuggled in our laps, and all of the other pleasures that pets can bring. In short, Gabi and Gretl became part of our family. And, they helped me settle into our new life in Lubbock.

Well, not so fast; it wasn't quite that easy. Gretl learned quickly to pee and poop on a large newspaper-lined tray that we had set out for that purpose. But Gabi simply could not learn to use that tray; she preferred the carpeting instead. After several weeks of cleaning up after her messes, we decided to return her to the breeder. In fact, I was flying to Austin on Southwest Airlines the next day and would take her with me. Oh no. Southwest didn't carry dogs. We'll have to wait until we had time to drive to Austin and back.

In the meantime, I planned to spend a week in our Colorado Springs condo working on a tedious project in uninterrupted solitude. To ease the burden of two dogs on Millie, I agreed to take Gabi with me. Once there, I set up her bed on the floor next to mine and her large toilet tray, which

I tried to coax her into using. Ho. On the second day, while I was working, I heard her little footsteps as she ran up the stairs and down the hallway to the tray and immediately peed and pooped in it. From then on, she used the tray without fail. As a reward, I allowed her to sleep in bed with me, which she seemed to enjoy. I did too. And, more importantly, Gabi continued to use the tray when we returned back in Lubbock, so we decided to keep her after all. Fate had been kind to her and to us in that regard.

The topic of dogs, by the way, brings up the topic of cats. One morning in Lubbock while driving into work, a cat taught me a valuable lesson that I have never forgotten. I had stopped at a Shell station along the way to fill up my car with gasoline. While I was waiting for the tank to fill, a gray cat emerged from the alley behind the station and walked to the busy street, with cars going 50 miles per hour in both directions. Clearly, the cat intended to cross the street. Oh no! "Don't try that" I yelled at the cat." Of course, the cat ignored me. I resigned myself to witnessing the tragic outcome of the attempted crossing. But, the cat waited, waited, and waited patiently until there was a brief pause in the traffic. The cat immediately took advantage of this opportunity and dashed safely across the street, scampering unscathed down another alley to parts unknown. I was greatly relieved at this unexpectedly fortunate outcome and thought that there must be a lesson to be learned from this episode. Indeed, there was: the importance of patience. To this day, whenever I encounter a situation that requires patience, such as crossing thick traffic to make a left turn, I remind myself of the lesson taught me by the "gray kitty": just be patient. In verb form, I "gray kitty" until the opportune moment arises.

My job was certainly less than inspiring. Few faculty members had federally-funded research grants. Many of them relied on Federal earmarks and state funds awarded to the university. Moreover, neither the provost nor the president showed much enthusiasm for the research mission. Only the chairman of the board of regents seemed enthusiastic about expanding the research activities. But that wasn't enough to make a significant impact. Furthermore, my senior associate vice president was a political patronage appointee with no faculty experience. I liked him personally, but I couldn't count on him to handle faculty issues knowledgeably. Fortunately, he sensed my concerns and found a good job at another university. He and I were both happy with his departure.

Now, with him gone, what could I do to get things moving? For starters, I needed a strong colleague from the faculty. Thus, I hired a faculty member, Karlene Hoo, to fill the associate vice president for research position. She was a professor of chemical engineering and associate dean for research in the college of engineering. Perfect. Right off the bat, she and I got along well together. She understood research administration and provided invaluable help in running the office. Plus, I enjoyed talking with her; we shared similar interests.

With Karlene's help, I decided to boost Texas Tech's research portfolio by developing its inherent strengths. Two possibilities stood out: wind power and cotton farming. Accordingly, we worked closely with two of the university's premier wind-energy researchers to craft a proposal for the university to build a large array of wind turbines that would provide not only a setting to study large wind farms but also 100 percent of the university's electrical energy. After about a year into the project, however, the local utility company quashed our plan, for it would deprive them of their largest customer, namely Texas Tech. So, the proposal came to an unceremonious end. That disappointed me, for I thought that this could have become a significant research stimulant.

How about cotton? About the time I arrived on campus, the college of agriculture had hired a nationally renowned cotton geneticist. With generous state and local support, the university offered her a huge start-up package of nearly $2.5 million, and I allocated prime space in the university's new biomedical research building for her laboratory. Despite this infusion of institutional and state support, the celebrated researcher had difficulties leveraging this support into research grants from external sources. In fact, she failed completely. I don't know why she couldn't obtain Federal grants, but she just couldn't. After a couple of years, her start-up money ran out, as did the university's enthusiasm for her research program. With little operating money, her research program sputtered to a stall. It was simply a matter of time before she was deprived of most of her laboratory space and, unfortunately, any further institutional research support. The investments in her research program simply didn't work out.

No wind, no cotton. I had few alternative ideas to stimulate Texas Tech research. Sure, there were individual faculty members with their own research projects, but there were no large-scale efforts that could significantly "move the needle," so to speak. The West Texas oil and cattle industries, of course, came to mind, but other Texas universities had long since asserted their primacy in these areas, leaving few if any openings for Texas Tech.

Despite these disappointments, I enjoyed my job. I enjoyed trips to Austin to chat with the governor's staff members and other state officials to discuss statewide research initiatives, meetings with various civic leaders to discuss potential economic development initiatives, visits to wind farms throughout the Panhandle, and so forth. I enjoyed meeting with oil-company executives and my counterparts at the University of Texas, Austin, Texas A&M, and the University of Houston to discuss potential research collaborations. And I enjoyed chatting with various faculty members about their research projects—none of which were in my own area of expertise.

However, despite my growing contentment with Texas Tech and Lubbock, near the end of my third year there, one event occurred that changed my attitude towards my job at the university: the university's accreditation was not re-affirmed. More specifically, the Southern Association of Colleges and Schools (SACS) accreditation association placed Texas Tech on probation. Quite simply, the provost had dropped the ball. Unfortunately, the president seemed reluctant to reprimand the provost, holding him accountable for this dire situation. I say unfortunately, because this allowed the system chancellor and the board of regents to hold the president solely responsible, making his life quite unpleasant. So unpleasant, in fact, that the president resigned his position and began looking for another job. He quickly accepted the presidency at another university.

Just before he stepped down, I came to the realization that I could no longer serve effectively—that is, with conviction—in the administration of a university that was on probation with its accreditation. Stated differently, working at a university that was on academic probation was not in my career plans. I began to think more and more about resigning my position. But to do what? Teach in the biology department? That didn't sound very appealing.

Fate entered the scene again. Coincidentally, just a couple of days before the president's departure, Millie received an offer to teach gross anatomy as a member of the faculty in the department of anatomy at the University of Heidelberg medical school. I would be welcomed as a visiting professor in the department without pay, and the department would arrange access to a laboratory where I could resume my research program on stem cells. This all sounded good. I had an excuse to resign as vice president at Texas Tech, and we had an opportunity to return to Germany, albeit Heidelberg and not Munich, which I would have preferred. No matter. Many very good researchers in my field worked in Heidelberg. Okay. We're going to Heidelberg.

I hastily submitted my resignation as vice president for research. Almost reflexively, I requested a one-year leave of absence without pay, thus preserving my tenured faculty position for a year as a safety net in case the Heidelberg position failed to materialize as promised. As he was leaving town himself, the president approved my request. I urged Millie to ask for a leave of absence as well, but she refused; she had no intention of ever returning to Texas Tech, which by now she disliked as much as she had disliked the University of Hawaii. That's a big mistake, I thought.

Prior to the move, I had to ensure continuity in my own office. My departure left a void in the vice president for research position. Until a permanent replacement could be hired, the obvious person for an interim appointment was Karlene. In fact, she took on the responsibility without hesitation. I had felt somewhat guilty about leaving the office after only three years, but with Karlene at the helm, I felt comfortable knowing that the office was in good hands.

As the moving date neared, Millie and I sold the Ransom Canyon house and her car, stored my car, our furniture, and other belongings in our Colorado Springs condo, and rented a furnished apartment in a Heidelberg suburb (Ladenburg) all in the period of three weeks. Of course, the dogs were going with us, so I had to arrange for the vaccinations and health documents required by the German authorities upon arrival in the country before our departure. That was the most difficult part of the move.

The traveling lingered over a bizarre incident that occurred in the chancellor's office a few days before I left. A generous donor gave Texas Tech stocks in his high-tech start-up company valued at $50 million. The stock transfer to the university occurred late on a Thursday afternoon.

Immediately afterwards, the chancellor instructed his chief investment officer to sell the stocks first thing the next morning (Friday). Well, that wasn't going to happen. The chief investment officer explained that he wouldn't be available to do it because he had promised to take his wife and kids out of town on a long-anticipated vacation weekend. But don't worry; "I'll do it first thing on Monday morning." The annoyed chancellor said: "Then have your assistant sell them first thing tomorrow morning." That wouldn't work either, because he had been given Friday off to visit family out of state. In fact, he wasn't even in Texas at the time. Uh oh. A cardinal administrative rule had been broken: the office was to be left completely unattended on Friday. The chief investment officer shrugged that off and repeated: "Don't worry; nothing ever happens on a Friday. I'll do it first thing on Monday morning." Which he did.

Unfortunately, the chancellor should have worried, because the value of the stocks dropped precipitously over the weekend due to a sector-wide correction: from a value of $50 million to a value of $38 million. Texas Tech incurred a $12 million loss because nobody was available to sell the stocks on the preceding Friday. Needless to say, the chancellor was livid. He fired the chief investment office and his assistant right after the sale was completed; they were escorted unceremoniously by campus security officers out of their offices and off campus. I witnessed this scenario with amazement, thinking: "Never put off until Monday what should be done on Friday."

Heidelberg

The eventful day came. With the dogs in a crate, we flew non-stop from Denver to Frankfurt. At the Frankfurt airport, we hired a porter to help us get our luggage to the curb where a van awaited us. But first, we had to clear the dogs for entry into Germany through the airport veterinarian's office. When we got there, early in the morning, the office was empty; nobody was there to inspect the veterinary paperwork that I had worked so hard to procure. I was prepared to wait for the veterinarian to arrive, but the porter had other ideas. Impatiently, he grabbed the luggage cart, dogs and all, and marched us out of the terminal past the security guards to the van waiting for us curbside. After giving him a generous tip, we took off for Heidelberg—technically for the nearby town of Ladenburg. Within an hour, we had arrived in our new home.

Ladenburg was a quiet little town on the banks of the Neckar River, about seven miles north of Heidelberg. Our apartment was sparsely furnished, but it had the basics: bed, couch, television, internet and other up-to-date electronics. On our second day there, we bought a car, a Mini Cooper S, which was just big enough to hold the two of us, the two dogs (in their cage), and a few bags of groceries.

Fortunately, there were several bicycle paths linking Ladenburg and Heidelberg, which Millie had learned about before coming to Germany. So, she had brought along a small fold-up bicycle (a *Klapprad*) specifically for riding to and from work. Thus, every morning, regardless of the weather, Millie rode her little bicycle into Heidelberg and back. That was good, for it allowed me use of the car during the day.

Oh, but the dogs. We were on the third floor of a four-story apartment building in a quiet neighborhood. Or, at least it was quiet until the dogs arrived. The move, the new home, the novel environment stressed the little creatures, and they reacted by barking. Not surprisingly, this unwelcome clamor bothered the other tenants in the building. The burden of assuaging the neighbors and controlling the dogs fell on my shoulders since Millie started work soon after our arrival. Instead of going to the department at the university, I spent my days walking the dogs, sitting with them in the Spartan living room to relieve their stress, and one way or another to squelch their barking. That helped the dogs (and neighbors) but left me feeling like a prisoner enslaved to Gabi and Gretel — dear dogs that they were.

  We had been in Germany for only three weeks when I concluded that this move was a big mistake for me; Millie was quite happy with her new job but I was quite unhappy with my role as an imprisoned dog-sitter. Furthermore, Millie seemed insensitive to my complaints about the situation. There was only one solution: Millie would stay in Heidelberg for the remainder of the academic year, but I would return with the dogs to Colorado Springs. So, I made the necessary arrangements. That evening, when Millie came home, she confronted the dog crate and my packed suitcases in the living room. The seriousness of my unhappiness struck her immediately, and she promised to help me find a solution. After further discussion, I agreed to postpone my return for a week or two. Of course, we were both relieved at this temporary resolution of the crisis.

  Later that week, Millie found a kennel, Rex Kennel Helfrich, on a back road midway between Ladenburg and Heidelberg where the dogs could stay during the day while I went into the university. So, I developed a new routine:

every morning, I dropped the dogs off at the kennel, continued to the university for the day, and picked them up on my way home. Both the dogs and I benefitted immensely from this arrangement. They could bark as much as they wanted at the kennel, and I could get out of the house. I was no longer a prisoner. We continued this routine for the duration of our stay in Heidelberg.

I now began to enjoy our stay in Heidelberg. The anatomy department treated me well. The department director provided me with an office, which I shared with Millie (who was nearly always in the teaching laboratory), and a small stipend to keep me happy. Initially, I was offered the use of a patch-clamp setup where I could record currents in stem cells that I had cultured. Unfortunately, the equipment was old and in need of repair. Frustratingly, it was impossible to achieve stable recordings, for the electrodes "drifted" (that is, moved slightly), disrupting their contact with the cells. Sensing my frustration, the director kindly arranged for the necessary repairs, but we soon learned that they could take as long as six to nine months. Whoa! No good. I would have nothing to do in the laboratory for that time.

    As a consolation, the director introduced me to a younger researcher in the department, an American expatriot (and Harvard graduate), Kerry Tucker, whose interests coincided with mine. Kerry generously offered me the use of his stem-cell laboratory until the equipment was repaired. Although he lacked the necessary equipment for an electrophysiology (patch-clamp) research program, I gratefully accepted. Soon, I befriended the other members of his research group, who also welcomed me into their fold. I enjoyed helping Kerry's students and just puttering in the laboratory, growing stem cells, directing their differentiation into neurons, and so forth. None of this was going anywhere scientifically for me, but it kept me occupied. My meaningful research career was coming to an end, but at least I was enjoying this final episode.

On weekends, along with the dogs, Millie and I explored the Heidelberg environs. This took us to quaint villages along the Rhine and the Neckar rivers and into the heart of the German wine industry along the French border, near Strasbourg. On weekends, we (including the dogs) would often go to one of the nearby restaurants or vineyards for lunch and a glass (or two) of local wine. On one long weekend, we even took the dogs on the train with us for a short visit to Munich.

Fortunately, as the dogs slowly adapted to their new home, their stress levels dropped. Yes, they still barked annoyingly but less often and for shorter durations. My stress levels dropped as well, partly due to Sunday morning long runs (ten or twelve miles) along the Neckar River to keep my marathon conditioning intact. I was happy. This trip to Germany was now working out quite well for all of us.

But wait! In early May, 2009, about nine months after our arrival in Germany, Millie announced suddenly that she had submitted her resignation and that we would return to the United States immediately. That is, within a week. The announcement stunned me. "Why?" I asked. She didn't answer my question, not then, not ever.

The suddenness of our planned return to the United States threw a kink into plans I had made for the next academic year. Most importantly, I had just arranged to teach in the medical school's physiology course during the year, and now I had to cancel that. Plus, Kerry had bought several new pieces of equipment specifically for my use in his laboratory. Now, with me gone, he would simply be stuck with them.

Nevertheless, in a rush, we sold the car to the dealer we had bought it from, arranged for transportation to the Frankfurt airport, packed our bags, and flew back to Denver.

Of course, my imagination wandered as I kept pondering what had gone wrong for Millie at work that prompted such a precipitous move. Without ever getting an answer to that question, we settled into our condo in Colorado Springs; it would be our new home for the foreseeable future. Although we had this home, this sudden return to the United States launched a very unsettled period in our lives.

Colorado Springs

Back in the United States, Millie was not yet prepared to retire. Accordingly, she applied successfully for a half-time job as an associate professor of anatomy at a recently established osteopathic medical school, Rocky Vista University, located in south Denver (Aurora, to be exact). In her opinion, this was an ideal job, despite the one-hour drive each direction on a very crowded highway (I25). To ease the driving, she bought a BMW X3 SUV. I seldom drove the car, but when I did I realized that she had made a good choice.

I was not yet prepared to retire either. But, I wasn't certain what I could do: return to Texas Tech where I still had tenure; apply for some faculty or administrative position in the Colorado Springs and Denver area; try to get a consulting job with some executive search firm? Without a good answer to these options, I decided to take my time and enjoy Colorado Springs. But, here I was, once again confined to home with the two barking dogs. I couldn't repeat this experience.

So, in late May, 2009, one day before the deadline, I hastily informed Texas Tech that I would be returning to my faculty position in the fall. That last-minute announcement caught the university off guard; they had not expected me to return. Thus, my salary money had been absorbed by other programs, and my laboratory equipment had been taken by other researchers for their own use. With some effort, these issues were sorted out before my arrival back in Lubbock that fall. Fortunately, the department chair didn't ask me to teach during the fall or spring semesters, allowing me time to prepare lectures and so forth.

This was not an ideal situation, for Millie and I would have to live apart. Neither of us relished that thought, but she adamantly refused to return to Texas and I adamantly refused to stay at home alone during the day with the two barking dogs. Thus, hesitatingly, we agreed that we would have to live apart until I was ready to retire in Colorado Springs. Now, I had only one other issue to resolve: where to live in Lubbock. We had sold our house, so I needed somewhere else.

Once again, fate intervened. Karlene had just arranged for a sabbatical at the University of California, Riverside starting that summer, and her husband Eric (at least I assumed that they were married) had taken a job in Maryland. Moreover, Karlene had arranged for her mother, who had been living with them, to move into a nursing home. So she offered me the use of her house for the academic year. Perfect. My plan was to live in her house in Lubbock and commute up to Colorado Springs on university vacations and occasional long weekends.

With these workplace arrangements in place for the fall, I spent the summer in Colorado Springs, where I found myself with free time on my hands. In my idle moments, I began to re-live my experiences as vice president for research at Texas Tech. One experience stood out in my memories: a series of conversations with Prins Nevhutalu, Deputy Vice-Chancellor of Research, Innovation and Partnerships at Tshwane University of Technology in Pretoria. He had been awarded an American Council for Education fellowship to study research administration in American universities, including Texas Tech University. While Prins was visiting Texas Tech, he and I had many question-and-answer sessions about various aspects of my job. As I answered his questions, I realized that I had learned many "tricks of the trade" through years of experience at three very different universities and that I enjoyed discussing them with him.

Pondering these discussions, it occurred to me that I should write a book documenting what I had learned about university research management over the years. I would base it on these conversations. Thus, I began writing the book, which I would call *Conversations with Prins*.

I soon discovered that writing a definitive monograph, as this was becoming, is a demanding undertaking, especially with two little dogs barking at every provocation outside. To control them, I bought small collars that released citronella upwards towards their noses whenever the dogs barked; ostensibly, the repugnant smell would deter them from barking. This helped a bit.

With them at my side and the lingering aroma of citronella in the air, I wrote every afternoon. Slowly, a book began to take shape. I was becoming an author.

Lubbock-II

Before I had finished the first draft of my book, summer came to an end, and in late August, 2009, I had to "report for duty" at Texas Tech. By now, Karlene had moved to California, Eric had moved to Maryland, and her mother had moved into a Lubbock nursing home. So according to my plan, I could move into her vacant house as soon as I arrived. This was a very nice, private place to live, located about a mile from campus. After settling in, I would drive back to Colorado Springs every two or three weekends and whenever Karlene or Eric came to Lubbock for one reason or another. To my surprise and great relief, Millie never objected to this planned living arrangement Indeed, anticipating these long drives (about 8 hours each way), she suggested that I trade my Jeep for a sports car, a BMW Z4M, to make the trips safer and more comfortable.

Ah, what a fine car that BMW was. It was bright red with a black convertible top, hugged the road, and had the potential to achieve mind-numbing speed. Of course, it was perfect "cop bait." Thus, I seldom drove more than three or four miles per hour above the speed limit. Only once, when driving through the Texas panhandle, did I lose my self-control, taking the speed up to at least 90 miles per hour as I passed a large truck. Oh that felt good! Until the policeman's red and blue lights started flashing in my rear view mirror, that is. I had no excuse, so I accepted the ticket and paid the $164 fine. From then on, I relied heavily on the cruise control to stay within the legal speed limit (usually about 70 miles per hour).

Lubbock-II

Fate disrupted my living plan in Lubbock. Early in the fall, Karlene returned earlier than I had expected from her sabbatical. Now what? I hadn't anticipated her to return so soon. Instead of "kicking me out" immediately, Karlene allowed me to stay in her house for a while. We worked out a living arrangement that we hoped would not raise eyebrows, so to speak. When I accompanied Karlene on her weekly visits to her mother (I carried and set up her wheel chair), Karlene simply referred to me as Doctor Smith, with no mention that I lived in her house. And, whenever Eric returned to the house for a long weekend or holidays such as Christmas, I would pack my belongings and drive up to Colorado Springs until he left. I was never sure whether he knew that I was living there, although I doubted it. Millie knew about Karlene's return but never registered a concern.

The two dogs, Gabi and Gretl, of course didn't care about any of this in Lubbock. All they cared about was my return to Colorado Springs, always welcoming me with their usual yapping. As I walked into the condo from the garage, they jumped up and down while running around and around my legs in apparent glee. All of this excitement, which could go on as long as five minutes, usually caused Gabi to pee uncontrollably on the carpet as she barked and celebrated my return. Delightful little dog.

In general, after returning to Lubbock I kept a low profile. Most of my previous colleagues — administrators and faculty members — never knew (or acknowledged) that I had returned. Every now and then, I would cross paths with one of them, but we never exchanged greetings or even knowing glances of acknowledgment. I didn't exist in their lives anymore. I no longer ran with my group every morning, as I had. Oh, I would encounter one or two of my former running partners at a race, but we usually had negligible interactions. My only social exchanges occurred in my department: faculty meetings, encounters in the hallway, et cetera. But those occurrences were infrequent. Thus, except for grocery shopping trips and other routine shopping chores with Karlene, after my return to Texas Tech I lived the life of a recluse. Of course, my pilgrimages to Colorado Springs brought me back into society. Curtis and Millie saw to that. But those visits lasted for only a few days each month. And, they became less and less frequent as the stress of the eight-hour drive each way (unending road repairs, frequent bad weather, and so forth) gradually eroded my driving endurance, even with the BMW.

In spring, 2010, I planned a trip to several Southern California universities to interview their vice chancellors for research for my book. Coincidentally, my visit to UCLA coincided with a campus visit that Long Beach State College had arranged for Karlene. We decided to get together in Long Beach, where, during a conversation about California, we talked about the two small dogs belonging to her landlady in Riverside. Although she had never owned a dog, Karlene had bonded with these two, walking and feeding them on a regular basis. "I miss them." Flippantly, I suggested that she should get her own dog. To my surprise, Karlene answered: "What kind should I get?" Well, I remembered how much my son Curtis liked his beagle, so I suggested a beagle. Okay, why not? We looked in the classified ads of the local newspaper and found a nearby beagle breeder with puppies for sale. The ball started to roll uncontrollably.

To make the story short, Karlene bought an eight-week old puppy that afternoon, naming it Barney. Early that evening, she was scheduled to fly back to Lubbock, so we bought a small cage to carry Barney on board with her. I flew back to Lubbock separately, intending to drive up to Colorado Springs straight from the airport but decided to stay in Lubbock for another few days to help Karlene with the little puppy: buying a pen, water and food bowls, a bed; cleaning up his messes; et cetera. Barney quickly destroyed his bed (and every bed since then) as well as the living room carpet which he chewed away along its perimeter and soiled regularly in several corners. In short, Barney was a typical puppy: undisciplined and destructive. Our immediate goals were to train him to walk on a leash and to poop and pee outdoors. The former took about a week, while the latter took about a month. The destructive chewing problem took much longer.

In November, 2010, a momentous event occurred. At least, for me it was momentous. I ran the New York Marathon. This certainly wasn't the first marathon that I had run; no, but it was to be the last. I had been looking forward to running this particular marathon, my fifteenth, for a very special reason. Up to this point in time, I had run four of the five so-called World Marathon Majors: Berlin, Boston, Chicago, London. With the New York City marathon under my belt, I would have completed all five, a noteworthy accomplishment in the marathon racing community.

The race day, November 7, was cold, very cold. Thus, I was uncomfortably cold going into the race. Nonetheless, along with 43,000 other runners, I took off over the Verrazano Bridge from Staten Island to Brooklyn and on through the other boroughs of the City. For some reason, perhaps the cold weather, I ran more slowly than usual. And, I sensed more fatigue than usual. So much, in fact, that during the final stretch uphill along the length of Central Park, a terrifying thought crossed my mind: Ho; I may not be able to finish this race. But, I suppressed that insidious thought and pushed onward to the finish line, finishing in an uncharacteristically slow time (about five hours). Nonetheless, I had now run the World's Five Majors.

While recovering from that grueling race, I decided to retire from running marathon distances. I was quite content with that decision. And, I was proud of my accomplishments. After all, I had achieved two noteworthy pinnacles of marathon racing: I had run the Boston marathon (twice, in fact) and had completed the World's Five Majors. Furthermore, my knees were still intact, but at my age (66 years old), it was just a matter of time before I ran one too many marathons and incurred a lasting injury. Or, at least, so I thought. Shorter races (for example 5- and 10 kilometers), were okay; they were less taxing on the knees. But no more marathons. With that decision, I let my base training level decrease from about twelve miles to about four miles.

In early 2013, less than three years after I had retired from marathon racing, fate cast a disruptive blow to my contentment. The World's Major Marathons, now sponsored by Abbott Laboratories, added a sixth race, the Tokyo marathon. Now what? No longer could I boast that I had run all of the world's major marathons. I would have to run the Tokyo marathon. But, I simply didn't have the necessary energy and commitment to get back in condition to run another marathon. No; I couldn't imagine getting up at 4:30 every morning for training runs that would take up to four or more hours at the longer distances. I much preferred to lie in bed until later in the morning. So, I had to adjust my contentment to having run five of the six world's major marathons. Furthermore, recently (2024) Abbott added a seventh marathon to the series (the Sydney marathon) and announced its intention to add two additional marathons to the world's majors in 2025. I still get irked by the expansion beyond the original five marathons, for I could easily have run the Tokyo or any other marathon if it had been included in that elite group prior to 2010. Oh well, so it goes.

Apropos training for marathons: after I had retired from marathon running, I came to a startling realization. Most, if not all, of my marathon-racing colleagues seemed to be running from some personal situation: a bad marriage, a seriously sick child, a troubled past of some sort, et cetera. The long-distance running provided an escape from these situations. Looking back, I questioned what situation I might have been trying to escape. The only reasonable answer was an unsatisfactory marriage with Millie. Could that be true? When I started running marathons, I wasn't aware of any serious problems in our marriage. Was I naïve? Was the marathon running a harbinger of problems to come in our marriage? Time would tell.

As time passed, I finished my book manuscript. The challenge now was to find a publisher. Ultimately, Oxford University Press agreed to publish it under the title *Managing the Research University*, with a 2011 release date. When it finally appeared, I was very pleased; the Press produced a beautiful book. Now, the challenge was to market it. Accordingly, I contacted the Society for Research Administrators simply to let them know that the book existed. To my surprise, the Society asked me to develop a series of webinars based on the book. I agreed readily. So, I prepared a series of 17 one-hour webinars (one for each chapter) using PowerPoint slides that I presented to Society members during the next year or so. Publication of the book and presentation of the webinars marked another inflection point in my career, from university administrator to author.

While writing *Managing the Research University*, I alluded briefly to the limits of a chief research officer's authority. I wrote no more than about a paragraph on the topic, but I had much more to say about it. Indeed, I had enough to write an entire book on the limits of authority at all levels of university administration. Certainly I had learned about these limits the "hard way" during my career as a chief research officer and executive vice chancellor. So, I began to write my second book in earnest, which I titled *Limits of Authority*. Pedagogically, I chose to make my points by citing anecdotal cases involving a fictitious provost.

The writing of this, my second book, went quickly. In about a year, I had completed the manuscript and submitted it to several university presses, including Oxford, for publication. The book was soundly rejected by all of them. They all agreed: it didn't have sufficient rigor. Stung by this rebuke, I decided to re-write the entire book, placing the anecdotal cases in a legal context. Suddenly, this became a challenging book to write. I would have to look up the legal foundations of each anecdote, citing judicial opinions and so forth. It was time for some serious scholarship.

Speaking of scholarship, in the fall of 2010, my honeymoon from teaching ended. The department expected me to teach a fall-semester course; I could choose the topic. I chose a three-credit graduate-level course on stem cells. Only two intrepid graduate students enrolled, hardly enough to warrant offering the course. But, nobody in the administration complained to me, so I taught it, satisfying my teaching obligation for that semester. The next semester (spring 2011), I taught another course on stem cells, concentrating on their use in regenerative medicine. This time, six students enrolled. Once again, I met my teaching obligations. And then again in fall, 2011, I taught the same course, but this time 13 students enrolled. I was pleased with the slowly growing attention to my topic.

    In the back of my mind, however, I knew that the university would not allow me to teach a single three-credit course per semester with such small enrollments forever. Sooner or later, I would be assigned a much heavier teaching load comparable to my colleagues' six to nine credits per semester. And, indeed, I was. Starting in spring, 2012, and every semester from then on, I was assigned to teach introductory anatomy and physiology, both in-person and online lectures, plus laboratory sessions, for nine credits total. Although I had taught introductory physiology at the University of Wisconsin to as many as 608 undergraduates in the class, I had a cohort of about six graduate-student teaching assistants and three full-time professional laboratory assistants to relieve my workload. All I had to do was to prepare and deliver the lectures. In contrast, this Texas Tech course wouldn't have teaching assistants or other help with the laboratories, grading, or anything else. I would have to do it all. Moreover, I would require significant time to prepare; I would have to learn the anatomy portion, refresh my lectures on the physiology portion, and arrange for the online delivery. I complained to the chair: "I need a semester to prepare for this course." But my complaints fell on deaf ears. So, I "went around" the chair to the dean, who had been one of my former running partners. He agreed that I needed a semester (spring 2012) free of any obligations to prepare for such a demanding course. Ah, I had one reliable friend from the "old days."

Even before assignment of this onerous anatomy and physiology course, teaching the small "boutique" three-credit courses in 2010 and 2011 triggered vague thoughts of retirement. And those thoughts triggered thoughts about the Registry.

What's the Registry? During the first several years at Texas Tech, I heard about several administrators (deans and so forth) from "the Registry." I didn't know what "the Registry" meant and paid little attention to the term until one day, out of curiosity, I looked up its meaning online. Aha: The Registry of College and University Presidents. It is basically an employment agency that places retired university presidents and chancellors into interim executive positions at colleges and universities. That caught my attention. I had now retired officially from the University of Hawaii, so, in early spring, 2011, I called the Registry and asked if I could join their roster of retired chancellors. Maybe, but not just anybody can join the Registry. First I had to undergo a thorough review of my qualifications, including recommendations from five peers (that is, other presidents and chancellors) and interviews by both a professional psychologist and the Registry's senior management team. In late spring, 2011, I received the good news: I was now a member of the Registry. They would be in touch with me whenever a potential interim job opportunity matching my qualifications arose. I wasn't retired from Texas Tech yet, but I thought that I would simply retire from the university if a Registry job opportunity did, in fact, come along.

Then, fate confronted me with three significant events that impacted the course of my life. The first occurred that summer (2011) when Karlene left Lubbock for a two-year position as a Program Director at the National Science Foundation (NSF) in Arlington, Virginia. I took off a couple of weeks to help her drive to Arlington, along with the dog. Karlene had arranged to live in a small apartment on the 17th floor of a building attached to the NSF building where she worked on one side and a Hilton hotel on the other side. Predictably, the 17th floor location changed Barney's routine; whenever he had to pee or poop, he had to travel down the elevator and across the street to the nearest available open space—usually ignoring a "No Dogs Allowed" sign posted on the lawn. Of course, this arrangement changed Karlene's routine as well, for she had to accompany Barney whenever the "urge" hit him—not only during the day but usually at least once in the middle of the night.

I flew back to Lubbock alone to face my teaching for the fall. I had enjoyed the several days in Arlington amidst the cultural milieu of the greater Washington, D.C. area. Moreover, I had the opportunity to re-connect with friends and colleagues who lived in the area. I wanted to return whenever I could get away from Lubbock—long weekends would be sufficient.

The second event occurred in late 2011 when Millie and I decided to get a divorce. This was not an easy decision. Indeed, it was quite difficult. Although I commuted every two or three weeks and on holidays to Colorado Springs, the strains of living apart began gradually to affect both Millie and me. We had worked and lived together compatibly for about thirty years, so the marriage had deep roots. But we both began to realize that we couldn't continue our marriage under these circumstances. What should we do? Over a beer at a downtown pub, we decided that a formal divorce might be in both of our best interests, although neither of us relished the idea. No lawyers; we'll fill out the necessary legal documents ourselves. So, we worked out an equitable division of assets; besides her share of our money, she would keep the two dogs, and I would buy her share of the Colorado Springs condo. Moreover, we would file the paperwork together with the local court. After so many years of working together in the laboratory, Millie and I had little difficulty working smoothly together as we went through the process. Even so, all of this took several months to complete, but eventually, on July 11, 2012, the divorce was final. I was in Colorado Springs when the formal decree arrived in the mail. We both looked at it, stunned at the finality of our thirty-year marriage.

Since I now owned the Colorado Springs condo, Millie decided to retire and move to Florida. Accordingly, she bought a townhouse in Palm Harbor, near Tampa. To help her with this bittersweet move, I agreed to drive her to Florida and set up her new home. So, we all piled into her new MiniCooper, which was stuffed with luggage, Millie's various household belongings, and the dogs in their cage. It was a tight fit, but the little car was certainly comfortable and "up" for the journey. Gabi and Gretl slept most of the way, although in the rearview mirror, I saw them poke their little heads up now and then to look around before going back to sleep. After that trip, I saw Millie only once—a short weekend visit two weeks later to help her with electrical and other minor repair issues in her apartment. I haven't seen her since. Our relationship was over. And that was that.

The third event: my resignation. During this time, I became less and less enthusiastic about the prospects of continuing at Texas Tech. Thus, coincident with the divorce, I decided to resign my faculty position. That was a significant decision, for it meant giving up tenure. But, I simply could not undertake the burdensome teaching load awaiting me in the fall. So, I informed my chair that I would resign effective July 1, 2012. Although he had only about six weeks to find a replacement to teach the onerous anatomy and physiology course, he immediately accepted my resignation. I sensed that the chair was glad to get rid of me and, more importantly, to recover my salary. I was now a "free man," so to speak. Divorced and retired.

Huntsville

Fate had other plans for my freedom. Within about a week after my resignation from Texas Tech, the Registry asked if I would consider an interim appointment as Vice President for Research at the University of Alabama in Huntsville. I knew a bit about the university. It had been founded as a research university to complement Wernher von Braun's work on the United States' efforts to put a man on the moon. That appealed to me. But, Alabama? I didn't relish the idea of living in that state, but ultimately I decided to accept the position. So, I made the move. In Huntsville, I rented a nice apartment about a mile from campus.

Right off the bat, I enjoyed work in Huntsville. The university was smaller than any I had worked at before, but I liked its "passion" for research. The city of Huntsville (nicknamed "Rocket City" for its role in developing rockets for space flight) shared this passion, proudly supporting its research university. I never had to justify the university's research mission on or off campus, as I occasionally had to do in both Wisconsin and Hawaii. The job required me to get "top-secret security clearance" (for what, I don't know), which required a very extensive background check by the FBI. Some of the FBI's questions profoundly disturbed Millie, for she let me know in very strong terms about her displeasure in answering them. She never told me what the questions were about, but she warned me: "Don't ever do that to me again." "Okay, okay. I had no control over that."

The job introduced me to NASA and the aerospace industry at nearby Marshall Space Flight Center as well as the adjoining Army's high command at Redstone Arsenal. I spent many hours in meetings about one thing or another with high-ranking NASA and military personnel, including about half a dozen Army generals. For the most part, the generals were quite affable and knowledgeable about their area of expertise (for example, helicopters). In that regard, and admittedly to my surprise, they certainly earned my respect.

Occasionally, the job took me down to Birmingham, Tuscaloosa, and Montgomery: the "Deep South." I experienced some emotional discomfort viewing relics of the antebellum and the more recent Jim Crow periods in United States history, especially in Montgomery. Indeed, I chose not to visit Selma (a short distance from Montgomery) and other flashpoints during the Civil Rights protests of the mid-1960's. Huntsville was enough of the Alabama experience for me.

Since I was now divorced, I felt comfortable flying up for an occasional weekend in Arlington to visit Karlene and Barney. I enjoyed my visits to Arlington, as did Karlene and Barney. In fact, they always greeted me at the top of the subway escalator when I arrived from the airport. And, as I knelt on one knee, Barney would always jump up against me nose to nose with tail wagging as if to tell me all about what had happened while I was away. I felt welcomed. Moreover, in neighboring Washington, D.C., I had lunch now and then with several former colleagues—mostly lobbyists—from both Hawaii and Texas Tech. I liked their company, for they kept me abreast of current sources of Federal funding.

For recreation in both Huntsville and Arlington, not surprisingly, I ran. But the distances seldom exceeded eight miles since I no longer trained for marathons. In Huntsville, I always ran alongside a small creek in a bucolic county park, the Indian Creek Greenway, located several miles from my apartment. Often I was alone on the path, enjoying the privacy and beauty of the landscape. The landscape certainly differed from the dirt roads through the cotton patches around Lubbock.

Whenever I visited Karlene in Arlington, I always ran on the Custis Trail, a well-trafficked footpath that stretched for 4.5 miles alongside a busy highway (interstate 66) and above-ground Washington Metro subway line. The trail was noisy, to say the least, but I enjoyed running through the adjoining Arlington neighborhoods. Moreover, in one direction, the trail extended to the banks of the Potomic River, where I overlooked Washington, D.C. I never tired of that view.

The year in Huntsville went by quickly. On May 31, 2013, my Registry assignment in Huntsville came to an end. Several weeks before I was scheduled to leave, the university's president asked me to stay on as interim provost for a year. I was tempted, quite tempted; he was a good president, and I enjoyed working with him. But, Karlene's appointment at NSF was coming to an end as well, and she would be moving back to Lubbock. I wanted to help her with this transition, especially moving the dog across the country again. After considerable handwringing, I decided to forego the opportunity to continue as interim provost and to return to Lubbock with Karlene and Barney. Besides, I wanted to work on my book, *Limits of Authority*, using the resources of the Texas Tech Law School library.

The logistics of moving back to Lubbock were complicated. My job (and lease) expired on May 31, but Karlene's assignment (and lease) expired on June 17. After considerable head scratching, we devised a plan to accommodate these separate dates. In late May, Karlene left Barney with friends in Arlington and flew down to Huntsville for a week to help me pack my belongings. Ideally, our plan was to drive the BMW from Huntsville to Arlington, where I would stay until she was ready to move.

Together, we would then drive both her car and the BMW to Lubbock.

The plan encountered two "snags." First snag: before we even left Huntsville, we realized that the BMW, a sports car with only two seats and a small trunk, was much too small to hold more than a couple of suitcases. Thus, we ended up giving away most household items. With a trimmed load, we drove comfortably up to Arlington, through the beautiful Southern countryside.

Second snag: how to transport the dog out to Lubbock. We had overlooked the fact that he was too frisky for one person to handle alone in either car. So, to solve this dilemma, we decided that after a couple of days in Arlington we would leave Barney with friends and drive the BMW to Lubbock. We would then fly back to Arlington in time to help Karlene move out of her apartment on June 17. Finally, we would drive her car, a roomy Honda Accord, to Lubbock with the dog snuggled in her lap.

Following this plan, the trip went smoothly with one costly exception. After checking into one hotel along the way, we discovered in the fine print of the room contract that pets were not allowed. No problem; we'll sneak our little dog through the back door. Nobody will know the difference. Except for one perceptive guest who saw us leading Barney into the room, that is. She reported this infraction to the desk clerk who promptly kicked us out of the hotel. And no! The hotel wouldn't refund our money for the night (more than $200). In disgrace, we drove on until we found a "pet friendly" hotel. Lesson learned: crime doesn't pay. Fortunately, with no further mishaps, we all arrived in Lubbock safely.

Lubbock-III

Upon our return to Lubbock in summer, 2013, Karlene and I acknowledged to ourselves that we were beginning to live openly as a couple. I was officially divorced from Millie, so I was much more comfortable living in the same house with Karlene. And sometime during the past year or two, Karlene's relationship with Eric dissolved. I never knew when or how that happened, only that he no longer came to visit her, and she seldom mentioned his name. Regardless, that relationship was over, freeing Karlene to live with me "in the open." Consequently, Karlene and I no longer hurried clandestinely when walking in public: through the supermarket or across campus. Furthermore, Barney matured into a young dog (no longer a puppy), and we frequently walked together through the neighborhood with him. In other words, we made no secret of our companionship.

Barney defined our family. Family? Yes; sharing the responsibilities of having a dog in the house brought Karlene and me together. During the day, he had the run of the house, and we played with him and cleaned up his messes. During the night, we put him to bed in a wire cage in the sunroom. Usually, he would make a huge mess of anything that we put in the cage, such as newspapers to pee on, dog beds, and so forth. Importantly, Barney seldom barked. What a change from Gabi and Gretl.

Put simply, Karlene and I bonded with Barney, who carved out a very special place in our affections. When he climbed into my lap for a nap while I sat in the easy chair, I could feel the man-dog bonds forming ever more tightly.

And Karlene took on the role as "the mum." She cared for his feeding and well-being and always had a morsel to offer the little guy, which became the core of their tight bond. From the age of eight weeks on, Barney never experienced anything but love under Karlene's and my care. Knit together by these bonds, we began to think of ourselves as a family unit: man, woman, and dog. Or, as we put it: Big Dog Daddy, the Mum, and Barney (also known as Mr. B).

Even with our now-public living arrangement, we continued to live reclusively. Karlene settled into teaching, which brought her into limited contact with colleagues and students on campus. But I maintained a much lower profile. In fact, my only exposure to other people occurred during my daily visits to the Texas Tech Law School library, where I studied the laws affecting authority in higher education for my book. And, even there, my only interactions consisted of my occasional hushed "Shh" to nearby noisy law students. Except for Karlene and Barney, I had no friends in Lubbock. None was leftover from my years as an administrator, and none was acquired after I returned from Germany. But, I didn't care. I was quite content, indeed happy, with my new home life.

Despite our happy home life, Karlene became restless teaching at Texas Tech. After 14 years on the faculty, she wanted to move into an administrative position at some other university. Ultimately, she accepted the position as dean of the graduate school at Montana State University in Bozeman, starting in early January, 2014. Ho, Bozeman? I had visited Bozeman several times in my past and liked the city: its mountains, Western culture, and proximity to Yellowstone National Park. Would I like to move up there with her? Buy a house together? Yes! I looked forward to moving up there with Karlene.

In preparation for the move, Karlene put her house on the market. We tidied up the place, but the chewed-on carpeting resisted our efforts. Luckily, fortune smiled on

Karlene. The house sold quickly to a family that didn't care about the tattered carpeting, for they intended to replace it immediately with hardwood flooring. They also agreed to a closing date far enough into the future to allow us time to find a house in Bozeman.

Other than these few details, the traveling seldom took me to Lubbock during this interlude between Huntsville and Bozeman. In retrospect, I'm not sure why, but I suspect that the overall environment simply lacked excitement, lacked memorable situations for my reclusive life. After all, I no longer worked for the university and seldom interacted with anybody on or off campus. And the ubiquitous cotton fields surrounding the city engendered only a very limited number of memorable occasions. Moreover, the oil pumps scattered across the countryside, amidst the cotton fields, engendered even fewer memorable occasions. They just went up and down, up and down, up and down. Face it: without the stimulation offered by working in the administration at Texas Tech University, Lubbock was fundamentally boring. I liked the ambiance of the West Texas culture, but that didn't translate into very many exciting memories either—certainly not the kind frequented during the traveling.

I was ready to move on. As Mack Davis (a Lubbock native) sang "I thought happiness was Lubbock Texas in my rearview mirror."

Bozeman

To help us get settled in Bozeman, I flew up there alone a couple of times looking for housing. Initially, I looked at typical neighborhood houses that we could easily afford. To my chagrin, they all looked about the same, surrounded by similar nearby houses. I was discouraged. So, out of curiosity, I asked my real estate agent to show me a million-dollar house, with no real intention of buying such an expensive property. She obliged by taking me to a relatively small house located on a twenty-acre lot along with about thirty other houses on an 800-acre working ranch located within a fifteen-minute drive to campus. The ranch had a barn, a herd of 15 to 20 horses belonging to the homeowners, a herd of about 50 cattle during the summer grazing months, and about 150 acres of hayfields, which were harvested for a profit every summer. The whole setup intrigued me.

When I walked into the house for the first time, I was stunned by the magnificent view of the surrounding mountains, the spacious fields of wildflowers, the tranquility of the place. The neighboring houses were all sufficiently far away to pose no intrusion into the privacy of any other home on the ranch. I was excited about this house, but $1 million? That night, I called Karlene to convey my excitement. She, too, expressed concern about the price. However, as we discussed our finances, we realized that we could afford the place by combining our resources. Okay, we'll buy it! And we did. We would close on the deal in late December, just in time to move in before Karlene began work at Montana State University in early January.

There was only one glitch to our moving plans: the weather. In November, a month before we were scheduled to close on the house, Bozeman was coated with over a foot of snow, and it wouldn't begin to melt until next April or so. We would need better cars for this kind of weather. The BMW would be of little use in deep snow, so we left it in the Colorado Springs condo garage until the snow in Bozeman had melted in the spring. Furthermore, Karlene's two-wheel drive Honda sedan would also be impractical in a Bozeman winter. So, we bought a Jeep (my car) and traded the Honda for a Subaru (Karlene's car). These cars would both be very capable in snow, and we were pleased with them. When we moved into the Bozeman house in late December, they handled our snowy driveway with ease. But, the moving truck, a big 18-wheeler, wasn't as capable. It hung up in the drifting snow when backing into our driveway to deliver our furniture. It took the company several hours to dig the truck out of the snow drift before it could drive closer to the house for moving our goods. Welcome to Bozeman.

In early spring, I sold the Colorado Springs condo and arranged to have the furnishings shipped to Bozeman. With the majestic Bozeman scenery, I reckoned that we would seldom wish to drive for eight hours to Colorado Springs to see mountains. After all, we saw them from our new house in all four directions. I included two items in the move that my brother had been storing for me: a baby grand piano inherited from our mother and the complete diary and extant short-story manuscripts written by our father. In my retirement, I hoped to resume playing the piano and to read my father's diary. In addition, with the improved spring weather, I could safely drive the BMW from its storage in the condo's garage to Bozeman.

We settled into our new home easily. It was a wonderful house, with many top-end appliances and other luxurious features. My favorite was a gas-fired potbelly stove in the family room, where I spent many hours reading and looking out the window at the mountains and wildlife. Moreover, the large yard provided a wonderful playground for Barney. To confine him, we installed an invisible fence around the house encompassing four acres of field inhabited by numerous mice, gophers, weasels, and other critters that brought out Barney's innate hunting instincts. He seemed happy, with his tail wagging quickly back and forth as he closed in on his prey. (In actuality, he seldom caught anything.)

We established a routine quickly. Karlene drove into work for the day while I stayed at home taking care of chores (cleaning the house, caring for the yard, and so forth). Daily, I walked Barney. Often we went to and from the barn (about a mile each direction), where he enjoyed exploring the haystacks, the barn cat's lair, the horse stalls, and the other sources of interest to a dog. In the winter, the walk to the barn could be viciously cold: near zero temperatures with a stiff wind. Nonetheless, we just pushed forward to the warmth of the barn or our house, depending on the direction. Occasionally, I would take Barney to some mountain trail for his walk, or we would drive through Yellowstone Park for a few hours, usually in the Jeep but occasionally in the BMW with the top down. On weekends, Karlene joined us on these sojourns into the surrounding mountains. One of our favorite places was Spanish Creek, about twenty miles outside of town. To get to the parking lot, the road passed through one of Ted Turner's ranches, the Flying D, where he raised about five thousand free-roaming bison. Karlene and I quickly became familiar with the huge creatures, learning to respect them, especially if we encountered them while walking along the road. More than once, we retreated hastily from a bison's (hopefully) faux charge. Barney was always oblivious to the potential danger. But, we sure weren't.

Apropos danger: one afternoon, Barney and I encountered a grizzly bear and her cub while walking on a trail not far from our house. We had just rounded a corner when a female grizzly bear appeared before us. She pushed her cub behind her and then charged us, stopping about 10 to 15 feet away. Barney tugged at his leash to approach the bear, but, of course, I restrained him. The bear paid little attention to the dog but looked at me squarely in the eyes. I looked back into her eyes, hoping to communicate that we meant no harm to her or her cub. As the bear continued growling viciously at us, we slowly backed away until we were around a corner, out of sight. We then turned around and quickly walked back to the safety of the nearest road. The next day, I bought a .45-caliber pistol and a can of bear spray to carry on our walks. I soon discontinued carrying the gun but not the bear spray. Several times each year, somebody is seriously mauled or killed by a grizzly bear in Montana; I was lucky, lucky, lucky to have escaped injury and didn't want to be caught without the spray if I ever encountered a bear again.

As a retiree, I had plenty of time to observe the workings of the ranch. For example, I watched the ranch manager harvest the yearly hay crop. It began in mid-April after the last of the snow had melted when liquid fertilizer was spread over the 150 acres of newly emergent hay grass (Timothy grass, mainly). By about July 1, the hay had grown to at least two feet tall: time to harvest. Using four different farm implements pulled by the ranch's tractor, the manager mowed the hay, raked it into neat rows running the length of the hay field, scooped it up, packaged it into 60-pound "small square" bales, picked up and stacked the bales, and, finally, hauled them to the hay barn. Ideally, all of this could be accomplished in about four days. Realistically, it usually dragged on for two or three weeks, mainly because of one equipment breakdown or another. I spent many hours looking over the shoulder of mechanics repairing the equipment. The traveling re-visited many more detailed aspects of the haying, such as bale size and weight, market price, and so forth. I suspect that few people would find this interesting, so I won't elaborate further on hay. Regardless, I enjoyed every aspect of the hay harvest; it was one of the high points of the year.

And then there were the horses and cattle. They were fascinating. The horse herd lived outdoors all year, including the sub-zero winter days and nights, in a pasture near the barn. As winter approached, they grew long shaggy coats, ate considerably more hay spread over the snow by the ranch manager, and huddled together to keep warm. In the spring, they shed their winter coats and spread out more in the pasture as they grazed fresh grass instead of hay. While Barney snooped around the barn, I watched the horses interact with one another. They appeared to have a well-defined social order with rules of behavior that I tried to understand with marginal success. When they were in the barn area for new horse shoes or a ride, I learned how to approach them, groom them, and feed them snacks such as carrots and so forth. In the latter case, I always ran the risk of being bitten by an overzealous eater. I'm sure that books have been written about horses and their herd behavior, and I intend someday to read one of them.

The cattle herd, comprised of about 30 cows with their newborn calves, grazed during the summer months in the fields behind our house. So, I could sit in my chair or on the deck and watch them go about their daily routines, including walking in single-file lines to the nearby water trough. My most striking memory is of their playfulness; they jostled each other and romped playfully. And, when a storm approached, they all ran at great speed downhill into the shelter of a group of trees. Karlene and I both spent many hours watching these entertaining animals. Cows; who would have thought that we would have found them so interesting? We were both saddened when they were rounded up at the end of the summer for delivery to a feed lot. We might see the same calves the next summer but not the adult cows. Their unpleasant fate was cast.

One other herd entertained us: elk. A herd of about 150 elk roamed in the surrounding area and passed through the ranch every two or three months. Elk are usually on the move, so it was a special occasion to see them. Sometimes they wandered through our immediate yard, allowing us the enjoyment of watching these beautiful animals up close. In the spring, several pregnant females would take refuge in a nearby willow grove to give birth to their calves. During this calving season, we always stayed away from the grove. Like the horses and cattle, the elk herd displayed a social structure, with the guards on the periphery, the females and calves in the center, and so forth. In late summer and early fall, the bull elk began their ritualistic bugling to establish their dominance and attract females. We could hear them from about a mile away. The bulls with their magnificent antler racks always were exciting to see.

Skiing became part of our routine for the first three years. One of Bozeman's main attractions is its proximity to two excellent ski areas: Bridger Bowl and Big Sky. Bridger Bowl is the more popular of the two areas for local residents. It is located only sixteen miles outside of town and has a variety of slopes ranging from easy to extremely challenging. Although Karlene wasn't an accomplished skier at first, she was enthusiastic about improving her skills. So, we bought new skis and boots, and, like most of our neighbors, season passes to Bridger Bowl. (We never went to Big Sky). For ten weekends in the winter, we would spend a day skiing. Karlene improved considerably, but I found myself disinclined to ski difficult black diamond slopes as I had in the past. I preferred to ski with Karlene on blue slopes of moderate difficulty. We enjoyed skiing together, but after three years of skiing at Bridger Bowl, our enthusiasm waned; we no longer wanted to go through the hassle of skiing: mounting the ski rack on the car, getting dressed in all of the paraphernalia, sitting in cold chair lifts, and so forth. So, we quit, putting the skis into storage where they still rest collecting dust.

Because of its proximity to Yellowstone National Park, Bozeman attracted visitors. Accordingly, we had visitors, always in the summer: Karlene's sister and brother-in-law, my brother and his wife, each of my sons, and several others. They all enjoyed sitting on our deck, looking out over the mountains and field of wildflowers. And, they enjoyed our nice, private guest bedroom with its own bathroom. Karlene and I liked their company. Indeed, we looked forward to their visits, as long as they didn't plan on staying more than a week or so. Which, thankfully, they never did.

My younger son, Corey, made several visits. Foremost, he enjoyed the fishing in surrounding rivers and the two ponds on the ranch. He re-introduced me to fly fishing, which I had enjoyed as a child but had not done for many years. Inspired by Corey and despite my reservations about inflicting pain on animals, I began to fish the nearby rivers and the ranch ponds regularly. The trout were large and plentiful, mainly due to the state's mandatory catch-and-release regulations. Often, Karlene and Barney joined me on fishing trips just to enjoy the wilderness. Bozeman and its environs had a lot to offer in that regard. I was very happy living there.

Within a year after our arrival in Bozeman, I finished my book, *Limits of Authority*, and began sending proposals to various university presses. Several of them rejected the book promptly for undisclosed reasons. That didn't deter me. Then suddenly three non-university academic publishers accepted the book within a two-week period. I accepted one of them, Rowman and Littlefield, which changed the title to *Understanding Authority in Higher Education*. Although I would have preferred a university press, I wanted to wrap this up before we embarked on a nearly three week trip to South Africa. Ultimately they produced a very striking book, characterized by a cover picture of an owl perched outside Karlene's Montana State University office window taken by a local newspaper photographer. I had worked hard on this book to give it the rigor missing in the first version. I remain very proud of this endeavor.

With that book in the publisher's hands, I now had free time to explore my father's diary and short stories. The most intriguing discovery in this trove was in the largest box, where I found 72 spiral notebooks containing his handwritten diary that spanned 12 years. Each notebook had 50 pages with hand writing on both sides of the page. I counted about 7 words per line and 36 lines per page. Multiplying all of these numbers yields about 1.8 million words. How could I possibly read all of this? Well, I did. To be sure, the reading was not always easy or pleasurable. Sometimes, he ranted unendingly about an event in his childhood, sometimes he harangued mercilessly about colleagues, exhausting my patience. Sometimes he wrote in abstruse metaphor, beyond my understanding. Sometimes I found myself gliding incomprehensively over the text, necessitating a re-reading, maybe two re-readings. At all times, he wrote deliberately, with well-constructed sentences, inserted after-thoughts, and no erasures. In fact, the writing didn't seem to have the spontaneity that I associate with a diary. I began to wonder if it had been written for some audience besides himself, with the thought of eventual publication in one format or another. Was I reading a draft memoir or a personal diary? Regardless, I began to look forward to reading the continuing episodes in this man's life, my father's life, his reactions to daily encounters with other people, his unspoken thoughts, his dreams.

As I read, I began to entertain the possibility of publishing salient elements of the diary, concentrating on his recovery from mental illness. There must be a compelling story in there somewhere, if only I had the talent to tell it. So, I began to flag noteworthy passages with Post-it notes. After I had finished reading the entire diary for the first time, I began to re-read it, concentrating mainly on the flagged passages. The volume of material in these passages overwhelmed me. I needed to be able to organize them somehow. To get the ball rolling, I began to type interesting passages about one thing or another into Word documents, with the hope of assembling them into a book. The massive number of flagged entries turned this into a daunting, time-consuming task. Furthermore, the tedium of typing in the diary entries slowed me down considerably. I needed frequent breaks from this boring task.

While working on the "diary project," I went through several boxes of musty folios with short stories. All of them were typewritten carbon copies on onion-skin paper under my father's pseudonym Ellis Worth. One small box had fifteen unopened envelopes, which, eventually, I got around to opening. Each contained an original typewritten short-story manuscript on bond paper along with a rejection notice from some small literary magazine. According to the postmarks, these must have arrived in the mail within three weeks after his death in 1972. In addition, one box contained at least twenty articles about the law, under his real name, Everett Ellsworth Smith. I knew that he had published five or ten legal articles, so I wasn't surprised to discover more. I set this box aside, thinking that they were probably out-dated. Besides, I'm not a lawyer and probably wouldn't appreciate these articles.

I hadn't counted all of the short stories carefully, but I guessed that there were at least fifty manuscripts. I was startled. I knew that my father had written short stories under the pseudonym Ellis Worth, but I had no idea that he had written so many. I knew also that he had never been very successful in publishing them; to my knowledge, only a dozen or so were published by small literary magazines. In fact, one particularly musty box, stained and misshapen due to water damage, contained about twenty magazines featuring a fictional short story by Ellis Worth or a legal essay by Everett E. Smith. This inauspicious box incarnated my father's dream: recognition as a writer.

As I curated these stories and the diary, fate intervened in a most unwelcome guise: health problems. While in Bozeman, Karlene and I decided to celebrate my 73rd birthday by taking a long-distance (about 100 miles over 6 days) walk through the Cotswolds in England. We booked hotel reservations through an English agency and arranged for air travel. Now, it was a matter of getting the needed physical conditioning. So, I began taking long walks up and down hills across the ranch with Barney.

    On one of these training walks, I noticed tightness in my throat and a slight pain in my upper left arm while walking uphill. Oh oh. I sat down on a bench, and the discomfort subsided. But when I resumed the uphill walk, it returned. Fearing angina, which I had read about many times over the years, I checked into the hospital emergency room. The usual tests were performed: electrocardiogram, echocardiogram, stress test, et cetera. Everything looked okay, with one exception: I still felt tightness in my throat while walking uphill during the stress test. The hospital cardiologist on duty sent me home with the directive to simply "watch and wait."

    Fate entered my life unexpectedly as I was preparing to leave the hospital. The discharge nurse asked me for the name of my primary physician. I didn't have one. So, the nurse assigned me to an internal medicine doctor, Michael Herring. When I looked him up on the internet, I discovered that he was a Harvard graduate. What a stroke of good fortune! Fate had treated me well. Indeed it had. Dr. Herring proved to be an excellent personal physician. Unlike so many physicians, he knew the science behind the clinical topics that he was talking about, which impressed me tremendously. Moreover, he enjoyed talking about Harvard as he checked my health. During our first session immediately after the heart tests, he suggested that I obtain an angiogram—the "gold standard" for cardiac health—just to be on the safe side. Okay, next Monday.

Fate had more in store for me. On Saturday morning, two days before the scheduled angiogram, I woke up to the unpleasant discovery that I could not urinate, no matter how hard I tried. As the bladder continued to fill due to urinary retention, it underwent occasional spasms. The pain from these spasms became more and more intense, certainly the most intense pain that I had ever experienced. Finally, Karlene took me to the emergency room, where the staff inserted a catheter to empty the bladder, thus relieving the by-now excruciating pain.

While I was there, an alert physician noticed that I was due for an angiogram in two days. He decided to keep me in the hospital until I could be seen by a cardiologist. Okay, why not? After examining me, the cardiologist chose to perform the angiogram during this hospital stay rather than wait until Monday. No point in checking in twice. So, after a fitful night in the hospital, I underwent the angiogram early Sunday morning, a day early. When I awoke from the anesthesia, I heard the staff discussing my stent. Stent? Yes, to restore blood flow through a blocked cardiac artery. I was quite surprised by this outcome. But, the cardiologist assured me that I would feel better immediately and could probably stick to my plans for the Cotswolds walk. All I had to do was take a statin and blood thinner every day to lessen the chances of any further complications.

Sure enough, I felt much better. And so, less than three months later, Karlene and I were off to the Cotswolds for our adventure. I never felt any hint of angina as we traipsed up steep hills. Since then, we have taken two other long walks with no recurrence of heart discomfort. Ostensibly, the stent did its job.

But, the other health problem—urinary retention—had not disappeared. Like a serpent in the grass, it lunged at me off and on. In the beginning, about once every three or four months, I would awaken in the middle of the night with the dreaded pain and bladder spasms. Occasionally, I could find relief by stretching, which somehow opened the urinary tract, but usually I needed a catheter to relieve the discomfort. What caused this problem? Prostate cancer? On the one hand, Dr. Herring noted that I had an unusually large prostate, characterized as benign prostatic hyperplasia, and marginally elevated prostate-specific antigen (PSA) levels—certainly not high enough to warrant serious concern about cancer. I probably needed simply to have the urethra enlarged by one of the several available procedures. Accordingly, he referred me to a urologist. On the other hand, my urologist recommended an immediate prostate biopsy to check for cancer, but I demurred because of the potential for damage to the pudendal nerve and, therefore, my sexual functions. Thus, I ignored the urologist's advice and found myself hobbling into the emergency room now and then for the dreaded but necessary catheterization. I was willing to pay that price for retaining my "manhood." And so, I put off any treatment of the underlying cause of my urinary retention, preferring to have a catheter inserted once every few months. The catheters were unpleasant, but they were tolerable for a few days now and then.

During this episode of unpleasant health issues in my life, fate cast a pleasant smile in my direction: Karlene asked me to marry her. Ho. Of course I would. So, we made plans for the glorious event. The more we planned, the more modest the plans became. After all, we had been living together for several years. Ultimately, we decided to get married in Las

Vegas: no big celebration, no family present, no whoopla of any sort. Within several weeks of our decision, Karlene was to attend a conference in Las Vegas. I went with her. On March 19, 2018, we took a taxi from the conference hotel to the wedding license office downtown, bought the license, and asked where we could actually "tie the knot." Marriage office, third floor in the neighboring building. So, we went to the marriage office and told the clerk that we wanted to be married. Right now. "Okay. That will be $35. Do you have a witness?" No; we hadn't thought about that. At the clerk's suggestion, I went into the hall and asked the first person to come along if he would please serve as our witness. "Sure. I'm waiting to witness my sister's marriage, but she's going to be late." The three of us went into the next room which had a wedding bower decorated with artificial roses. The clerk came into the room with a Bible, read a couple of verses, and then pronounced us husband and wife. "You may kiss the bride." She took a few pictures of us with Karlene's cell phone and wished us well. We thanked the witness and took off to catch a taxi for the ride back to Karlene's conference. We were now husband and wife. Although our living arrangements didn't change, I felt a great sense of happiness about this. Karlene was (and still is) a wonderful companion, a wonderful wife.

After about five years on the job, Karlene's happiness as graduate dean faded. She no longer enjoyed going to work in that capacity, so she resigned her position as graduate dean. Fortunately, she was a tenured faculty member. Thus, she returned to her professorship in the chemical engineering department. For a semester (spring, 2019), she taught in the department. But she had no enthusiasm for teaching. So, she searched for a new administrative job working with students and faculty members. And that took her to Gonzaga University in Spokane, Washington, where she accepted the position as dean of engineering and applied science, starting on June 17, 2019.

Hmm. I had heard of Gonzaga's fabled basketball teams but nothing about the rest of the university. Nor did I know anything about Spokane. I had never been there, so this would be a new experience.

Spokane-I

Once again, I drove alone to our new city, Spokane, to search for housing. And, once again, I began at the low end. Before long, however, I was looking at much more expensive properties. Eventually, I found a place nearly a half-hour's drive from the Gonzaga campus. It was a magnificent house, situated in the midst of a ponderosa pine forest and adjacent to conservation and agricultural land with a creek running nearby. Moreover the yard was replete with beautiful irises, which were in full bloom at this time of year. With the anticipated proceeds from selling our Bozeman house, we could afford this place without much concern for its cost. Karlene joined me in Spokane to look at the place. She liked it as well, so, after some haggling we bought it.

The move went smoothly. The weather was pleasant, and the movers were efficient. At the day's end, we had a houseful of boxes ready to unpack. Slowly but surely, we unpacked our things, hung pictures, arranged furniture, and so forth. Amidst this work, I had an invisible fence installed around the yard to keep Barney from wandering away. No stranger to these fences, he learned his boundaries quickly. Although Karlene had begun her work at Gonzaga during the weekdays, we managed to complete the move by July 4th. Our new home was ready to enjoy.

But, then the evil serpent reappeared. In the middle of the night of July 4, I had another case of painful urinary retention. We hadn't been in Spokane a week, so I had to search the internet for the nearest hospital emergency room where I could get a catheter. I ended up at what looked like an old, inner-city hospital with seedy-looking patients in the hallways. That didn't matter much; all I wanted was relief from the pain, which they provided skillfully. While I was there, the hospital assigned a primary care physician, who would replace Dr. Herring. I was quite saddened at losing Dr. Herring, but this was Spokane, not Bozeman. Unfortunately, the next day the catheter plugged, so I had to return to the hospital.

On this second visit, the hospital referred me to a local urologist. Begrudgingly, I went to see him. He recommended a transurethral resection procedure (TURP) to enlarge the urinary pathway. Again I demurred out of concern for my sexual functions. That proved to be a bad decision on my part, for I experienced urinary retention more and more often after that. I began to keep records of the occurrences, trying to ascertain the underlying events (for example, late-night martinis, jet lag, and so forth). If I could identify an event common to most occasions, I could hopefully control the retention behaviorally. Unfortunately, no single event stood out as a probable cause.

The retention problem reached its apex in February 2020, during a flight to Frankfurt, Germany, en route to Cairo, Egypt, where Karlene and I had planned a vacation. Midway across the Atlantic Ocean, the serpent struck; I could not urinate nor could I sit still because of the consequent pain. After landing in Frankfurt, I realized that I could not continue the flight; I needed medical attention—and quickly. We were escorted to the airport medical clinic for catheterization, but the young resident physician was unable to insert the catheter. Thus, he ordered my transit to the university hospital via ambulance. Fortunately, within less than an hour, the hospital's staff urologist effortlessly inserted a catheter and sent us on our way. We returned to the airport and successfully re-booked a flight to Egypt for that evening. The trip was rescued, so to speak, although it wasn't as enjoyable as we had hoped. How could it be with an uncomfortable, chafing catheter tube hanging out of me and a large urine collection bag attached to my belt everywhere we went?

When we returned to Spokane, Karlene insisted that I get the medical treatment needed to resolve this retention problem. No more putting that off. With little resistance, I visited the hospital urologist who had treated me before to get treatment. I told him that instead of a TURP, I preferred a non-surgical procedure, Rezum, which enlarged the urethra by injected steam; just the cells lining the urethra were killed by the steam and then they were sloughed off, leaving the rest of the prostate intact. According to advertisements, Rezum would have minimal effect on my sexual functions. The only clinic nearby that performed that procedure was in Coeur d'Alene, Idaho, about 45 miles away from our house. The drive wasn't that far, so I made an appointment with their specialist on Rezum. However, after an initial examination, he said that my prostate was too large for that procedure; I required the dreaded TURP. This time, I had little choice in the matter, so I consented to the surgery within the next three weeks. In the meantime, I wore a catheter to relieve what had now become persistent urinary retention. Before the operation, the urologist performed a biopsy on twelve tissue samples taken from my prostate; fortunately, they were all benign. Good news: no cancer. Following a COVID-19 related delay of several weeks, the urologist performed the operation. After a night in the hospital, I went home, and after a few days, I had no further bleeding or other side effects of the surgery. And, I no longer had any urinary retention. I found myself wondering why I had waited so long to solve this problem.

But the serpent had not gone away. It came back with a vengeance in a different guise. Several days after the surgery, the urologist told me the bad news: tissue samples removed during the TURP were cancerous—of the worst, very aggressive kind (Gleason score 9). A subsequent positron emission tomography (PET) scan revealed metastasis to the lymph nodes surrounding the prostate and my left hip bone (specifically, the acetabulum). To control the cancerous growth, the urologist immediately prescribed two drugs (orgovyx and XTANDI) that shut down testosterone function throughout my body and one monthly injection of XGeva that strengthened my bones against the damaging effects of the cancerous growth on my hip. With greatly diminished testosterone, my body reacted accordingly: lost body hair, increased head hair, reduced genitalia size, hot flashes, and so forth. In effect, I lost my "manhood." I protested to Karlene that these side effects were not in my plans for old age and threatened to discontinue these drugs. But she insisted that I continue taking the medications to control the cancer. "I don't want to be a widow," she proclaimed.

    The cancer diagnosis took its toll emotionally. The primary impact deprived me of any certainty about my future. When I asked the urologist about the prognosis—"should I be arranging my affairs?"—he merely shrugged, as if to say: "Who knows?" Similarly, when I asked how long I would be taking these medications, he replied: "Until they don't work any longer." I appreciated his terse candor, but it provided little soothing consolation.

    I felt as if I had nobody to talk to about the illness. Not my brother, my sons, or, for that matter, my urologist. Certainly not my primary care physician, who merely said that my urologist should be providing more emotional support as he scurried out the office door to see his next patient. Karlene provided warm comfort, but her main concern concentrated on my continuation of the medications, for I made no secret of my desire to discontinue taking them.

    A profound loneliness settled in. "My heart is a lonely hunter that hunts on a lonely hill." (William Sharp.) It was not the loneliness of a solitary man seeking the company of others. Nor was it the loneliness of a man walking in a quiet forest or wandering around in a quiet house. It was the loneliness of a man confronting his mortality. Of course, I was not the first person to experience this kind of loneliness; numerous literary classics delve deeply into this topic with much greater insight than I could muster. Furthermore, I must confess that I had never been old before (I was 76 years old at the time), so I didn't know if the loneliness might have occurred despite the cancer diagnosis. Regardless, I realized that I alone must deal with this emotional solitude, the confinement to a present here and now.

Under this cloud of uncertainty, I resolved to stay active, to enjoy life one way or another. In that maudlin frame of mind, I bought a Porsche 911 Carrera 4S—the kind of car many older men buy. I enjoyed driving it to and from Coeur d'Alene for medical treatments. And, Karlene enjoyed driving it to work on occasion. Yes, this was an expensive pleasure, but at this stage in my life, it was certainly worth the expense.

A few words about cars, by the way. The traveling often meandered to memories of fine automobiles that I have owned. I'm not talking about my Dodge, Pontiac, Volkswagen or the like. I'm talking about Porsches, Mercedes Benzes, and BMWs. My interest in these high-end cars goes back to my teenage years (1960) working in a gas station. I worked alongside another teenager, Jim. He knew a lot about all cars, but his favorite was the newly introduced Porsche 356. There were a couple of them in Colorado Springs. Once in a while, Jim and I would see one driving past the gas station. "Wow! Did you see that?" Jim told me all about the Porsche's legendary performance. "These cars can make a nearly right-angle turn when going

60 miles per hour." His enthusiasm infected me. From then on, I took a special interest in Porsches.

Two and a half years later, I heard more about the Porsche 356 from classmates at Harvard. After returning from Christmas break, several of them living across the hall from me were swapping tales about their Christmas presents. One of them said: "I got just what I wanted. A new Porsche 356." They all discussed the virtues of this car as if they had first-hand driving experience with it. I just stood and listened, thinking that these Harvard classmates certainly live in a fantastic world of privilege.

Twisting the clock forward about thirty five years to 1997, I bought my first Porsche in Honolulu: a used 1986 Carrera 911. Oh, I enjoyed that car. Of course, in Honolulu, there are very few opportunities to drive fast; in fact, the constantly congested roads precluded going faster than about 45 miles per hour at any time of day or night. But that didn't matter. Even at slow speeds, the car handled curves in an exhilarating way. I enjoyed my Porsche.

After several years, I decided to trade the Porsche for a used Mercedes Benz SL 500. Although I liked my Porsche, I couldn't resist this magnificent beauty with its shiny black paint job, convertible top, and beautiful handling. In most regards, it was superior to the Porsche for Honolulu daily driving. But it had one flaw: an orange "Check engine" light that could not be turned off. The light didn't affect the car's outstanding performance, but it bothered me immensely. Something in my personality could not tolerate this constant reminder that something deep within the car was not right. I complained and complained to the dealer, who spent many hours trying to determine the cause of this light but never discovered what triggered it. Finally, in frustration he offered to buy the car back from me. "Okay; I can't stand the light so I'll take the money." I had owned the car for only six months. During that short time, despite the annoying light, I developed an appreciation for the true luxury of a top-of-the-line Mercedes Benz.

One other top-end car brand captivated my interest: BMW. This began in Munich, where the BMW headquarters are located. During coffee break at the institute, my colleagues would often discuss the virtues of a BMW compared to a Mercedes, which (like the Porsche) is made in Stuttgart. They were quite partial to the hometown product (the BMW) with its superior performance and handling, et cetera. Okay. I had to buy one, which I did shortly after arriving in Madison. I traded in the Scirocco for a two-door BMW 320i. We took the only 320i on the dealer's lot, a bare-bones model. Jane and I liked the car so much that we traded it in for a new one loaded with various features (sunroof, leather seats, and so forth) the next year. These were good cars, to be sure; in fact, I drove this BMW for twelve years. But it didn't match the Porsche or the Mercedes in handling or luxury. But then again, the BMWs weren't as expensive either. In the long run, I ended up buying three more BMWs: two X3 SUVs and a Z4 M sportster. I was quite happy with each of them. Will I ever buy another BMW? No. They're good cars, but I'm tired of them. Five are enough.

In retrospect, these fine automobiles have brought me great pleasure. Currently I own three Porsches: the Carrera 4S, a Cayenne S, and a Macan S. And, to this day, I am always happy driving them. I continue to look at various top-end cars online, seldom with the intention of buying them. Occasionally, I contact a dealer about some detail of a particular car. These calls predictably trigger their sales pitches, which generally fall on my deaf ears. In that regard, I am their worst customer. But, I simply enjoy fine automobiles: driving them, talking about them, and writing about them.

The traveling takes me back to another fine automobile that I bought but never owned: a 1982 Ferrari

308 GTSi convertible. The car belonged to Alan Jay, who had been so kind to me when I arrived in Honolulu. Before Alan, it had belonged to the famous actor Richard Burton; indeed, it had a brass plate on the dashboard certifying his ownership at one time. For Alan, this was his "daily driver." I was concerned about that, for Alan was about 90 years old and more than a bit careless when he drove. But, so far he hadn't been involved in any accidents. I should know, for I carefully inspected the car whenever he and I got together (usually Sunday mornings for breakfast at the Outrigger Canoe Club). Alan could easily tell that I appreciated this classic beauty.

Then, one Sunday morning, fate cast a broad smile in my direction: Alan offered to sell me his Ferrari for $10,000. Ho! That was a bargain. "I'll take it." He would prepare the deed and I would get a cashier's check; we would finalize the deal late the next morning. That evening, Alan called me, saying that he had changed his mind; the price was now $18,000. That was still a bargain, so I agreed to go ahead with the purchase tomorrow morning.

But, early the next morning, fate's broad smile turned into a frown. Alan's daughter, who lived on Maui, called me with bad news: "My father has no right to sell that car. I took ownership of it a year ago, and it's not for sale." End of discussion. The deal was off. I never heard from her again, and Alan never mentioned the sale again.

Incidentally, several months later, Alan parked the Ferrari in a no-parking zone, and the police put a boot on the front wheel. When Alan saw the boot, he was enraged. In his anger, he jumped into the car and tried to drive it away with the boot still on the wheel. Naturally, this damaged the vehicle in several ways: the wheel, the front end chassis, the alignment, and so forth. The car was towed away for many repairs. I never saw it again—the Ferrari that I nearly owned was gone. Oh well, it was too good to be true. Besides, I reasoned in my disappointment, the car was impractical for it required ethyl additives in the gasoline and was, therefore, not "street legal" in California and many other states where ethyl-containing gasoline was no longer allowed.

    Oh well. Enough about cars. I could bore people for hours on end discussing them. But this isn't the venue.

More noteworthy, during this post-cancer-diagnosis epoch in my life, I began to write a new book on university finances—a topic that I had often thought about. This proved to be an enjoyable task, for I took the opportunity to describe the many accounting and budgeting principles that had perplexed me during my years as an administrator. The book was replete with numerical tables, calculations, and models. When I had finished, I sought a publisher. This is never an easy task, but this time, Johns Hopkins University Press showed an immediate interest. The Press published it in 2021 under the title *University Finances: Accounting and Budgeting Principles for Higher Education.*

    Before I had submitted the final version to the Press, my editor asked me to write another, shorter book on university budgets. Sure; I welcomed the opportunity to expand on what I had written in *University Finances.* So, I began working on the second book. Again, I enjoyed the research, the thinking, the writing on this topic. The final manuscript was finished within less than a year, and the Press published it under the title *How University Budgets Work.*

    Now, with two books on university financial matters under my belt, the Press began to promote me as an expert on higher education finances. Me? I'm a physiologist, not an accountant. But, their publicity campaign resulted in invitations from various sources such as *The Chronicle of Higher Education, The Conversation, USA Today,* and so forth to write articles on university finances and in interviews by reporters investigating one aspect or another about the topic. And, now and then I am called upon by the *Chronicle* for comments about some university's financial condition. In each case, I am referred to as an "expert on university finances" or an "expert on higher education." What a surprise! With every invitation, I had to study university finances and budgeting more and more and thus, indeed, became an expert. And, all of this was on top of the recognition generated by my first two books on university administration.

Within a period of a few years, in my late seventies, I had established a rewarding second career, borne primarily of my two books on accounting and on budgeting. Unlike my first career as a university professor of neuroscience, this career is free of competition with colleagues. I never care who reads what I have to say or writes a better book or essay. Moreover, I never bother to document these contributions on my curriculum vitae. At my age, I feel a professional freedom that I hadn't felt before. It is a wonderful feeling.

With the publication of the two books on finances and budgeting, I could now return to the planned book based on my father's diary. Gradually, I made progress. The first milestone was a completed book based on the diary, which I titled *Ascent from the Maelstrom: Dynamics of Recovery from the Trauma of War*. I was pleased with it, for I had woven together segments of the diary with my father's short stories (written under his pseudonym Ellis Worth). That year (2020), I submitted the book to numerous academic publishers and literary agents, but none showed an interest. In fact, only one editor made constructive comments: "Put more of yourself into the narrative." Hmm. Okay, I can do that. So, I began to rewrite the book, making change after change, putting more of my personal growth as a teenager and young man into the narrative. Moreover, at the editor's suggestion, I removed most of the Ellis Worth short stories that had been incorporated into that original version and streamlined the format by deleting the dates of the diary entries. After considerable thought on the matter, I decided that he was right about this major emendation.

Removing the short stories bothered me, for I had hoped to honor my father's desires to be a published writer by incorporating them into this book. And, I liked the way the stories interacted with the diary. Somewhat discouraged, I set the book aside indefinitely. Although it was nearly ready for publication in this revised version, I needed time to adapt emotionally to the changes. As Melanie Safka sang, "Look what they've done to my song, ma."

As an alternative, I decided to publish many of the short stories in two separate anthologies, *The Sonora Springs Tales: A Collection of Ellis Worth Short Stories* and *Once Upon a Farm: Tales of Discovery*. I didn't bother trying to line up an agent; instead, I decided to publish them myself. That proved to be more complicated than I had anticipated, but ultimately both books were published (Annandale Press, 2021). Thus, my writing avocation took a decisive turn, away from technical books to creative literature—even if I hadn't done the writing. I was simply the editor of my father's writings. I doubted that many people would read these two anthologies; after all, few editors had accepted these stories for publication even in small, esoteric literary magazines. Regardless, I took considerable pride in memorializing my father in this way.

While all of this writing was going on, fate cast a dismal spell on all of mankind—not just me: the COVID-19 pandemic. Within weeks after our return from Egypt, the COVID-19 pandemic erupted worldwide in March, 2020, disrupting nearly all aspects of normal life. Face masks became a necessary accoutrement outside of the house, college campuses shut down, classes and meetings of all sorts were conducted online. It certainly disrupted ours in Spokane. Karlene set up a home office, where she worked eight to ten hours per day. Both Barney and I enjoyed having her at home, although we had to adjust our habits to accommodate her need for a quiet working environment. For Barney, that adjustment was particularly challenging. At the onset, we had no idea how long these precautions would be necessary. But, as time wore on, we realized that this would not be a short-term inconvenience.

Fortunately, in early 2021, vaccines against the virus became available. Karlene and I took the first opportunity to get vaccinated. And the first opportunity to get the booster shot several months later. Although we still had to wear face masks and avoid large crowds, we felt a sense of relief. Step by short step, Gonzaga began to resume on-campus activities, and Karlene eased her way back into her campus office. But, it took about two years to restore "normal" operations.

In January, 2021, about one year after the onset of the pandemic, I received an invitation from the Registry to serve as interim vice president for research at Northern Arizona University (NAU) in Flagstaff for a sixteen-month period. I had turned down a handful of other Registry offerings during the past few years, but this one caught my attention because of its location. I had driven through Flagstaff several times and liked what I saw. Because of COVID-19, the first four months would be strictly remote. I wouldn't visit the campus until June. So much the better. Although I had reservations about the university's capabilities in research (the University of Arizona and Arizona State University dominated the state's academic research enterprise), I decided to accept the invitation. If this assignment didn't work out for any reason, my contract with the Registry allowed me to cancel the assignment with thirty days' notice.

The job began in February, 2021. Within a few weeks, I realized that my reservations were well founded. At the outset, I discovered that only several professors had significant, well-funded research programs. A credible research university required many more funded researchers. I adapted to that limitation by concentrating on the infrastructure needed to generate more faculty participation in sponsored research. That's a tough challenge at any university. But it became even more challenging when trustworthy rumors emerged that the governing board purportedly planned on de-emphasizing NAU's research designation within the state system. Consistent with those rumors, the university hired a new president who made public comments even before arriving on campus in June about supporting NAU's commitment to undergraduate education with no reference to research. As I became more and more apprehensive about the university's future as a research institution, my enthusiasm for the job diminished.

But then, fate intervened unexpectedly as it had so many times in my life. An old friend of mine who worked as an executive search consultant (that is, a "headhunter") asked me if I would consider serving as interim provost at the University of Tulsa for a maximum of six months. He explained that the university had just hired a new president, starting July 1, 2021. A lawyer by training, the new president had never held an executive-level position in higher education. Thus, part of my assignment as interim provost would be to provide helpful guidance as he learned the job. Now, this position appealed to me. Every aspect of it, even if it meant moving to Tulsa for several months. So, I agreed to accept it for three months, extendable to six months.

Of course, I had to resign my position at NAU to take the Tulsa position. So, I gave the Registry the required thirty days' notice with no explanation about why. I could do that according to my contract with the Registry. But, I did mention that I had accepted another interim position, without giving any details. This angered the Registry for two reasons. First, they had counted on me to remain at NAU for the entire 16-month duration and second, my contract with the Registry stated that I could not accept any interim position that they did not broker. After a handful of scathing e-mails, the dispute calmed down, and I remained a member in good standing with the Registry, despite my pending position at the University of Tulsa.

Tulsa

With all of that kerfuffle with the Registry settled, I flew to Tulsa to arrange for a place to live. I found housing with little difficulty: a ground-floor one-bedroom apartment located close to an expansive park where Barney could enjoy the outdoors. The apartment even had a small fenced garden in front, suitable for the dog to raise his leg or wag his tail straight up and down but not much more. Furthermore, the apartment complex was only about one mile from the campus, so I could easily come back home over lunch breaks to care for Barney. The only drawback to the location was the large number of vagrants in the park. Although they looked menacing, they seldom seemed to pay attention to strangers walking in the park. So, I assumed that we could all get along together.

Fate continued to work in my favor. Because of the COVID-19 pandemic, Karlene was still working remotely. As a result, she was free to join me in Tulsa, where she could set up a makeshift office on the kitchen table to work. So, over the July 4th holidays, the three of us — Barney, Karlene, and I — drove to Tulsa in Karlene's Subaru. This would be our new home for at least three months. Everything went smoothly for Karlene and me. I flew back to Spokane now and then for medical treatments and Karlene flew back now and then to look into her campus office and school research buildings, making sure that they remained in good condition during the pandemic-related closures.

Things didn't go so smoothly for Barney, however. Despite the new smells, a few saucy neighborhood cats, and other novel dog attractions, he seemed uncomfortable much of the time. His walks were often rushed because I had to return to work. I seldom allowed him to sniff too long at garbage receptacles along the pathways in the park, and I limited how closely he could approach a neighbor's cat. The very hot summer weather added to his discomfort. He missed his home in Spokane.

Indeed. During one of our walks in the park, he pulled out of his harness and ran away from me at top speed. I chased after him as he ran up a hill towards the freeway. He paid no attention to my whistling and calling; he just wanted to get away from this dreadful place. He was heading back to Spokane. Fortunately, fate stepped in. A vagrant sitting under a tree with his scruffy white dog caught Barney's attention. Barney suddenly turned away from the freeway and approached the little dog. The vagrant heard my calls and restrained Barney until I caught up with him. I credit the vagrant, whom I never saw again, with saving Barney's life, for surely he would not have survived the freeway traffic. This traumatic experience made me realize how unhappy the dog was. I felt pressured to get him back to his home in Spokane but also had to complete my three-month commitment in Tulsa. Somehow, Barney would have to adapt to this temporary arrangement.

I enjoyed my role as interim provost. The president, my boss, was an agreeable, energetic man who often sought my advice—at least for the first several weeks, that is. After that, he struck out on his own, running the university competently but not always as I would have recommended. Little by little, he stripped the provost's office of various reporting lines, such as the dean of students, faculty development, and several other functions. Most notably, he moved management of the academic budget from the provost's office to his office. In short, he was concentrating power in the president's office at the expense of the provost's office. I expressed my concern that he was slowly marginalizing the provost. But, it didn't matter much to me; I was a "short-timer." I would always point out his mistakes (at least in my eyes), but I would leave it to my permanent successor to right these wrongs.

During my first week at the university, when the new president was still listening intently to my advice, I told him that the university had a structural deficit. For several years now, it had been generating less revenue than it had been spending and had been making up for this operating deficit by borrowing millions of dollars regularly from a line of credit with a local bank. Of course, those loans had to be repaid with interest, which added to the deficit. Consequently, until the university eliminated this deficit, it would always be strapped for the discretionary money needed to grow in new, innovative directions. The president understood this financial limitation immediately and asked: "What shall we do about it?"

I suggested that he launch a "1/2/3 plan" to reduce expenditures: each unit's operating budget would be reduced by one percent, two percent, and then three percent for the next three years, respectively. Those cuts, totaling six percent of each unit's operating budget, would be sufficient to eliminate the deficit and restore health to the university's finances. The president agreed to the plan with one major modification: it would be a 3/2/1 plan instead, with the administrative offices' (such as the provost's) budgets cut by five percent (instead of three) in the first year. Remembering the trauma of the 4/4/4 plan at Hawaii, I recommended that he stick with a more gradual reduction, but the president persisted. And so, the 3/2/1 plan went into effect about two months after I arrived. For the most part, I sat back and watched the president's office implement the reductions with the deans.

My most pressing issues in the office operations involved personnel. In my opinion, the assistant to the provost could do no right. I had to replace her, but for reasons that I could never understand, human resources dragged its feet. So, I was stuck with her. Worse still, my very competent associate provost got into a tiff with the president over working conditions, so he told her to return to the faculty—no matter what I said. I would miss her expertise and industriousness. But returning to the faculty was, in fact, just as well, for she was an assistant professor, which limited her future in higher administration. In her place, at the president's suggestion, I hired an English professor who had been working for him as a special assistant. She caught onto the requirements of the job very quickly, which pleased me. Two other key personnel in my office resigned for one reason or another, but I didn't replace them. Those unfilled positions would be available for my successor to fill.

Another perplexing issue in the office operations involved telephones. Or, more appropriately, the lack of them. Instead of standard telephone landlines, the university used an online messaging application, Teams. This program rivaled Zoom for video conferencing, but the university relied on it for one-to-one conversations as well. Thus, to "telephone" somebody, I had to use Teams. Okay, that's not so bad if I wanted to initiate the call. But, any incoming calls had to come straight to me; they could not go to my assistant who could filter them and, if appropriate, then forward the call to me. Furthermore, my assistant could not place a call for me and then forward it to me after the recipient had answered.

All of these limitations to standard office telephone procedures annoyed me, for they disrupted the management style that I had learned many years earlier. For example, my first boss at Wisconsin, Bob Bock, taught me always to let my office assistant answer the telephone and ask the caller what the call was about. Then, after putting the caller on hold, the assistant would tell me who was calling and what the topic of the call was, thus allowing me time to collect my thoughts. If I needed more than a minute or so to think over the pending discussion, I could always be "out of the office but would call back." When I complained to the University of Tulsa telecommunications office about these limitations, I was told that: "Curious. You're the first person to complain about this." Hmm. Well, at best, I had to endure only three months of this annoying inconvenience.

Notably, I got along well with the deans. During our first meeting, where we all sat far apart, fully masked due to COVID-19, I told them that I expected them to be strong deans, as I had told the deans at the University of Hawaii. "Don't come to me with problems; come to me with solutions. If I'm asked to solve a problem for you, then you are ceding your authority." Furthermore, I assured them that I would always support them in public; we would resolve any disputes privately. In fact, the deans seldom came to me with an issue they couldn't handle on their own. Sometimes I didn't agree with their decisions, but I never overrode or criticized them. The deans liked these assurances of their leadership primacy.

Likewise, I got along well with the faculty senate. Stereotypically, faculty senates and provosts often disagree on one thing or another, resulting in a sense of animosity between them. The senates' usual complaint is that they were not consulted on a particular decision. I learned the hard way at the University of Hawaii always to respect the senate's sensitivity on this issue, since it meant so much to them. Accordingly, at the University of Tulsa whenever any topic arose that might vaguely interest the senate members, I sent it to them for their consideration before I took any action on the topic, even if the topic was not in the conventional purview of the senate. Of course, that slowed down the decision-making process considerably, but it certainly pleased the senate members and, ultimately, generated positive "buy-in" from them. At one point, the senate president referred to me as the senate's "guru." I considered that a flattering compliment.

As my initial three-month commitment approached its end in late September, the president asked me to continue until he had recruited a permanent replacement. That search would most certainly stretch out to next summer. I couldn't agree to stay in Tulsa for another three months; I had to get Barney back to his home in Spokane. When I told the president that I couldn't continue, he said plaintively: "But I need to have a provost." He did, indeed. I knew that. As a compromise, I agreed to continue for another three months, to the end of the year, but I would work remotely from Spokane. During that time, I would train my associate provost to handle most of the critical tasks of the job so she could take over as interim provost in January when my appointment would come to an end. The president agreed reluctantly on one condition: I would be in Tulsa for the board of trustees' meeting in November. Okay. We had a deal. Neither of us was particularly enthusiastic about the arrangement, but at least the university would have an experienced provost for a while longer.

On the first of October, when my apartment lease expired, Karlene and I packed our possessions into the Subaru, with Barney snuggled in her lap, and began the long drive back to Spokane. Despite the tedium of the drive, Karlene and I enjoyed the time together. We talked and talked about nothing in particular and looked out onto nothing but the endless, lonely expanses of Kansas, Eastern Colorado, Wyoming, and Montana. Although we are both solid Democrats, during this drive we developed an appreciation of the conservative voters in those states; in their relative isolation on the vast prairies, the farmers had to be self-reliant. Yes, the Federal government might provide some relief when nature dealt the farmers a devastating blow (severe drought, major storms, and so forth). And, they gladly accepted Federal-government money for any other reason. But that was an unreliable source of income. Unimpressed by any of this, nobody enjoyed the conclusion of our trip more than Barney when we pulled into our driveway. Home at last.

Now, from the comfort of my home office in Spokane, I returned to work as interim provost at the University of Tulsa. Although I had considerable experience working online with NAU, I had an array of difficulties working online with Tulsa. I still faced the inconvenience of using Teams for telephone calls and an incompetent front office assistant.

Beyond those difficulties, meetings with the deans were more difficult online. Those meetings are challenging under the best of circumstances, and the limitations of online dialogues exacerbated those challenges. Neither the deans nor I were particularly happy with this arrangement. We missed the opportunity to assess nuanced communications via eye-contact and body language. Slowly, however, I adapted to the task of meeting with the deans online.

In November, I returned to Tulsa for the board of trustees meeting and stayed a week to assert my authority as provost in person. Fortunately, my associate provost had taken on more and more of the responsibilities that required the provost's attention. By the end of the year, she was ready to step in as my replacement. And, I was ready to step down; my contractual term was over. The president thanked me profusely for my help during the past six months, but I suspected that he felt relieved to get past having his provost working remotely. If I were in his position, I certainly would want the provost just down the hall—not 1800 miles away.

Spokane-II

As the new year, 2022, began, I faced a lull. No more Tulsa. What would I do in this next phase of retirement? One thing I did was take a lot of naps. Funny. The more naps I took, the more I wanted them. They were addictive. But, I didn't want to get into the habit of taking so many naps; I wasn't ready mentally for that harbinger of old age. Moreover, the naps induced the traveling, so much that I began to lose my way in the past. I had to find something to occupy my mind, to break this habit of napping so often, to anchor myself in the present.

The best option was to resume working on the book based on my father's diary. So, I plunged into the effort: writing, rewriting, and rewriting. And once again, I immersed myself in the tedium of digitizing key sections of the diary and writing précis for inclusion in the book. Within about a year, I declared the manuscript ready for publication. To distinguish it from my unsuccessful previous version (*Ascent from the Maelstrom*) I changed the title to *The Man I Didn't Know: My Father's Hidden Struggle with PTSD*. Ultimately, I had a new, revised version that I resubmitted to a handful of publishers and agents, but none of them responded. Sadly, I was on my own. Okay, no point in feeling sorry for myself. Accordingly, I prepared the text files, the cover, and various other items needed for a self-publishing firm. Despite my previous experience with the short-story anthologies, all of these preparations took longer than I anticipated. But, finally, in the fall, the book was published (Annandale Press, 2023). It was a beautiful book. I was (and still am) quite proud of it. Most probably, few people will read it, but at least I have memorialized another aspect of my father's legacy (in addition to the short-story anthologies). I felt a great sense of accomplishment and satisfaction after working ten years on this project.

Then, there were also the Harvard interviews. Besides cold weather and snow (except in Hawaii), each winter brought another cohort of Harvard applicants to interview. These interviews had become a rite of winter, so to speak. Since 2001, over the past 23 years, I interviewed applicants in six states and three countries. The winter of 2023 was no different. I looked forward to these interviews, for they introduced me to the "best and brightest" high school students in the world.

Some aspects of the interviewing process had changed with time. Notably, prior to the COVID-19 pandemic every applicant received an in-person interview. I would drive to them, or, more often, they would drive to me. During the pandemic, however, the interviews were by Zoom. It took some adjustments on my part to structure the interviews to this new format, but the students seemed to have little difficulty with online communication. The use of Zoom has continued after the pandemic; in fact, Harvard has replaced in-person with Zoom as the "official" interview format.

Another significant change has been Harvard's limitation of interviews to only a select fraction of the applicants—usually those most likely to be admitted. This change became necessary as the number of applicants skyrocketed during the past several years (the 2020s), reaching nearly 60,000 for a class of only 2000 admitted students. As a corollary to this triage, with rare exceptions, each applicant selected for the interview had straight A's, very high test scores, and exemplary extracurricular activities (for example, first violin in the all-state orchestra, state tennis champion, class president, and so forth).

Consequently, since they all looked about the same "on paper," I was forced to consider more nuanced aspects of the candidate's suitability for Harvard. If I had to specify two qualities that I sought, they would be: first, the applicant is a "thinker" and second, has achieved state or national recognition for some activity.

The most significant change in the Harvard applicants has been a dramatic shift in gender and ethnicity. When I began interviewing, most applicants were male. Nowadays, a slight majority of the applicants are female. I don't know the exact application percentages by gender, but the admitted class remains close to 50 percent female (53.6 percent in 2023). The ethnicity has changed as well, although it depended on the location of the interviews. In Hawaii, the applicant ethnicity was mixed: some Whites, some Asians (including South Asian), a few Pacific Islanders. When I moved to Texas, the applicant ethnicity was primarily White, with an occasional Hispanic. Now, in Spokane, their ethnicity is often Asian, and now and then Hispanic. Less than half of them are White. Harvard's admissions for the past several years reflect this ethnic mix of applicants; last year's (that is, 2023) freshman class was 40% white, 30% Asian, 17% African-American, 12% Hispanic, and 1% Pacific Islanders. These percentages differ dramatically from the ethnic mix of the United States population as a whole, which is about 60 percent White. Regardless, I have been left wondering: Where are the White males? I'm not alone in that regard, as this question has been raised throughout higher education during the past several years. Of course, pundits posit various explanations (for example, other career opportunities have emerged), but certainly I have no astute answers to this question. From my perspective as an interviewer, the White males simply aren't applying.

All of that aside, I interviewed another ten students this winter (2023-2024). There were only three males and four White applicants (male and female combined), as had become the norm nowadays. With Harvard's new triage system, each applicant was superb: wickedly smart and highly talented. I enjoyed my conversations with them, wishing that each of them would be admitted. But, the odds were stacked against them; this year, Harvard would admit less than four percent of the applicants. The fate of privilege would favor only a very few fortunate applicants again this winter. Ironically, one white female that I interviewed was accepted, but she turned down Harvard in favor of Brigham Young University. I was stunned by this decision. She must be a very devout Mormon to forego this coveted opportunity to attend Harvard.

During the traveling, I remembered occasional comments by one person or another about how difficult it is to get into Harvard these days. "It's not like it was when you went to Harvard," implying that it was much easier "back then." Well, I seldom responded to these comments, which I considered quite ignorant, with anything more respectful than "Yeah, yeah." But, did they have a point? After all, the total number of applicants had risen dramatically, but the number of admitted students had not changed significantly. My unequivocal answer, however, is that admission to Harvard was no easier when I applied than it is today — at least as far as I can tell. I was valedictorian of a large high school class, a member of various musical, athletic, and service organizations, and an avid reader. And most of my Harvard classmates had comparable credentials. Nowadays (and during the preceding 23 years), very, very few of the applicants I have interviewed have credentials of that breadth and quality. And, those rare individuals who do have them are usually admitted to Harvard. Restating my point, my classmates and I were admitted to Harvard in 1962 and, in all likelihood, would be admitted to Harvard today.

Now, as I look at Harvard after my eightieth birthday, I'm disappointed by the purported anti-Semitism and pro-Palestinian demonstrations triggered by the ongoing war between Israel and Hamas in the Gaza strip. They certainly disrupted normal campus activities, but protests of one sort or another have occurred at Harvard many times in my lifetime.

Indeed. At Harvard, as elsewhere in the northern hemisphere, springtime means a time for rising temperatures, melting snow, getting outdoors, enjoying the end of a long cold winter; the time when every man's thoughts turn to love. The time to release all that pent up energy after the long winter. And what's a most effective way to dissipate that energy? The annual spring riot.

Yes, the spring riot. Okay, sometimes the students couldn't wait until spring, and the riots began earlier in the school year. But they were still college riots, nonetheless. They are a tradition on all but the most moribund campuses. But a lively place like Harvard has always had a good riot, usually in the springtime.

My traveling took me back in history to apocryphal riots in the past. For example, as freshmen we were told about Harvard's legendary "great butter rebellion." According to the lore, it occurred in the late 1700's, probably 1768. Historians can't agree on the exact date, but they tend to agree on the events. In the dining room, an excitable student picked up a piece of butter, pronounced it rancid, and threw it across the hall. Then the trouble began. The riot began. Skipping forward past many other riots, we come to the year before I entered that hallowed institution, spring 1961. The university announced that henceforth all diplomas would be written in English instead of the traditional Latin. Oh, the students didn't like that at all. So, they rioted to express their displeasure. According to an urban legend, students even welded a streetcar to the tracks in Harvard Square. What better way to express their outrage? (In fact, that didn't really happen during this particular riot; it happened at MIT sometime in the 1930s). Of course about ten years later, Harvard students joined their counterparts at universities across the country in riots protesting America's involvement in the Vietnam War. The only problem was that the rioting at the University of California, Berkeley and the University of Wisconsin totally eclipsed Harvard's attempt to grab the public's attention.

During the "off years" when there weren't any momentous events to catalyze a good riot, Harvard students would riot by storming the nearby Radcliffe campus on a "panty raid." Oh yes. With great vigor, they marched en masse into the dorms and stole the panties from the Cliffies, who were squealing in outraged delight. The panties were usually retrieved the next day from the nearby tree branches.

Well, all of this brings us to the 2024 unrest on campuses nationwide. Spring riots against the Zionist state of Israel. Hmm. That's as good as any other reason to join the action. After all, it's spring, and final exams are still several weeks away.

Am I irreverant? Perhaps. But, as I age, I am less and less inclined to take events like the pro-Palestinian riots on college campuses very seriously. Naturally, I must be cautious about sharing these light-hearted thoughts about weighty issues; not everybody appreciates my lack of respect for the plight of either the Israelis or the Palestinians. But that conflict has simmered since my early childhood and from what I can tell will continue to simmer indefinitely, no matter how this current war ends. What a sad state of affairs for the people whose fate was to be bound to this troubled part of the world.

The traveling in the unconstrained realm of fantasy came to an abrupt end when fate delivered a most unwelcome blow: the death of my brother on July 12, 2024. The traveling now entered the realm of recollections constrained to my only brother—some sad, some happy. Curt's death wasn't entirely unexpected. His health had been deteriorating slowly over the past year or so. His mental acuity remained sharp, but his physical strength, his core and limb muscles, had degenerated to the point of feebleness. "I'm so frail," he commented to me in our recent conversations. Oh, he could walk from his Lazyboy chair in the bedroom to the couch in the adjoining living room but not much farther without a lengthy rest along the way. And, most importantly, he could walk from either of these places to the nearest bathroom, which he did with frequent regularity. These signs didn't presage his imminent death; other more ominous signs did, though.

The portentous signs of Curt's health issues appeared first in 2011 or so when he suffered a pulmonary embolism: a blood clot migrated from his leg into his lung (and fortunately no farther into his heart or brain). I was in Lubbock when I received a phone call from him while he awaited medical attention in the emergency room for shortness of breath. He hadn't even told his wife yet. I drove up to Colorado Springs and found him in the hospital, where he stayed for nearly a week. This was serious. The doctor placed a filter in his vena cava to halt the progress of any further clots into his heart and prescribed warfarin to thin his blood. According to Curt's doctor, he would be taking warfarin indefinitely to reduce the chances of life-threatening blood clot formation. Gotta keep that blood moving. A few other health issues arose during the next few years, but none threatened his life.

Then, in early summer, 2024, a strange event occurred. While walking into his kitchen, he tripped on a carpet and fell face first onto the floor: a classic "face plant." He managed to get up and "shake it off," but he emerged with two telltale black eyes. A few days later, he developed a serious nose bleed that lasted five hours. That's a long time, a very long time for a nose bleed. He called me midway through this ordeal, and I recommended that he seek medical help immediately. He refused. Before he had finally stanched the flow, he declared that he was taking his healthcare into his own hands: "I'm going to stop taking warfarin." So, he did just that. I worried about that decision, because the warfarin had greatly diminished the likelihood of another embolism. I worried further when Curt commented almost daily about occasional dizzy spells. Finally, a couple of days before he died, he had brief mini-seizures and "blackout moments." Something was wrong. Indeed, after one of these dizzy spells, Curt dozed off in his easy chair and never woke up.

When I heard the news of his death, a profound cloud of grief settled about me. I lost my only brother! We had shared our lives together. I went through several days of intense grieving, unable to control waves of tears. I lost my only brother! Gradually, however, the passage of time has blunted the impact of this loss, but occasionally I still shed tears when I think about him. I lost my only brother!

The traveling inevitably visited and re-visited memories of my brother, my only brother. I recollected Curt's amazing talents. They were unique, very unique. Piano playing, for example. Like me, he grew up immersed in music, playing various instruments, learning to read music, and so forth. The piano was always the core instrument for both of us. Like me, he didn't practice, and like me, he hopped from one piano teacher to another. Thus, like me, he didn't really excel at piano playing. Until his sophomore year in college, that is. Then his piano playing talent blossomed.

At this point, the story requires some elaboration to appreciate Curt's talent playing piano. In high school, he had many interests, which did not include academics. They did include ping pong. In a short time playing at the local YMCA, Curt became very good, winning several local championships. In fact, his nickname among rival players was "King Pong." But then his interest in ping pong suddenly waned. Bowling took its place. And, soon he became a very good bowler, winning several local championships. Once again, however, his interest in this sport suddenly waned, and he took up golf. Yes, quickly he became an expert golfer. And so it went. These intense interests took their toll academically, however, and Curt graduated with no distinction whatsoever. He managed to get into Southern Colorado State College on probation and to finish his freshman year precariously close to flunking out.

During the summer between his freshman and sophomore years, two things happened: he grew by several inches to well over six feet tall and his interest turned to the piano. Why the piano? Maybe he perceived that at the time he didn't have any other options in life. I don't know; he may not have known either. His interest in piano just happened. And so, Curt began to practice eight or more hours every day and became a very good pianist by the end of the summer. This interest in piano persisted much longer than his other interests; indeed it lasted throughout college and for many years afterwards. Three years later, he graduated with distinction in music from Southern Colorado State and went on to get his master's degree in music at the prestigious Eastman School of Music in Rochester, New York. From then on, music, piano in particular, became his profession, his passion.

The traveling took me to a time when, using the nickname "King Curt" and wearing a set of white tails, Curt went on a solo concert tour at various venues in the West playing pieces composed by John Cage and other avant garde composers on a "prepared" piano with sounds altered by knives, forks, screws, rubber erasers, and other objects inserted between the strings. Everything but a dead mouse. He enjoyed telling about the musically conservative audience members whose reaction to the boings, sprocks, and other strange sounds verged on the profane: "What the hell is this noise?" Curt loved playing this modern, non-classical music. It wasn't Beethoven, that's for sure. But, he certainly could play Beethoven and the other classical composers beautifully. I always enjoyed listening to him play whatever piece by the classical composers that he had "in his fingers" whenever I visited his house. Ah, the traveling took me to many other memories of Curt that skipped fleetingly through my mind, evading capture for this chronicle. But they form a silent reminder that I lost my only brother. What a painful loss.

As time passes and days on the calendar fly by, I remain in Spokane. It is my home for the foreseeable future. In fact, I am tethered to this city because of my need to visit my urologist about twice monthly. Moreover, I am tethered by Barney. In his advanced age (approaching 15 years old), Karlene and I are less and less inclined to disrupt his routine by placing him in a kennel while we travel or, after the Tulsa debacle, to move him to another home. Karlene takes occasional trips out of town, but I stay here, keeping Barney company, "holding down the fort," so to speak.

I don't mind this sedentary life. During the past 67 years, I have visited many parts of the world. I don't have a "bucket list" of places to see or exotic things to do before I'm too old to get around easily. No; I'm quite content.

Of course, who knows when fate might intervene once again.

Epilogue

The traveling hasn't come to an end, but my telling of it nears its end. Every day, every night I continue to revisit unrecounted memories in my past, to be sure. They could be told. Eventually, however, this story, as life itself, must come to an end, brought to a conclusion. Before adding that final punctuation mark to this chronicle, though, I am compelled to touch upon several topics of noteworthy relevance or irrelevance to my life.

The first topic is my legacy. Professionally, my scientific contributions have disappeared into the shadows of time. Few people remember me as a neuroscientist. I take no umbrage in that. After all, very few people (including nearly all of the applicants to Harvard that I have interviewed) remember who J.D. Watson is, much less the myriad other Nobel Prize winners of the past few years. So it goes. Fame is fleeting.

Personally, my two sons constitute the core of my legacy. Both have earned their Ph.D.s and are distinguished professors in reputable universities. I am very proud of them. Moreover, I have three grandchildren: Christof (son of Curtis and Alexia), River (son of Corey and his former wife Laura), and Hannah (daughter of Corey and Laura). During their youth, I saw them with some regularity but not often enough to develop the kind of bond that many grandfathers have with their grandchildren. Quite simply, we all lived too far apart for extended time together.

Nonetheless, I keep in touch with Christof who has a Ph.D. and M.D. from the University of North Carolina and holds a position at Harvard Medical School's Dana Farber Cancer Center. Harvard! I wept in joyful pride when he announced his position at Harvard. I exchange emails now and then with River, who changed his name from Adam. He is studying for a master's degree in counseling at DePaul University in Chicago. I'm immensely proud of these two boys as they contribute to my legacy as an academic. Then, there's Hannah, whom I remember as my joyful little granddaughter. Over the past ten years or so, I've lost contact with her. All I know from Corey is that after graduating from college, she has worked in Cleveland at one job or another. Even Corey, her father, has limited contact with her. I'm not proud of this estrangement; she's my granddaughter after all, carrying some of my genes. Why don't I take the initiative to re-establish our relationship? I've tried to contact her on numerous occasions over the years, but she seldom answers e-mails, birthday cards, or letters. Nor has she ever contacted me. I suppose that I could try harder, but sadly I've given up. Very sadly.

Memories of my children and grandchildren evoke lyrics from a classic song:

> Sunrise, sunset
> Sunrise, sunset
> Swiftly fly the years
> One season following another
> Laden with happiness and tears
> One season following another
> Laden with happiness and tears.

On occasion, as I have become older, I return from the traveling "laden with happiness and tears."

The second topic is politics. In retrospect, the traveling seldom took me to memories of politics. I now wonder why not. After all, most of my professional colleagues had well-formed political opinions. In fact, pollsters estimate that about a third of all Americans are what they call "highly engaged" in politics. Surely I must have had some thoughts on the subject. Oh yes, I disapproved of the wars in Vietnam and Iraq. But, I simply didn't share the anti-war fervor of my colleagues. And yes, more recently, I disapprove of the disgustingly vulgar Donald Trump. Bluntly put, I consider him to be a horse's ass, not fit to be a role model for anybody but the most depraved scoundrel. However, my intense dislike doesn't extend deeply into his decisions made as president. No, I rarely spent much time thinking about political affairs unless they affected me personally.

Despite my general disregard for politics, I voted in every election for a national or state office. In my younger years, I probably voted mostly for Republican candidates. I say "probably" because I don't remember how I voted even in the most consequential elections. For example, did I vote for Richard Nixon or Hubert Humphrey in 1968? Did I vote for Ronald Reagan or Walter Mondale in 1984? I simply can't remember. But, my upbringing in ultra-conservative Colorado Springs shaped my early political viewpoints, even though my father was a staunch Democrat, so I probably voted for the Republican candidates. In my older years, from about age 60, I most assuredly know how I have voted: entirely for Democrat candidates. My decisive turn to the political left resulted from the increasingly annoying intrusion of evangelical Christian values into the Republican's political platform. I'm not inclined to debate political or ideological matters; that is like engaging in a pissing match with a skunk. With that crude simile, I'll discontinue this discussion of politics; I've made my point.

The third topic is personal integrity. In my youth, my parents had contrasting influences in this regard. On the one hand, my mother always encouraged me to seize every material advantage, even at the expense of somebody else's material disadvantage. For example, if a grocer erringly gave me a dollar too much in change, she would congratulate me on my good fortune. Now, I must add that she never suggested that I should break the law; don't steal the dollar or a dollar's worth of goods. Never break the important laws, like murder, larceny, and so forth. Less important laws were a different matter. For example, she never hesitated to allow me to drive the car before I was old enough to have a drivers' license. Nor did he hesitate to allow me to drink beer before I had reached the legal age for alcohol consumption in Colorado. On the other hand, my father always encouraged me to uphold the most righteous behavioral standards—to follow the Golden Rule, so to speak. He set good examples. I remember one Saturday lunch when the waitress gave him ten cents too much in change. My father discovered this several blocks down the street. He promptly turned around, walked back to the restaurant, and gave the waitress the dime. Likewise, he insisted on following the law—all laws—strictly. He disapproved of my driving and drinking beer before the legal ages. That would never happen when we were with him.

Throughout my life, my personal behavior has tended to follow my father's guidance. Oh, if a store clerk gave me a dollar too much in change, I might not walk back to return it as my father would have done. But in more consequential situations, if I detected a monetary error in my favor, I would point it out for correction. For example, Millie underestimated the amount I owed her in our divorce settlement by about $200,000; I promptly told her about the error and corrected her arithmetic. Or, as happened more than once in airport lounge chairs, when I found a wallet with lots of cash in it, I would track down the rightful owner. In these and numerous other examples, I always imagined how I would have felt if I had incurred such losses. The Golden Rule always prevailed.

The topic of personal integrity was quite important in my scientific career. As a research scientist, I faced tremendous pressures to achieve publishable results, with numerous temptations to "fudge" data to improve the credibility and impact of a particular set of experiments. I resisted these temptations, adhering to the Harvard-based proposition that my accomplishments did not depend on any form of dishonesty. Unfortunately, some of my colleagues failed to resist these temptations. I noticed falsification in scientific data over the years: some blatant, some subtle. I never confronted these colleagues directly, but, of course, my respect for their research contributions sank. I'm now retired and no longer actively keep an eye on research integrity, although I certainly read with sadness about the recent high-profile accusations of academic fraud by presidents Claudine Gay and Marc Tessier-Lavigne of my alma maters Harvard and Stanford Universities, respectively. Obviously, they could not resist the temptations earlier in their professional careers, and I do not respect them for these lapses. By and large, I look back quite proudly on my record of integrity in my research program.

I do not profess to be a paradigm of unblemished integrity. I suspect that very few human beings my age can. Too many things happen; too many decisions must be made. But the traveling bypassed any egregious lapses, sparing me the necessity to document them in this chronicle, to explain myself. When the traveling comes to an end, barring any unforeseen circumstances, I can truly "rest in peace" on that account.

The fourth topic is friendship. When reflecting on memories from the traveling, I realized that I made few lasting friendships during my lifetime. Oh, I got to know various classmates and, of course, my roommates and girlfriend Ruth while at Harvard. And, I made a couple of friends at Stanford and later in my career. But, usually, we went our separate ways in pursuit of our career goals. I have not kept in meaningful contact with any of them. Well, I should say most of them.

A priori, one friend requires special attention: man's best friend, my beagle Barney. Understandably, dogs differ from humans. Thus, I cannot logically consider him a friend, a colleague to discuss deep thoughts with or share a glass of fine wine with. No. But I cannot understate the comfort he has brought me during the past 14 years. Indeed, during the daytime traveling, Barney often lies beside me in the recliner chair, most probably doing the traveling in his own universe.

Numerous books, essays, and other media have extolled the comforts offered by pets. I concur with all of them. So, I will limit my contribution to this voluminous collection to only a few remembrances from the traveling.

My memories of this wonderful dog go back to his earliest puppyhood. Barely eight weeks old, he moved to Karlene's house where he ventured into the backyard now and then. I remember watching him navigate through grass as tall as he was (about eight inches or so); occasionally he would bump into a single blade of grass that knocked him off balance. As he grew into an adult dog, he displayed typical beagle traits: he loved to hunt small rodents, chase rabbits and deer, and bay whenever he encountered a strange animal such as a porcupine, opossum, or coyote. Otherwise, he seldom barked unless he needed somebody to open the door for him to go outside or come back in. In that regard, we had a deal: he wouldn't pee or poop in the house but we had to open the door immediately when he had an urge to go outside.

Apropos wild animals: the coyotes were a problem, a very threatening problem. For them, Barney would make a great meal. And we knew that. Barney's first encounter with a coyote occurred in Bozeman while he was out in his yard hunting rodents. Then, we heard him bay. Uh oh. Karlene

Epilogue

saw the coyote closing to within about three feet from Barney, opened the door, and yelled, distracting the predator. Meanwhile, I raced outside with a shovel, which caused the coyote to retreat. His second encounter occurred in Spokane while Barney was walking around in his front yard. Again, we heard him bay. I rushed to the front door and found Barney at the doorstep with blood flowing from wounds to his ear and neck. While Karlene distracted the retreating coyote, I quickly cleaned the wounds and took him to the pet emergency hospital downtown. The wounds were not deep, fortunately, but he still has a scar on his ear. Barney's third encounter was also in his front yard in Spokane. This time, he did not bay. He simply walked silently up the sidewalk towards the front door, with a coyote about three feet behind him. I just happened to look out the front window as Barney approached the door, with a traumatized look in his eyes. I quickly raced outside in my bare feet and stepped between the coyote and Barney. While I negotiated a retreat with the coyote, Karlene pulled Barney into the house. Although Barney was unscathed physically, he was affected emotionally by this traumatic experience. For the next several months, Barney never ventured more than about twenty feet from the front door. And to this day, he is very cautious out there, sniffing, looking, and listening for any sign of danger. Furthermore, as a precaution, I now always accompany him as a bodyguard whenever he needs to go outside. I will not lose Barney to a coyote on my watch.

Barney is now fourteen, going on fifteen years old. That is about the expected lifespan of a beagle. Sadly, he can no longer jump into the car or onto the bed without help. But, despite his physical limitations, Barney remains my faithful, comforting companion: my best friend. Oh yes, I should emphasize that Karlene shares my love for this dog; he is her best friend as well. Needless to say, we will face a tragic episode in our lives when Barney takes the final sojourn while doing his traveling.

In the human realm, two of my longest-lasting friends have been a married couple, Arnold and Ann Weinstein, whom Jane and I met at Harvard when he was a graduate student in Comparative Literature. Our friendship began when we all lived in Peabody Terrace, where Ann and Jane worked together in the superintendent's office for a short while. Arnold and Ann had a daughter about Curtis's age, which catalyzed informal chit-chat in the office and on the playground. Our friendship grew over gourmet food, which Ann and Jane prepared and served with all of the pretentious ceremony of the finest dining. Getting to the point, we all enjoyed each other's company. Our lives have interlaced for many years, and we continue to remain in contact.

During my senior year, Arnold and Ann went to Lyon, France, where Arnold would study at the University of Lyon. We would miss them, but not entirely, for they generously allowed us to move from our rather starkly furnished eleventh-floor apartment into their more spacious and comfortably furnished fourth-floor apartment while they were in Lyon. For us, that was a luxurious upgrade. By the time they returned, we had just left that wonderful apartment for Stanford. They had one year to go at Harvard; Arnold received his Ph.D. the next year and took a faculty position at Brown University where he has been a professor ever since.

After leaving Harvard, we next met Arnold and Ann during our summer at Woods Hole when we drove to Providence and stayed at their house for a long weekend. Fate cast a smirking smile on Jane and me, because Ann was preparing a classic seven course French meal for several of Arnold's faculty colleagues and their spouses that Saturday evening. Now, Jane and I were no strangers to elegant French meals after our round-robin dinners at Dudley House and our evenings with Arnold and Ann in Peabody

Terrace. So, we looked forward to this special treat. The gala event began early in the afternoon when Arnold served me a glass of fine Amontillado sherry while Ann and Jane arduously prepared the meal in the kitchen. Correction: Arnold served me several glasses of this delicious aperitif. Before the meal had even begun, I felt the alcohol starting to make its claim on my senses. As soon as the guests arrived, of course we all had another glass or two of welcoming sherry, followed by a couple of flutes of champagne. And then the dinner began, accompanied first by generous glasses of delicious white Burgundy and then by several equally generous glasses of delicious red Burgundy—all premier cru wines from France. By the time the salad was served (near the end of the meal in classic French style), I was quite inebriated. Indeed, only a rushed dash to the nearest bathroom averted a most unpleasant moment at the table. On my return to the table, we continued with a fine port to accompany the cheese course. And then, of course, the evening wouldn't be complete without a snifter or two of VSOP Cognac as a digestif at the end of the meal. By the time the last guest had departed, I was ready for bed. Really ready!

    Our paths crossed several times while Jane and I were in Europe. While we were in Sweden, Arnold and Ann rented a farmhouse in the countryside near Bayonne in Southwestern France for the month of August and invited us down for a week. Hooray! We looked forward to this visit and bought train tickets. We made two big mistakes in our hasty planning for this trip. First, we had not anticipated how crowded the trains would be with tourists flocking to the Basque region of France during the classic European vacation month of August. Quite simply, the trains were packed. Packed! Second, we didn't know that in Europe, a train ticket doesn't guarantee a seat; that required a separate reservation. So, we were packed into the train car with no seats for the entire distance from Gothenburg to Bayonne.

Nonetheless, we arrived as scheduled and settled in for the week.

But then, while we were enjoying bottles of Bordeaux wine in the cool evening, disaster struck. More specifically, it struck Curtis as he was playing in the dark with Arnold and Ann's daughter. He ran right into a barbed wire fence, which inflicted a serious laceration on his upper lip: cut it right open. Jane and I stanched the bleeding while Arnold drove to the nearest village about ten miles away to fetch the local doctor. He arrived with no anesthetics; only a small kit of routine doctor's tools. Curtis's lip continued to bleed profusely, so the doctor decided to stitch the laceration on the spot, with no anesthesia. Arnold, Ann, Jane, and I held down Curtis as firmly as possible while the doctor stitched the lip. Curtis healed quickly, but he still has a permanent scar on his lip as a reminder of that unpleasant experience.

A year or two later, Arnold and Ann bought an isolated farmhouse near Irun in the Pays Basque region of France, near the Spanish border. Again, they invited us to visit them for a couple of weeks in August. Having learned our lesson, this time we reserved seats on the train ride from Munich and back. Although the train was packed with vacationers, at least we had places to sit and sleep amidst the overall chaos outside our compartment doors. At the farm, the time went by quickly with no mishap. We enjoyed the local foods and wines, which we bought at the nearest market, and took occasional sojourns to visit historical sites in the region. A highlight of the vacation occurred when the local sheep ranchers invited all of us to a traditional Basque feast with a sheep grilled on the spit, freshly baked bread, locally produced cheeses, and, of course, lots of local red wine. All in all, we were sad to leave such an idyllic environment.

Despite their enjoyment of the place, Arnold and Ann sold the farmhouse less than a year later due to the local political instability. As they were packing up to leave at the end of their second summer there, members of the local Basque National Liberation Movement asked to use their farmhouse during the winter. Whoa. Arnold and Ann faced a serious dilemma: if they refused, the movement might damage or even destroy their farmhouse; if they agreed, the local government might damage or even destroy their farmhouse. The only solution was to sell the property rather than risk alienating either political group.

Notably, Arnold and Ann lived in Stockholm during the year when Jane and I lived in Gothenburg. So, of course, we drove to Stockholm to meet with them on several occasions. On one of those occasions, we continued by ferry to the island of Gotland, where we stayed in a cottage they had rented. It had been built several hundred years ago when Visby, the main city on Gotland, was a member of the Hanseatic League. During those medieval times, people were shorter, and accordingly, the doors to their houses were shorter. So short, in fact, that Arnold and I had to lean over to avoid hitting our heads going through them. Forget to do that? Not so pleasant. Of course, at each of these meetings, we partook of the great 1962 Bordeaux wines being sold-off by the Swedish government.

I could go on and on describing occasional get-togethers with Arnold and Ann over the years. But, they all sound predictably the same: lots of good food and scandalous amounts of wine. Now, Arnold and Ann have aged just as I have. They still live in Providence, with a summer house on Block Island. I have visited them there a couple of times, and we continue to correspond via e-mails. In retrospect, he is my only close friend who is still alive.

I suppose that I should mention one other good friend, Paul Grobstein. I say "suppose" because Paul came and went very quickly through my life. But he left memories that the traveling took me to on many occasions. I'll explain that presently, but first the context. I met Paul at Harvard, where he was two years behind me. We were in a couple of classes together but were never good friends. Just classroom acquaintances. After final exams, I never expected to see him again.

But I did. During the beginning of my second year at Stanford, while walking down the hall in the biology building, I encountered Paul who was sitting in an office with books piled high on his desk, smoking a pipe. He was a first-year Ph.D. student in Donald Kennedy's laboratory. Since his office was just down the hall from mine, we got to know each other quite well, often reminiscing about Harvard. And, on numerous occasions, Jane and I joined Paul and his girlfriend at the time for dinner at a local restaurant. We enjoyed Paul.

While we were in Europe, I lost track of Paul. But I surmised that he had completed his Ph.D. and postdoctoral studies. Indeed, he had. About the time of our return, he wrote me a letter explaining that he had accepted a position as assistant professor at the University of Chicago, which is only about a two-hour drive south from Madison. I was glad to renew our friendship, so Jane and I drove down to Chicago on numerous occasions to spend long weekends with him and his wife. Despite their chain smoking and reluctance to wash the pile of dirty dishes after a festive meal (Jane and I would usually do that for them after they had gone to bed), we always enjoyed those visits.

After Millie and I began to live together, we continued the visits to Chicago. Paul readily accepted her as my new wife. And, with him and his wife as a foursome, we continued to enjoy big dinners together with the usual overabundance of wine. Importantly, Millie didn't mind staying up with me after they had gone to bed to wash the pile of dirty dishes.

But then, bizarre things happened that disrupted our friendship. First: his wife entered the Ph.D. Program in Paul's department at the University of Chicago. No problem

Epilogue

yet, for she joined the laboratory of a young colleague. Now for the problem: Paul and this colleague, who was single, engaged in an affair. That abruptly ended Paul's marriage, and his soon-to-be ex-wife found another Ph.D. advisor. And, now at Millie's stern insistence, it abruptly ended our visits to Paul in Chicago. In fact, it ended our frequent telephone calls. Paul and his colleague soon married and had two children.

I never saw them together mainly because the next bizarre thing happened: Paul didn't get tenure, but his new wife did. Now what? Paul landed on his feet by getting a job as chair of the biology department at Bryn Mawr College in Pennsylvania. His new wife faithfully followed him, giving up her tenured position at the University of Chicago for a professorship in biology at Bryn Mawr, her alma mater. This job ended Paul's research career and, for some reason, ended his interest in maintaining our close friendship. Quite simply, we suddenly went different ways with divergent career goals and interests. Within a couple of years, his new wife died of cancer, leaving Paul to raise the two children. Then, not long after they had "left the coop" as young adults, Paul died unexpectedly at age 65. The obituaries didn't say anything about the cause of death. To this day, I don't know the cause.

In short, Paul had been a good friend. A very good friend. We had enjoyed many hours over a cup of coffee or a nice dinner and bottle or two of fine wine discussing our mutual interests: our time at Harvard, Peter Ray's wine course at Stanford, Donald Kennedy's career, the Vietnam War, and so forth. Bizarre circumstances simply brought all of this to an abrupt end.

I had one other noteworthy long-lasting friend, namely Ron Kalil. In many ways, Ron was a classical tragic character. (I say "was" because he is now dead). A graduate of Harvard (three years ahead of me), Ron was an assistant professor of anatomy at the University of Wisconsin when I arrived in Madison. As a neuroscientist, he was quite successful, but as an anatomist he was quite unsuccessful. Indeed, he became an influential founder of the university's neuroscience training program but failed to attain tenure in the anatomy department, mainly because he refused to teach his assignment in gross anatomy. Fortunately, many of his neuroscience colleagues championed his case for tenure, and ultimately the ophthalmology department agreed to accept him as a tenured associate professor, although as a basic scientist Ron had nothing to offer in this strictly clinical department. Thus, he continued to run his productive research program and administer the training program without any other departmental distractions. Not a bad deal.

Because of our common Harvard backgrounds, Ron and I became close friends, sharing tales of our undergraduate experiences. And, as we got to know each other better, we began to share more personal stories about our lives. He and his wife divorced at about the same time as Jane and I did, and we both ended up marrying a former student from our laboratories. We seldom talked about that aspect of our lives. But we did talk about money on many occasions. Ron studied the mutual fund market assiduously, so routinely I sought and followed his advice on money management: where to invest my savings, my pension accounts, and so forth. At one point when I asked where to invest, his answer was simply "Anywhere but where I just did."

After I moved to Hawaii, I continued to interact professionally and personally with Ron. Besides our scientific collaboration, I appointed him to the advisory board of one of my large NIH grants, paying him generously for his services. In that capacity, I also paid his full expenses for several annual trips to Honolulu for board meetings. These pecuniary benefits amounted to tens of thousands of dollars, and I could easily perceive his gratitude. And for me, it provided the opportunity to visit with my good friend.

As time went by, Ron became increasingly more acerbic as the medical school administration tried to reclaim much of his laboratory and office space for younger faculty members. Ron steadfastly refused to relinquish any excess laboratory or office space despite his slowly shrinking research program and negligible teaching. I tried to convince him to yield to the younger generation, but he refused to listen to me on that matter. By the time I had moved to Bozeman, this persistent jousting with the administration caused Ron to become irritable, grouchy, and, frankly unpleasant at times. Regardless, our friendship ran deep, so to speak, and we could still talk about "things" in depth: personal thoughts, science, reactions to growing old, for example. I valued his friendship.

During one of my last telephone conversations with him, Ron asked if I had ever thought about death. I wasn't sure what he meant: an experimental animal's death, another person's death, or his own death. Without seeking clarification, I muttered "Yes, off and on," and let it go. That was the last time I spoke with Ron. He died several months later at the age of 79 from causes not mentioned in the obituary. I chose not to pursue the cause of death. I'll never know. Oh, I could find out from his first wife or his children, but I prefer not to probe into this private matter. Regardless of his quirks, I miss Ron. I lost a very good friend.

The final topic: Ron's death brings up the topic of "the end." Of course, like everybody else, I have no idea when the end may occur. At age 80 with my heart disease and metastatic prostate cancer, an actuary may declare me to be closer to the end than a healthy nineteen year old male might be. I don't dwell on the actuarial realities of the matter. After all, regardless of what the actuary declares, the nineteen year old could encounter an enraged grizzly bear, a drunk driver, a falling tree, or any number of other fatal catastrophes. It happens all the time, regardless of age. Unlike my fictional, much younger counterpart, however, I surely think about the end more than he does. And, my outlook on life reflects these thoughts.

The major difference between the nineteen year old man and me nowadays is that I have lost a long-term sense of the future. The nineteen year old man may dream about someday getting married, having a family with two children, eventually buying a Porsche 911, and so forth years into the future. But, I no longer have those or any other aspirations beyond the near term. My health has seen to that. Indeed, my future extends forward about as far as the next prostate serum antigen (PSA) test. Currently, every three months my PSA level is tested. If the value rises, then I must promptly confront further, more intrusive (and probably less pleasant) therapeutic measures to control the cancer: X-rays, chemotherapy, immunotherapy, and so forth. If the value stays undetectable, as it is now, then I can look forward to the next PSA test. Those three month interludes between PSA tests comprise the timeframe of my future.

Yes, these health issues limit my view of the future. But maybe the actuary has played a role: maybe the loss of a long-term sense of future is an unwelcome corollary to my advanced age. At my age, I'm considered an old man. I've never been this old before, so I don't know what to expect. Is a limited view of the future quite normal, regardless of health concerns? Maybe; after all, actuarial data pretty much tell the tale. If that's the case, then I join a large crowd of similarly fated people my age and older. That is, I'm normal.

When I spend too much time thinking about my limited view of the future, my thoughts can turn morose. For example, the traveling may lead me down a path into a dark place, a deep woods, a cave, a well, or something like that. Or, I may even be simply lying in bed in a dark room. These dark places harbor unpleasantness: often an illusory, poorly defined person, a nefarious stranger, tugging at me, trying to pull me farther into the darkness. I resist. In my resistance, I may cry out, awakening Karlene. Or I may somehow silently elude the pursuer for the time being. But I know it will return. Moreover, the traveling may simply follow a path to darkness just far enough to invoke a sense of depression. Occasionally a profound depression. In that dark realm, I find myself questioning the innate compulsion to continue my journey. Stated far more bluntly, I question the desire to continue living. "To be, or not to be, that is the question." Again, I resist being pulled deeper into this darkness. Thoughts of my wife, my children, and yes, even my dog counteract the forces of depression, pulling me out of the darkness.

Enough of these maudlin thoughts. They are no way to end a chronicle of my life. I have enjoyed the journey, and fate has granted me a life of privilege. I am secure financially; my children are secure in their professions; my grandchildren are at various stages of professional maturity. Most importantly, I have a wonderful wife, Karlene, who provides loving comfort and companionship. I appreciate the fates of privilege. Moreover, when I look at the beautiful world surrounding me, I marvel at the wonders of nature and think about how lucky I am to be here. Make no mistake.

At the end of this chronicle of the traveling, do I have any particularly insightful wisdom to pass onto future generations? Not really. Oh, sure, I could come up with some pithy platitudes: "Enjoy every day as if it were your last," and the like. At best, however, I pass on the wise advice offered by the singer "Baby" James Taylor when asked about the secret of life: "The secret of life is enjoying the passage of time." Oh, so true.

www.ingramcontent.com/pod-product-compliance
Lightning Source LLC
Chambersburg PA
CBHW021951160426
43209CB00030B/1909/J